POLITICS
The
Japanese W

Books by Jon Woronoff

WEST AFRICAN WAGER

ORGANIZING AFRICAN UNITY

HONG KONG: CAPITALIST PARADISE

KOREA'S ECONOMY, MAN-MADE MIRACLE

JAPAN: THE COMING SOCIAL CRISIS

JAPAN: THE COMING ECONOMIC CRISIS

JAPAN'S WASTED WORKERS

INSIDE JAPAN, INC.

WORLD TRADE WAR

JAPAN'S COMMERCIAL EMPIRE

THE JAPAN SYNDROME

ASIA'S "MIRACLE" ECONOMIES

POLITICS, THE JAPANESE WAY

POLITICS
The
Japanese Way

by
Jon Woronoff

M
MACMILLAN

First edition (Lotus Press Ltd, Tokyo 1986)
First edition (Macmillan) 1988

Published by
THE MACMILLAN PRESS LTD
Houndmills, Basingstoke, Hampshire RG21 2XS
and London
Companies and representatives
throughout the world

Printed in Hong Kong

British Library Cataloguing in Publication Data
Woronoff, Jon
Politics the Japanese way.
1. Japan — Politics and government
— 1943–
I. Title
320.9′52   JQ1615
ISBN 0–333–45307–7 (hardcover)
ISBN 0–333–45947–4 (paperback)

Contents

PART FOUR: THE OUTCOME

Foreword

Ever since I started writing my "crisis" books about a decade ago, I intended to do a book which would be entitled *Japan: The Coming Political Crisis*. But this effort was constantly put off. Partly, I was too busy exploring and demystifying other aspects of this supposed uniquely successful country, especially the economy. The other cause for delay was that the ins-and-outs of politics are even more obscure and carefully hidden.

It has taken a long time to discover, first of all, what Japanese politics is not. It was necessary to realize that much of the activities, the parties, programs, elections and so on that appear on the surface are just a facade. Then it took more time to figure out what was going on underneath. This is much less documented and harder to grasp, but certainly every bit as important. Finally, I wanted not only to describe the mechanisms but show how they affected virtually every aspect of Japanese life.

The result is *Politics, The Japanese Way*. It is an attempt to examine Japanese politics in its own context, discarding as much as possible the Western slant (since adopted by the Japanese) of what should be studied and looking at those things that make it function, whether regarded as possessing academic merit or not. This has taken me in very different directions from most other authors on the subject. And it has frequently led me to draw radically different conclusions.

Unlike the other "crisis" books, I do not pause often to scrutinize what others have written and confound their more preposterous claims. I do not set out to dispel the innumerable myths and illusions that prevail. Yet, in nearly every page, I go against the current and refute (or ignore) much of what is regarded as the conventional wisdom. I also, once again, end up criticizing the system more than others.

While this book may not be as glossy and uplifting as desired, it does have an essential redeeming feature. For, by getting away from the existing literature and seeking a new path, I can do what the political scientists should have done years ago. Being scientific is not to extrapolate from what one's peers have said, to approve or condemn it, and then to add a minor flourish of one's own. That is mere quibbling.

The scientific approach is to look at reality, draw conclusions and come up with a hypothesis. This should subsequently be tested by comparing it with reality again. If it does not tally, it should be scrapped. If it reflects what is actually happening to some extent, then it can be refined. I have therefore gone to the events, the facts and figures and tried to make sense of them. If my conclusions differ from those of others, that is regrettable but of no great importance.

Only if they deviate from reality am I seriously concerned. By giving this book so much more time than the others, and tracing events as closely as I could, I think I have come up with a tolerable reflection of reality, of the Japanese way of politics. I do not doubt that I have made occasional errors or drawn some mistaken conclusions, that is only natural. And I should be more than willing to correct them if they are pointed out. But at least I have not wasted my time scribbling about things that do not matter just because it is expected.

As I do not apologize for differing on the contents of the system, I do not regret my censure of its deviations from the ideal. As shown repeatedly in the book, the Japanese people are perfectly aware of how imperfect and flawed their "democracy" is. Stating this candidly is not really to go against their views so much as to break with the mores of the country in that one does not openly criticize if one is part of the group. As an outsider, it is much easier for me. Indeed, as an outsider it is almost my duty since the internal sources of criticism are so weak.

This exercise is increasingly urgent for, by shunning criticism while reveling in the praise of foreign syco-phants, the Japanese find it easier to convince themselves that things are perhaps not so bad. This is a tempting conclusion for then it would not be necessary to make the unpleasant effort of improving them. But no objective analysis of the political system could possibly find it either morally admirable or mechanically effective. And the longer the Japanese wait to do something about it, the worse the system will get and the closer they will come to the impending crisis.

JON WORONOFF

PART ONE

THE RULES

1
Revamping The System

Things Are Seldom What They Seem

Japan is a model democracy, you say.[1] A Western-style
parliamentary system based on the separation of powers.
Is that so? What! A fascist dictatorship? A capitalist
regime of exploitation and oppression? Well, maybe so.[2]
And maybe not. Maybe it is some of those things, or all, or
none. But probably it is something quite different. After
all, the Japanese system evolved for centuries on its own
or moderately influenced by China and Korea before it
was "discovered" by the first Westerners. It took a long
time for alien ideas to penetrate and, even today, any
influence is only partial. So, there is no reason to assume
that Western labels would be very appropriate.

Ethnocentrism, as we are constantly warned, is the
most insidious threat to the objective study of other
societies. We all have our national biases and preconcep-
tions which distort our understanding and even perception
of foreign countries. This, as any reputable scholar will tell
you, makes it extremely difficult to properly assess what is
actually happening elsewhere. And, so it seems, this has
been a particularly vexatious bane in dealing with Japan.

Scholars (and even amateurs like myself) are therefore
admonished to see and understand things in terms of the
country concerned. It would appear that they do make an
effort, at least in their more abstract analyses or in foot-

notes. Yet, the basic presentation of Japan's political system, say, is little different from what is done when portraying that of the United States, Great Britain, France, Germany or any Western country. And even when it is admitted that the likeness is not yet perfect in all respects, it is assumed that it must ultimately be so due to broad and inescapable currents imposing a convergence.

Thus, you start with the institutions, which are neatly divided into executive, legislative and judiciary, neither more nor less, and see how they should function. You consider the people, since the more fashionable systems (liberal, socialist and even dictatorial) emanate from the people nowadays, and see how they influence events. Then, of course, you look at the political parties, which should transmit the people's will and run the state machinery, to determine their policies and ideologies and conceivably, although not always, what they actually do.[3] Finally, there is a special concern for democracy. Just how democratic is Japan? Is it as democratic as our countries? If less so, why? If more so, aren't there lessons for us?

In so doing, it is once again reality which is squeezed into the artificial schema that were originally derived from Western systems and may—or may not—apply to some other country. When they do not apply, it is immediately assumed *not* that the other schema are simply different but that they are either worse (in most cases) or better (on rarer occasions). Still, if we are really so anxious to avoid ethnocentrism, would it not be wiser to look at reality first, examine how the system works in practice, and then come up with any comments about how good or bad it may be?

This is the attempt that will be made here. There is no guarantee that it will succeed entirely or even be more than an interesting intellectual exercise. But it is absolutely essential to pay closer attention to what is actually happening in Japan than has been done in most instances.

This might lead us to a Japanese path, a Japanese way of doing things, that is quite different from what is ordinarily presumed.

Finding it, obviously, will not be easy. Not only is it hard for an outsider to jettison personal views and experiences, the Japanese make it hard. For they also tend to present their political system in the very same terms, according to the very same schema and with many of the very same value judgments that exist in the West. They also talk of a separation of powers, political parties, human rights, freedom and democracy. And they love comparing Japan's achievements to those of other countries (especially Western ones).

What does one call this? It is not ethnocentrism for they are not viewing Japan from without. It may be othercentrism, since they are certainly describing and evaluating it in terms which are alien to their culture or which have been poorly assimilated.

Regrettable confusion arises inevitably from the use of apparently safe and familiar words, even when there is no intent to mislead. Most of the terms used to describe Japan's political system were borrowed from the West and have been assimilated more or less inadequately. Some were painstakingly converted into ideograms, using existing characters which, more likely than not, had slightly or even substantially different nuances. Others were more wisely left in *romaji,* so one can plainly see their foreign origin and realize that they are not truly indigenous and may not be applied in quite the same way. Yet, even then, it is impossible to speak of democracy, freedom, rights and duties, political parties and electoral campaigns, capitalism, socialism, Marxism or almost anything as if the same words have even roughly the same meaning.[4]

Moreover, even if the words did have the same meaning, if *demokurashii,* for example, signified exactly the same thing in both societies, there would still be no guarantee that they would result in the same or similar behavior. It cannot simply be assumed that the highly positive value attached to certain concepts in the West is as favorable in Japan. Nor can it be assumed that people will have the same feelings for them or a willingness to make the same sacrifices to attain them. In a cold and abstract sense, they may look alike. But the emotions they evoke and, more so, the actions they elicit, may be poles apart.

This shows how great the difficulties can be even when a serious and honest effort is made to resolve them. But we cannot forget that as soon as some institution or practice is seen as inherently good those concerned will wish to be regarded as being on the side of the angels.

This is particularly important in Japan where a very clear distinction is made between *honne* and *tatemae,* between things as they are or realities and things as they should be or ideals. When describing actual events, an ordinary Japanese may reveal the *honne* and express dismay at certain practices. However, as soon as it comes to evaluating Japan as compared to the rest of the world, even a trusted informant is likely to slip back into a *tatemae* that makes Japan look very fine indeed.

There is also a disconcerting propensity to apply several divergent standards, switching from one to the other as conditions dictate. This is facilitated by the underlying ambiguity of the Japanese language and also Japanese mores which make it possible to abide by one set of rules in certain situations and another set of rules in others. Or whereby one behaves in one way with superiors, another with inferiors, and yet another with equals. And, most notably, the different morals that govern relations within a group and those that apply toward outsiders. This double (triple, quadruple . . .) standard makes it possible both to practice—and not to practice—democracy, parliamentarianism, and so on at one and the same time.

Finally, it is amazingly easy to be misled due to the strange gift of mimicry that prevails. The Japanese have shown an extraordinary ability to adopt a broad range of external behaviors while only internalizing some, and those to varying degrees. Looking at them go about electioneering, holding Diet sessions, or attending international conferences, it would be assumed that there is little difference. This is especially true since they are dressed like their foreign counterparts, make similar gestures and often use the same fashionable jargon. But this may be nothing more than an illusion.

It is therefore essential to consider substance more than form, deeds more than words. In fact, it would be wisest as much as possible to just forget about form and words and see what is actually happening.

The Old Game Ends

What is this country which has twice been invited to enter the select circle of modern democratic nations?

For the longest time, it was the scene of what was once regarded as "glorious" deeds in which ruthless leaders and their brutal warriors defeated older groups which had grown weak and effete. There was much warfare and bloodshed, a good show of loyalty, but also betrayal, and an incredible amount of misery and suffering for the ordinary people. While this took place in many parts of the islands, what was happening in the central area around later-day Kyoto and Osaka is what has come to be recognized as national history. The following is the briefest possible rendition, yet enough to set the tone.[5]

In 587, the Soga family defeated the Mononobe, only to be undone by the Fujiwara in 645. Despite internal intrigues and revolts by the Taira, there was no major change until the Minamoto, after destroying most rivals, took over in 1185. The new era lasted, despite periodic revolts, until a trusted general, Ashikaga Takauji, turned traitor and established his own rule in 1338. This regime was relatively shaky and thus civil strife spread throughout the country for over a century. Then, in 1568, Oda Nobunaga set out to conquer the nation, such as it was, defeating the Ashikaga and destroying the Shin Sect in Osaka. Assassinated by a trusted follower, he was replaced by basely-born Hideyoshi who resumed the struggle and later sent an expedition to Korea. After he died, Tokugawa Ieyasu, who controlled the eastern Kanto region, took charge and finally subdued his enemies at the Battle of Sekigahara in 1600.

It was only then that one could begin to speak of a history of Japan, for most of the earlier events took place in relatively independent domains that had been created and reshaped by local lords whose allegiances were loose and shifting. Even the wars that pitted "eastern" against "western" chieftains involved a small portion of the central island of Honshu. It was not until 801 that the Ainu were defeated in northern Honshu. Kyushu remained relatively autonomous until Hideyoshi's day and Shikoku was largely ignored. Unification of a sort took place under the Tokugawa who created a more structured system. But even this *Bakufu* was clearly divided between their own family, the trusted "hereditary *daimyo*" and the "outer *daimyo*." These *daimyo,* or lords, ruled over their own domains *(han)* pretty much as they liked and merely owed fealty to the Tokugawa *shogun.*

Then, in 1868, many of them turned against the Tokugawa Shogunate when it proved too timorous to expel the Western "barbarians" who entered the country despite an

official policy of seclusion. Having had a longer acquaint-
ance with these outsiders, and learned some of their
military techniques, leaders in outer *han* like Satsuma and
Choshu were able to defeat the *shogun*'s forces in a rather
short civil war and reinstall the emperor. This is what
actually united the nation since men with strong links to
more peripheral regions now controlled the center and
thus, for the first time, could adopt decisions covering the
whole country. Among their earliest acts were the aboli-

The past invades the present and future. Samurai on the march.
Credit: Foreign Press Center/Kyodo

tion of the old domains, suppression of the regional frontiers, and creation of a unified state. At the same time, Hokkaido was firmly brought in.

During the whole preceding period, there was a dual system of rule with the emperor remaining sovereign "for ages without end." However, while reigning, the emperor rarely ruled aside from brief periods until a new military leader emerged to take control. The actual rulers were the various warrior families which adopted titles such as regent, *kampaku, shogun* and others. Engaged in almost constant strife, they found it hard to create a very solid state structure. With the Tokugawa, who ruled for almost three centuries, this was finally initiated. Like the others, a bureaucracy based on Chinese models was appointed, taxes were collected and public works were undertaken. Any suspicious activities throughout the land were carefully watched by an elaborate spy system.

Under the Shogunate, the social hierarchy was consolidated and then rigidified, again in a Confucian mode. On top were the emperor, the shogunal family and the lords and lesser nobility. Then came the warriors *(samurai),* so essential in earlier periods but slightly supercilious in times of peace. Many were thus turned into bureaucrats. Beneath them were the peasants and artisans, who did useful things. The merchants, whose activities were less highly evaluated, came under them (although with enough money they could enhance their position somewhat). Lastly, there were the outcastes (*eta* or, nowadays, *burakumin*) who performed certain unclean tasks.

While the new regime that began with the "restoration" of the Emperor Meiji to power in 1868 could have continued along these more traditional lines, it was resolutely decided to break with the past.[6] This was partially because those who most ardently supported his cause were younger, less influential *samurai* from the outer domains who obviously wanted a sweeping change in the power relationship. But they had also been deeply impressed by the military might and technological superiority of the Westerners, whom they could not possibly defeat or safely cooperate with unless Japan adopted a more modern posture. Just to remind them of this need, various unequal treaties were imposed which could only be repealed when it did appear a more civilized place.

Thus, a vast number of reforms were initiated. Some were to unify the nation as regards administration (turning the *han* into *ken* or prefectures), trade (ending the regional customs controls), police, army and bureaucracy. There was an attempt to learn from the West as concerns science and technology, military tactics and equipment, industry and commerce, medicine, philosophy and so on. To expedite this process, Japanese were sent to study abroad while foreigners were invited to Japan as teachers. The educational system was hastily expanded and gradually renovated.

The riskiest experiment, one about which there were somber misgivings in high places, was to introduce a system of parliamentary government based on democracy. This was hinted at by the emperor as early as 1868 in the Charter Oath, when he spoke loosely of establishing a deliberative council and giving the people a part in decisionmaking. This was not forgotten by those out of power, especially disgruntled *samurai* and people from the former "inner" prefectures. They pressed hard, and it was announced that a constitution would be promulgated in 1889. Ito Hirobumi, one of the more conservative leaders, was promptly sent abroad to study the matter. Not surprisingly, he set upon the Prussian system as the ideal model, and this was further adapted to Japanese conditions as the ruling oligarchy saw them.

Nevertheless, the Meiji Constitution was a big step

forward and, once taken, events were no longer entirely in the hands of the emperor or those who advised him. Sooner than expected, political cliques and parties were founded by popular leaders who wanted a share of power, sometimes even by Imperial advisors who had been temporarily eclipsed. These formations attracted more followers as they began to play a role in national affairs, especially the apportionment of funds and allocation of public works. However, not until Takashi Hara, in 1918, was a "commoner" and party-man chosen as prime minister. Meanwhile, slow and fitful progress was made in expanding voting rights. Due to age and wealth limitations, only about 1% of the population voted for the first House of Representatives. It took until 1925 to attain universal male suffrage, with women still excluded. And there remained the House of Peers, largely hereditary or appointed, which had equal strength in the Diet.[7]

The heyday of the political parties occurred under the reign of the Emperor Taisho, Meiji's less distinguished successor, from 1918 to 1932. In this era of "Taisho democracy," there was an alternation of parties, sometimes a very rapid and abrupt one, as groups rose, fell, split, merged and so on and ambitious politicians tried to remain on top.[8] Alas, this game was terribly expensive, so it was the budding economic concerns (zaibatsu) which financed the parties and ultimately influenced and used them. This eventually reached the point where the two main parties were widely regarded as subservient to the two main zaibatsu, Seiyukai to Mitsui and Kenseikai (later renamed Minseito) to Mitsubishi.

All this while, and quite independently of what the constitution said, there was a parallel government. For, given the crucial position of the emperor in the system, it was possible for those surrounding him to have a decisive influence on many matters. The most privileged initially were *samurai* from Satsuma and Choshu who not only counseled the emperor but filled key posts in governments and ministries with their allies and protégés. Some of the peers also enjoyed a special relationship. Within the Privy Council, by pulling strings in the official organs, or through a word with the emperor, these advisors *(genro)* were usually a stronger force than the parties and politicians in Meiji days.

In Taisho days, just as the political parties reached their peak, another category of extra-parliamentary advisors and string-pullers arose. This was a less cultivated and more aggressive group, the military. During much of the period, military men exercised direct control over the army and navy, not letting the politicians interfere. They influenced decisions which resulted in wars against China and Russia and the annexation of Korea. When they did not get official permission to advance further into Manchuria, young officers acted on their own. Some were particularly militant and nationalistic, even turning on the generals and admirals and twice assassinating civilian leaders. With the country drifting toward war, the military eventually took over the government formally as well. It was General Tojo Hideki, prime minister as of 1941, who made the fateful moves along with his military colleagues.

What is most intriguing about this past is how the Japanese could turn this way and that, adopt a multitude of strikingly different regimes, yet always let control slip into the hands of those who, even with no formal status, possessed the real power. First the *genro* ruled, and then the politicians, and finally the military, all without amending the old constitution, which had no significance whatsoever as of 1940, when all parties were disbanded and leftists were arrested while the population was driven into an Imperial Rule Assistance Association (Taisei Yokusankai). This knack also permitted a very neat transition after the war when the office of the Supreme Commander for the Allied Powers (SCAP) decided how Japan should be run until a new constitution could be adopted.

Given the past performance, SCAP's primary function was to find a political format that would enable Japan to become—and remain—a democracy. This was not likely to be easy for, as events clearly showed, the foundation was not as solid as had been hoped. Despite a century of supposed democratization, only a brief period even vaguely resembled what in the West was regarded as democracy. And even that period was marked by abuses that dismayed the local populace and brought the whole concept into disrepute. It was this disillusionment and reconsideration, as well as a return to older traditions and nationalistic ideologies, that led to the sapping and undermining of the essential institutions.

Reaching beyond the formal political structure, there were reasons to doubt that the groundwork was much firmer now. The Japanese adhered to a number of religions, none of which attached much value to the sort of attitudes and behavior needed to buttress democracy. Shinto, whatever its original thrust, was turned into a tool of the militarists as it justified emperor worship, distinguished the Japanese from others, and heightened nationalism. Buddhism, which could not be twisted in this direction, much to the contrary stressed a looking inward, an otherworldliness and a disconcern for the things of this world. Confucianism, increasingly the state ideology under the Tokugawa even if eclipsed thereafter, remained deeply embedded in most social and political institutions, with its stress on hierarchy, centralism, etc. No matter how admirable in some ways, none of this was really designed to contribute to good citizenship in the modern sense.

Admittedly, there were Western currents which quickly

–24–

mixed with the existing religions and philosophies. There were a modest number of Christians and many more who were affected, to one degree or another, by Christian teachings. Democracy was quite popular among the intellectual elite, the students and many ordinary people. Alas, the less one benefited from it, the more it was desired, while those in power tended to disregard it. Socialism and communism were absorbed much later, in equally adulterated forms, and in different ways both supported—or undermined—the former. What proliferated most, however, was capitalism. The idea appealed immensely to the business elite, which never tired of praising it, although the system that evolved was based almost as much on traditional techniques which had little to do with rational management and even less with free enterprise.

While religion and ideology were big concepts, for use on special occasions, lesser folk customs and practices were far more effective in shaping action. They have been summed up in many ways and often brought under the heading of Nihonism. Despite divergencies, a primary element has always been proper relations between individuals, along the lines of obligations and human feelings *(giri-ninjo)*, which could elicit allegiance to the emperor or simply a return of favors.[9] This prevailed over more transcendental things like abstract principles or written laws. It also created a definite situational ethic since proper relations depended so much on the relative status of the parties, with relations between men and women, young and old, superiors and inferiors, insiders and outsiders, varying tremendously.

A second element is a taste for hierarchy. It arose partly out of personal relationships, strongly shaped and supported by Confucianism, and the whole order of traditional society. While the earlier classes had been formally abolished, they were quickly replaced by the emperor, a new nobility of peers, men of considerable political or economic influence, and then the bureaucrats whose ethos was often expressed as "revere the official, despise the commoners" *(kanson minpi)*. Beneath them were the ordinary people, many of them still peasants, craftsmen and petty merchants, plus an increasing number of factory workers. There was also a nascent middle class and some intellectuals whose position was hard to define but not overly impressive. Just as a new class structure arose after the Meiji Restoration, another one could develop after the MacArthur reforms. It was simply a question of determining where the real power lay for, once that was decided, any lesser groups could be brought into line, willingly or unwillingly.

The emphasis on personal relations and hierarchy had a subsidiary result which was doubtlessly linked to another apparently typical phenomenon, namely groupism. Due to the need for one-on-one relations, groups usually grew as magnetic leaders attracted a personal following over the years. They could only expand so far given an individual's limited time and contacts unless, as Chie Nakane indicated, his subordinates then formed their own subgroups. Thus, "parent" groups spawned "child" groups and by accumulating more and more such units quite extensive entities could be constructed. But the larger they grew the more they displayed a tendency to splinter.[10] Moreover, they were based essentially on mutual interest and not abstract principles or formal goals.

Among many other elements, the urge for consensus should not be overlooked, particularly because it is influenced by personal relations, hierarchy and groupism. While decisions within one group are relatively easy to attain those between different groups, with different goals and constituencies, are much harder to reach. They are rarely sought through open assemblies and rational debate but rather by one group or leader aligning the rest on its position, partly through compromise, partly by offering compensation or helping them in other ways. The process can be long and painful, especially since the ideal is unanimous approval as opposed to mere majority support. That helps explain why the outcome is more often a vague understanding than an explicit agreement and it remains uncertain whether this is actively supported or just tolerated by more peripheral backers.

Brief as this sketch may be, it must be evident that neither Japan's historical record nor its cultural background were inherently propitious for modern democracy in Meiji days and the progress had been quite limited and rather patchy even into Taisho times. The prewar and war period marked a disturbing relapse. Thus, although SCAP had the authority to impose a new constitution and to resume the democratization process, it would be hard to insert the right graft in the existing stock. The match was likely to be poor and democracy might not take. Even if it did, it was impossible to tell what forms the new branch would assume as it grew.

But such thoughts did not put off the reformers and their admirers. Idealistic or naive, they assumed that a fresh page had been turned and their efforts had irrevocably pointed the people in a new direction.

"Viewed within the centuries-old sweep of Japanese history, the Occupation was only a fleeting and adventitious circumstance. But its revolutionary achievements were enormous. It brought to the country popular sovereignty, fundamental human rights, free elections, responsible government, and respect for the worth of the individual. These are the essence not only of democracy, but of Japan's new society as well."[11]

Imposing New Rules

The new constitution under which Japan functioned as of May 3, 1947, was a drastic change from the former Meiji Constitution. It marked an even sharper break with the *de facto* government system of the nationalist and wartime periods. It was, without a doubt, a very fine and admirable document drawn up by intelligent and caring people who wanted to put the Japanese back on the right path. It contained some of the cleverest mechanisms and loftiest principles, drawing both from American and European precedent.

In that sense, it could be regarded as a very big step forward. However, unlike its predecessor, it had not been framed so much by the Japanese themselves. Prince Fumimaro Konoe, who directed the initial studies on constitutional revision, and the Shidehara Cabinet, which drew up the final version, would never have gone that far. The only reason the constitution took the shape it did was that SCAP presented the so-called "MacArthur draft" to the government which took the hint and continued its work along the same lines.[12]

The MacArthur proposals and the advice of American scholars were even further removed from Japanese experience and practice than the Prussian model had been in Meiji days. But it was hoped that the people would have learned something more about democracy and its workings during the Taisho era and that the military defeat would have shattered many of the pillars of the old system. Just to be certain, a number of directives were issued by SCAP, including the arrest and purge of war criminals, dissolution of the *zaibatsu,* emancipation of women, encouragement of labor unions, and effectuation of land reform. Even then, there was a definite risk in imposing a constitution that was so alien "it looked as if it had been translated from a foreign language."

The major difference with the earlier constitution is that the emperor, having already denied his divinity, merely became the "symbol" of the state while sovereign power resided in the people. In what was doubtlessly regarded as an essential section, thirty (and not just ten) articles laid down a bill of rights which enumerated many points that are missing from European constitutions and some that are not even included in the American one. While the section also refers to "duties," they are not indicated with anywhere near as much detail or emphasis.

While these rights are rather conventional ones for the Western world, they are highly innovative or even revolutionary for Japan. There is, naturally, equality under the law and freedom of assembly, association, speech, press, religion and so on. In an American vein, there is the right to life, liberty and—why not?—the pursuit of happiness. Taking into account the Japanese context, there is also reference to the right to education and work as well as equal rights of husband and wife. The right of workers to organize and bargain collectively is specifically guaranteed. And there is even a rather strange catch-all provision ensuring the "minimum standards of wholesome and cultured living." The most unusual article, coming even before the rights and duties, is one renouncing war.

The Diet is the highest organ of state power and the sole law-making body of the state. It consists of two houses, the House of Representatives and House of Councillors. The functions of both are quite similar, as are the method of election and privileges. But the lower house clearly retains the initiative and can pass legislation over the opposition of the upper house by adopting it a second time with a two-thirds majority. For two crucial items, budget and treaties, the House of Representatives is in an even stronger position since its writ becomes law even if rejected by the House of Councillors.

Executive power is vested in the cabinet which is headed by the prime minister. It has broad authority to control and supervise the various administrative branches and handle general administrative tasks, including affairs of state and foreign affairs, administration of the civil service and preparation of the budget. It is expected to resign if a non-confidence resolution is passed by the House of Representatives or if it refuses a vote of confidence. The alternative is for the prime minister to dissolve the House and call new elections.[13]

Thirdly, there is a judiciary consisting of a Supreme Court and other inferior courts as may be established. No organ or agency of the executive can have higher judicial power and all judges are independent in the exercise of their conscience and bound only by the constitution and laws. Going further than most European countries, again in an American mode, the Supreme Court can determine the constitutionality of any law, order, regulation or official act.

Finally, to promote decentralization, special stress is laid on the organization of local self-government. In keeping with the principle of local autonomy, local public entities are entitled to establish assemblies and representatives of the communities shall be elected by direct popular vote. They possess the right to manage their own property, affairs and administration and to enact their own regulations.

The Constitution of Japan (Nihonkoku Kenpo) is thus a splendid document. It is based on the classical separation of powers between executive, legislative and judicial branches. It is rooted in the sovereignty of the people. The essential checks and balances are carefully adjusted. And its 103 articles specify very clearly how each of the organs should operate and what the relationship between them should be.

Nevertheless, even the best laid plans can go awry and the noblest intentions come to naught. This comment is not made because of any petty deviations here or there which might lead one to believe that the transition from theory to practice was not flawless. There are any number of major, quite glaring defects which immediately strike the eye. They are so evident, indeed, that the average Japanese can grasp them with no training in political science or constitutional law.

In fact, the whole system is called into question by a compelling bit of folk wisdom which was admirably summed up by Chitoshi Yanaga and would probably be confirmed by anyone familiar with Japanese politics.

Voting in the Diet. What could be more democratic?
Credit: Foreign Press Center/Kyodo

Comparing the situation to the children's game of *janken*
in which paper is stronger than stone, stone stronger than
scissors, and scissors stronger than paper, he wrote:

"There seems to be general agreement among students
of Japanese politics that the nation is governed jointly by
organized business, party government, and the administrative bureaucracy. As to which of the three groups is
more powerful, there is no agreement. . . . Professional
politicians believe that the administrators are running the
country. Businessmen are quick to assert that the party
politicians determine national policies. Administrators are
convinced that organized business, working through the
party in power, is in control of national policies."[14]

For the moment, there is no need to decide which of the
three is stronger, that will be dealt with later on. What has
to be done now is much simpler. It is merely to assert that
the formal political system, as set forth by the constitution
and many scholarly theses, cannot possibly reflect reality
if it is so widely felt that the bureaucracy and business
community are not only major actors on the political scene
but two of the three most important ones. For neither of
them are provided for in the initial script. That is not
surprising, given the circumstances. But it was clearly a
misreading of the Japanese cultural situation.

The bureaucracy has played an extremely significant
part, officially and unofficially, for centuries. Many of the
early bureaucrats were actually *samurai,* members of the
nobility, who assumed administrative tasks for reasons of
prestige (and also need) in the imperial, shogunal and local
courts. Their stature was greatly enhanced after the Meiji
Restoration, since they were directly responsible to the
emperor and not the Diet. While sometimes used as a tool
of the politicians first and then the military, they always
retained considerable influence because they were the

ones who knew how the administration worked and their cooperation was essential. While now formally subject to the will of the government, they still know best how to make the state machinery run smoothly. And that has ensured them a continuing and prominent role in the nation's affairs. The fact that things have not changed so much is already reflected by the tendency to continue calling them *bureaucrats* rather than *civil servants,* which they are not.

Businessmen also performed crucial functions during the Tokugawa and ensuing eras by financing the emperor, *shogun* and lords. These loans were sometimes paid back in coin, but more often in favors, which heightened their status yet further. "Democracy" did not eclipse this power. If anything, the endless needs of contending political parties and striving politicians only increased their leverage since more funds were required than ever. By the late Taisho period, it was broadly felt that the business cliques dominated politics. In recent decades, business made a phenomenal comeback in politics as well. Whether strictly true or not, it is obvious that the business community is regarded as a formidable force by the right, the left, and the common people.

There are a number of other features that are perfectly visible to the naked eye and which have deep roots in the Japanese political culture. Critical decisions have frequently been influenced by figures in the shadows, men with no official position but who give advice or pull strings. They can be knowledgeable advisors, illustrious elder statesmen or more dubious middle-men and power brokers. There has also been a continuing tradition of respect not for the aged but for seniors, with such mentors remarkably present. And, while not a recognized political formation, there has always been a tendency toward factionalism and factions abound in political circles as well.

Perhaps even more decisive, and this also has roots in Japanese customs, there has been incredible stability in the relationship between the political parties. The Japanese system, indeed every democratic system, assumes an alternation between two or more parties with the "ins" periodically replaced by the "outs." This is not written into the constitution; it cannot be. For the people's will might be to return the same party forever. But the fact that the Liberal Democratic Party has been in office for three decades, and the conservatives more broadly defined for four, must have far-reaching and stultifying effects on what is generally understood as democracy.

Thus, and this much can already be sensed, the Japanese political system is bound to be strikingly different in practice from what is set out in theory. Moreover, it is bound to be significantly different from that in other countries, including those at similar economic or social levels and even those which boast a very similar constitution. This means that the system must be studied very carefully to see just what the differences are and what the consequences of these differences are.

*   *   *

This done, further along the line it will be possible to indulge in comparisons and assessments. The Japanese system can be measured against other systems or the ideal. It can be judged in terms of moral value or sheer efficiency. Its strengths can be praised and its weaknesses condemned. One can consider whether it will get better or worse and what might be done to improve the situation. There is no need for anyone else to agree with the author's conclusions, but at least there will be a firmer basis for such attempts.

NOTES

1. Ezra Vogel claimed that "Japan is now a more effective democracy than America" and Edwin O. Reischauer found its system of democratic rule was "not notably inferior to those of the West and perhaps stronger in some respects."
2. Justification for such views, very widespread among many Japanese writers, can be found in J. Victor Koschmann, *Authority and the Individual in Japan.*
3. This is the case, for example, in Koichi Kishimoto, *Politics in Modern Japan.* Even when it is less clearly structured, the same approach is adopted by most commentators.
4. For special insight into this confusion, see Earl H. Kinmonth, *The Self-Made Man in Meiji Japanese Thought.*
5. Much longer versions are available in Whitney Hall, *Japan: From Prehistory to Modern Times,* and Sir George Sansom, *History of Japan.*
6. On the modern period, see among others W.F. Beasley, *The Modern History of Japan,* Hugh Burton, *Japan's Modern Century,* Richard Storry, *A History of Modern Japan* and Chitoshi Yanaga, *Japan Since Perry.*
7. See Robert Scalapino, *Democracy and the Party Movement in Prewar Japan.*
8. See Bernard S. Silberman and H.D. Harootunian, *Japan in Crisis, Essays on Taisho Democracy.*
9. See Ruth Benedict, *The Chrysanthemum and the Sword.*
10. See Chie Nakane, *Japanese Society.*
11. John M. Maki, *Government and Politics in Japan,* p. 68.
12. This process and early experimentation with democracy is dealt with in Nobutaka Ike, *Japanese Politics,* Maki, *op. cit.,* and Harold S. Quigley and John E. Turner, *The New Japan.*
13. On the workings of the Diet, see Hans H. Baerwald, *Japan's Parliament.*
14. Chitoshi Yanaga, *Japanese People and Politics,* p. 27.

PART TWO

THE PLAYERS

2
The Politicians

The One-And-A-Half Party System

If Japanese democracy were to succeed this time, few things could be more important than a sound and effective party system. The first indications were very encouraging. No sooner had political parties been authorized than some of the former units which had been suppressed during the war sprang back into existence. Three were regarded as basically conservative, irregardless of their names, the Japan Liberal Party, Japan Progressive Party and Japan Cooperative Party. A Japan Socialist Party (JSP) arose out of the remnants of three prewar groups, the Socialist People's Party, Japan-Labor-Peasant Party and Japan Proletarian Party, reading from right to left. And the Japan Communist Party (JCP) came out of hiding and held a congress.[1]

Not surprisingly, after a long lapse in political activities, it took some time for the parties to select their leaders and be consolidated. The first postwar decade was quite tumultuous, with formations splitting or merging, new ones cropping up and old ones disbanding. Within the parties there was almost as much jostling as ambitious leaders formed groups of followers, tried to gain power or decided to cooperate with others and then perhaps bolted the party to join another or create one of their own.[2]

This was further complicated by the eclipse of some

politicians who were initially purged by SCAP, mainly those accused of collaboration with the Imperial Rule Assistance Association, some of them irredeemably reactionary, others much less so. But this purge did not last long and many returned to politics in the early 1950s. They joined the conservative parties as did numerous depurged bureaucrats. Meanwhile, reacting to strikes and leftist agitation, another purge was ordered by General MacArthur in 1949–50. This time "Communists" were put out of operation for a while. But none of the parties were crippled by these measures and there was a broad range of choice for all elections.

There was also a noteworthy alternation of parties in power with most cabinets lasting quite briefly. The bulk of them were conservative. The team with the most strength was the Japan Liberal Party, although it was wracked by internal dissension and had to form minority governments. In 1954, it was replaced by the Japan Democratic Party (successor of the Progressive and Cooperative Parties). During the whole period, there was only a short interlude when the Japan Socialist Party ruled, namely from May 1947-March 1948. And then it was in a coalition with conservative parties. Still, one could be pleased with the results and speak of a lively multiparty system.

One of the reasons why the Socialists had done so poorly was that there was continual feuding betwen right- and left-wing elements which led to a split in 1950, which was quickly healed, and then a bigger one in 1951, that seriously handicapped its efforts. In October 1955, the Japan Socialist Party was reunited again and looked as if it might get back into power. Faced with such a threat, the conservatives overcame their own differences and founded the Liberal Democratic Party (LDP) in November. This time it appeared that Japan had opted for a two-party system. It was often referred to as the "1955 setup" in following years.

However, one side of this structure proved less solid and lasting than had been assumed. The Socialists soon fell out again over sensitive political issues like the Japan-U.S. Security Treaty. In 1960, the right-wing faction broke away to establish the Democratic Socialist Party (DSP) and, in 1978, another splinter group set up the Social Democratic Federation. Meanwhile, in 1964, a new political formation came into existence, the Clean Government Party or Komeito. This absorbed voters to the right of the JSP. And the JCP continued pressing it from the left. The LDP, although losing a small contingent to the New Liberal Club (NLC) in 1976, was still in reasonably good shape.

This meant that, rather than a multiparty system or a two-party system, Japan had what was facetiously called the "one-and-a-half party" system in which the LDP perennially dominated politics and the JSP remained so feeble that there was little chance it might come to power. On this basis, the LDP kept winning elections throughout its three decades of existence and, aside from one short interval, the conservatives were in office for just about the whole postwar period. This is a unique and baffling case of democracy which already makes one think very hard about its meaning in the Japanese context.

While admitting that much of Japan's contemporary history is actually the history of the LDP and its predecessors, it is worthwhile briefly recounting the various governments and their main achievements.

The Shidehara Cabinet, introduced when it was finally admitted that Japan could not win the war, agreed to surrender to the Allies and then cooperated with the Occupation forces in purging undesirable elements and revising the constitution. A first Yoshida Cabinet in 1946 promulgated the constitution and, returning to power somewhat later in 1948, worked closely with the United States in restoring the economy and, with greater glee yet, containing the Communist influence. Taking advantage of the American "reverse course," Shigeru Yoshida made strenuous efforts to roll back some of the Occupation reforms, especially for labor, police and education. He was more successful in enhancing Japan's international position with the adoption of the San Francisco peace treaty and, with more difficulty, the Japan-U.S. Security Treaty. Not given to easy compromise, Yoshida's stringent rule was interrupted by periodic dissolutions of the Diet and ran through five different cabinets before he was ultimately replaced in December 1954.

The administrations of Ichiro Hatoyama and Tanzan Ishibashi were equally hectic, if much shorter, marked by the restoration of diplomatic relations with the Soviet Union and admission to the United Nations. Under Nobusuke Kishi, from 1957–60, there was greater stability of leadership but the turbulence continued. Part of this arose from his continuation of the rollback, more particularly a frustrated attempt to strengthen police powers. An even bigger crisis erupted over the revised Japan-U.S. Security Treaty, which was pressed in a high-handed way and sparked massive popular demonstrations that forced Kishi to postpone President Eisenhower's visit to Japan. Still, the treaty went through, the demonstrators dispersed and things calmed down.

The change resulted largely from the action of Hayato Ikeda, in office from 1960–64. Adopting more conciliatory methods, he was able to get along better with the opposition. He also realized that there was much less variance among Japanese when it came to economic matters and directed the nation's energies toward further development and promises of coming affluence with his "income doubling plan." Eisaku Sato, who remained in power for an unprecedentedly long stretch from 1964–72, reaped much of the fruit. He obtained the reversion of Okinawa, the Japan-U.S. Security Treaty was automatically extended in relative peace and quiet and the economic boom continued. But he also had to reap sour fruit as well, like the mounting environmental problem.[3]

By the 1970s, a new generation of leaders started coming to power, men with little or no prewar political experience. The first was Kakuei Tanaka (1972–74), who normalized relations with the People's Republic of China and tried to reignite development with his plan of "remodeling the archipelago."[4] But he was forced to resign amidst charges of corruption and "plutocracy." Takeo Miki (1974–76), appointed to clean up the party and restore confidence, was abruptly discarded. Takeo Fukuda (1976–78), complaining that economic problems had been neglected, took steps to stimulate the economy, albeit with only moderate success.

With budget deficits ballooning, Masayoshi Ohira (1978–80) sought to introduce a general excise tax which was roundly rejected by the electorate. His successor, Zenko Suzuki (1980–82), tried the opposite tack of holding down expenses through administrative reform. As of 1982, this reform was continued by Yasuhiro Nakasone, who added educational reform, tax reform, and new foreign policy and defense initiatives during his relatively activist term.

Thus, the conservatives ruled over Japan in good times and, more surprisingly, in bad. They presided over the conclusion of peace treaties with former enemies, the return to full sovereignty, reconstruction of the economy and rapid growth, expansion of social welfare and coming of relative affluence. They also witnessed the oil shock and sharp decline of the economy, a sluggishness in personal purchasing power and consumption, endless trade conflicts and then the winding down of welfare and explosion of national debt. Whether claiming that things couldn't be better or that things were much worse elsewhere, they managed to get reelected into the 1980s and no one knew how long this winning streak would last.

This upset all the prognoses of how the political situation would develop. Rather than alternating in power, the LDP held on alone. Admittedly, the conservatives had attained the peak of popularity as far back as the 1949 election, when they were three separate parties. From its first election, in 1958, the trend was for the LDP to win an ever smaller number of lower house seats and it dropped as low as 248 in 1979. It periodically picked up or lost a bit thereafter and was no longer in the comfortable position it once had. It became increasingly difficult to get a "stable majority" which permitted it to hold the chairmanship of all Diet committees. But this did not necessarily mean the end of one-party rule. Nor did it preclude occasional LDP gains, as in the 1986 "landslide" election when it won 304 seats.

Still, it did usher in the period of conservative-reformist parity *(hokaku hakucho)*. The opposition as a whole continued boosting its share of the House of Representatives, rising as high as 244 seats in 1979. But this was oddly distributed. During much of the period, the JSP kept losing strength, as a result of attrition and also splits, and had only 107. The DSP, with whom it rarely cooperated, had another 35. The JCP fared poorly as well, losing more than it gained, and not staying much ahead of the DSP. Where real progress had been made was with Komeito, with some 57 seats, and periodically the NLC, which experienced sharp ups and downs.

At this point, many Japanese political analysts, news

The LDP's elusive majority.
Evolution of Diet representation over the years.

	1958	1960	1963	1967	1969	1972	1976	1979	1980	1983	1986
LDP	287	296	283	277	288	271	249	248	284	250	304
NLC							17	4	12	8	6
Komeito				25	47	29	55	57	33	58	57
DSP		17	23	30	31	19	29	35	32	38	26
Shaminren								2	3	3	4
JSP	166	145	144	140	90	118	123	107	107	112	86
JCP	1	3	5	5	14	38	17	39	29	26	27
Other	13	6	12	9	16	16	21	19	11	16	2
Total	467	467	467	486	486	491	511	511	511	511	512

commentators and politicians as well as foreign academics and journalists began insisting that the LDP must continue losing ground which would be picked up by the left. After all, that was happening in Europe and, logically considered, the population was more educated, more urbanized and more liberal. Both the JSP and JCP predicted that the LDP would be ousted by "popular" forces by the late 1970s. Instead, losses were made on both ends and it was the middle which did best.

Thus, discounting a swing from right to left, the experts spoke glowingly of an "age of coalition." But which coalition? The JCP, JSP, DSP, Komeito and NLC put forward very different proposals ranging from leftist to centrist-dominated fronts. However, there could just as well be a conservative coalition revolving around the LDP.

While there is no iron rule as to what will happen in politics, and countless mistaken forecasts bear that out, it is interesting to observe what was occurring on the local scene. There, too, there has been a shift away from the LDP which easily controlled most towns, cities and prefectures during the first and even second postwar decades. Then the Socialists and Communists began working more actively and cooperated with other parties when necessary to take over from the LDP. The most notable achievement was to have Ryoichi Minobe elected Governor of Tokyo in 1967, but there were similar successes in Kyoto, Osaka, Yokohama and other heavily urbanized, relatively proletarian or middle-class areas. Often candidates came not from one party but instead represented the so-called "reformist" (kakushin) and "progressive" (kyushin) camps, depending on whether they were more centrist or more leftist.[5]

Once again, there was much talk of a turning point and predictions that the LDP would first be defeated in the cities and then the country as a whole. Yet, quite to the contrary, by the late 1970s the conservatives had made a startling comeback and the opposition lost many of the big cities and key prefectures. This was not so much because of any renewed popularity of the LDP but an admission that central government support was highly desirable and the reformists had not performed as well as hoped. Moreover, the LDP also learned how to form loose coalitions with other parties and was in a better position to have them win. Many of these tie-ups were with the NLC and Komeito, but also the DSP. Other candidates were sponsored by an extremely broad grouping that went as far as the JSP. And some leaders called themselves "independents" and accepted support from virtually anybody. A fair number actually ran unopposed.

This might be regarded as the era of "no-party" government where popular figures were supported by a mixed bag of political formations and collected votes from a cross-section of voters. They were not pledged to any particular program, neither that of the right, nor the left, nor in many cases one of their own making. They were simply elected because people seemed to have confidence in them as persons. That, by the way, is how many of the party politicians won their own elections. It was all the more logical when one considers that the parties had already shed much of their ideological baggage. The LDP was much less reactionary or hawkish than before, the Socialists and Communists less revolutionary and dovish. Along with the centrists, everyone was huddling in the middle, trying not to stand out too much.

This resulted in a country with amazingly little change and movement. The most prominent party has been in power for thirty or forty years, depending on how you count, and the other parties have been in the opposition for just as long or at least since they came into existence.

They no longer try to show how different they are from one another to gain points but rather stress their agreement with a common consensus which remains sufficiently amorphous and ambiguous. Since this sort of situation usually favors the incumbent, the *status quo* could continue, with minor modifications, indefinitely. While not forbidden by the rules of democracy, it is a rather odd way of playing the game to have one party in almost perpetual power and the others meekly allowing it to stay there.

An Eternal Ruling Party

Since the Liberal Democratic Party (Jiyu Minshuto) was so instrumental in shaping postwar Japan, it is essential to take a closer look at it. Traditionally, parties are defined by their programs and policies. But that is not easy with the LDP for these are rather nebulous and rarely put down in writing. As a start, it makes little sense to cling to the words enshrined in the name of the party or its predecessors, such as "liberal," "democratic," "progressive," or "cooperative." These are tags from prewar days when perhaps, given the conditions of the times, they were indeed appropriate. Nowadays, the most suitable term is quite simply "conservative."

In its original program, adopted on unification in 1955 and basically reconfirmed in 1985, several political ideals are expressed. One is to follow parliamentary democracy and reject the use of violence, destruction, revolution or dictatorship, implicit criticism of previous usages as well as the leftist threat. There is also reference to support of freedom, respect for the individual and rejection of absolutism and classism, another swipe at both right and left. But little is said concretely about what the party intends to do. The platform simply consists of six policy objectives of the broadest nature: to secure national morality and reform education; to reform the political and administrative systems and practices; to achieve economic autonomy; to build a welfare community; to evolve a peace diplomacy; and to consolidate national sovereignty.[6]

The only point which was spelled out more precisely relates to national sovereignty, namely to seek the autonomous amendment of the current constitution and reexamine assorted Occupation legislation, revising and abolishing those parts where necessary so as to fit the circumstances of the country. This was quite enough for the LDP to win a reputation as more than a conservative party, a reactionary one. But, aside from periodic threatening noises, this has been a lesser part of its activities with the big exception of the creation of a self-defense force. Otherwise, its primary concern has been with practical domestic issues. In fact, the most decisive step ever came in 1960, when Prime Minister Ikeda launched his "income doubling plan" designed to make the Japanese think more of economic matters that united them and less of political questions that divided them.

Admittedly, there is still no party to the right of the LDP and it did absorb most of the wartime nationalists and militarists—including some who had been purged. But many of these were older men and their hold on the party has lessened as they passed from the scene. There was a flurry of alarm in 1973, when a group of rambunctious young politicians, led by Yasuhiro Nakasone and Ichiro Nakagawa, formed the "Blue Storm Society" (Seirankai), promising to sacrifice their lives to achieve daring nationalistic goals. Yet, they also mellowed and their "bond of steel" cracked. Meanwhile, most of the newcomers were quite humdrum politicians, with few strong convictions, drawn mainly by the greater chances of success in the ruling party. Thus, while its membership starts on the (almost) far right, it goes well beyond the middle and overlaps with other supposedly "centrist" parties.

What is more indicative of the LDP's action, and what it is likely to do in practice, is its clientele. For, basically, its function is to look after the interests of certain major groups. First and foremost is big business, which urged the merger and supports the party financially. It also represents some sectors of small business and petty trade as well as many of the self-employed. Due to its cooperative wing, it also has solid roots in farm districts. Finally, it has cultivated part of the new urban middle class, those without much political consciousness or ideology and who just want calm and stability.

While the LDP periodically adopts new platforms or explains its present policies, this is not done too precisely because of the party's structure which is not that of a unified political formation embedded in common ideals but of closely related, yet partially autonomous factions which back specific leaders. There is no distinct political hue to the factions even if some of the heads are regarded as a bit more to the right or left, hawkish or dovish on certain issues. The membership, arising out of personal attachment, can—and frequently does—stretch across the whole spectrum, and it would be exceedingly difficult to achieve much agreement on policy.

Factions have been created at different times by different leaders and have waxed and waned as the boss rose or fell. Some have divided or disappeared, others were merged, and increasingly factions are inherited. One initial impulse for factionalism was that the various parties which formed the LDP were not fully integrated and, for decades, there were those who never quite forgot that they came from the liberal, democratic or cooperative wing. This was only exacerbated by the fact that many of the former were ex-bureaucrats and the latter professional politicians. Rather than give their undivided allegiance to a common party, they tended to orbit around strong figures, none being more dominating than Shigeru Yoshida. The "Yoshida school," including Ikeda, Sato, Tanaka, Fukuda and Ohira, is still with us today. This ancestry basically defines what is regarded as the "conservative mainstream" *(hoshu-honryu)* as opposed to the smaller, less influential groups which formed the "sidestreams."

The inevitable outcome was factional politics *(habatsu-seiji)* which strongly affected how the party operates. During the recent period, the predominant factions were those of Kakuei Tanaka, Masayoshi Ohira (succeeded by Zenko Suzuki), Takeo Fukuda, Yasuhiro Nakasone, Takeo Miki (succeeded by Toshio Komoto) and Ichiro Nakagawa, in that order. However, since Tanaka was obliged to give up his party membership after the Lockheed affair, his team could not come to power but remained active behind-the-scenes. In any contest, it is certainly not good ideas or wise policies which count but how many backers a faction could field when it came to a showdown. Given the shifting alignments, since some of the major factions were continually bickering with others, lesser factions could also make their weight felt and be rewarded for their support.

The purpose of factions is obviously not just to rally around popular leaders, nor is it entirely attributable to Japanese customs which encourage small groups. Rather, the factions are handier tools for helping Dietmen with their principal needs. Moreover, since the LDP cannot give everyone electoral support or cabinet posts, one joins a faction which will make a special effort. In return, it is necessary to promote the faction head's ascension in every possible way. After all, it is only when he is in a position of authority that he can really come through. Such positions include ministerial portfolios and LDP executive posts, especially secretary-general. But nothing is more coveted than party president (and prime minister).

With this double patronage, the leader can select both ministers and party executives. He generally places his own members in crucial posts and shares the rest out among those from allied factions or who must be wooed for some reason. This is done on the basis of factional balance *(habatsu-kinko)*. But there is evidently less concern among the "leadership factions" about what happens to those in "non-leadership factions." This generates frustration and friction as the "outs" mobilize to replace the "ins" and even some of those backing the leadership become restless if the president remains in office too long since this restricts their own chances to rise. Meanwhile, as prime minister, he may call a snap election in order to increase the strength of his faction over against the others.

In one sense, this is party democracy since there is some alternation in office, perhaps even too much considering that between Sato and Nakasone changes were made every two years. But it is hardly based on democratic principles. While the number of backers is important, this can be overcome by the amount of money that is made available by each camp since campaign funds are the main way of attracting new members or getting them to switch factions. And it is possible to buy votes in party elections. This would perhaps not matter as much if it were just a question of picking the party president. However, since he automatically becomes the prime minister as well under the prevailing circumstances, this implies short-circuiting the national elections and restricting the choice of the nation's leadership to a small number of LDP Dietmen and dignitaries.[7]

These abuses sparked virulent criticism at the election of Tanzan Ishibashi in 1956 and Kakuei Tanaka in 1972, in both of which cases votes were frantically bought and sold.[8] Even during the other party elections, where less money flowed, politicking and influence peddling were painfully evident. Thus, back in 1963, amidst much controversy over such behavior, the LDP asked its Organization Research Committee under Takeo Miki to propose ways of modernizing the party. Two years later, Kakeui Tanaka (then secretary-general) submitted a concrete plan. But nothing ever came of it. When Miki became prime minister in 1974, he again traced the party's ills to factional influence and suggested two cures: one was to dissolve the factions; the other to make the elections broader and more open.

Periodically, under Fukuda, then Suzuki, the factions were formally disbanded. But they continued to exist through personal contacts and so-called "study groups." Eventually, it was admitted that factionalism was just too strong to be uprooted and, in its defense, it had some positive features as well. One was that by having several party leaders it was possible to obtain a wider variety of views and satisfy diverse segments. It was equally possible to drop one president whenever public clamor erupted and appoint another. In fact, the range was so broad that the LDP could offer hawks or doves, straightforward or cautious men, party pros or former bureaucrats, those known for getting things done no matter what and others whose hands were relatively clean as the mood shifted. The alternative to a change of party was thus a change in party leadership.

The attempt at enhancing party democracy was not much more successful. As of 1977, a primary was to be held in which party members and associates could vote. This election by the rank-and-file would preselect two candidates and a runoff election, this time limited to LDP Diet members, would make the final choice. Attracted by catchy phrases like "you can chose the prime minister and party president" and a nominal membership fee, large numbers of ordinary citizens joined. But many were really just friends or supporters of the politicians and factions or representatives of pressure groups and lobbies. It even happened that factions paid the membership fee and apparently registered fictitious members. So, the conflicts and vote buying merely assumed larger dimensions. In the 1978 and 1982 elections, the winners were those with the strongest factional backing anyway. Partly for this reason, and because they did not want the power to slip out of their hands, the party leaders found various excuses to call off or prevent elections and take the real decisions in small circles of faction heads and advisors (like Kishi) or leave the solution to an individual kingmaker (like Shiina).

Before the "reform," LDP membership stood at only some 300,000, not much more than lesser parties and mediocre for a huge country like Japan. Once paying dues brought the privilege of selecting the next prime minister, membership expanded to over 3 million. As the system went into eclipse, the figure slipped to about half-a-million. The same artificial inflation occurred each time an election appeared imminent, followed by a notable deflation. Thus, despite more than three decades of rule, the LDP never progressed from a coterie of hardened politicians to a truly "popular" party.

With this background, it is much easier to understand LDP history in spite of the many twists and turns. And, it must be remembered, this is also an integral and essential portion of Japan's political history per se.

The principal point of origin for many of the ensuing events was the decision of Ichiro Hatoyama, then president of the Japan Liberal Party, to have himself replaced by Shigeru Yoshida when he was purged in 1946. It was thus that Yoshida came to power, and stayed there until 1954, ignoring an apparent understanding (at least to Hatoyama) that he would step down later. For years, Hato-yama fought to make a comeback, first splitting the Liberal Party and then forming the Japan Democratic Party to that end. Hatoyama was later succeeded by two associates, Tanzan Ishibashi and Nobusuke Kishi, who ruled through a still unsettled LDP. Kishi, who took over in 1957, fell from power almost as much due to internal rivalry as opposition pressure.

With Hayato Ikeda, as of 1960, the Yoshida line was again in the ascendency and, despite assorted party squabbles, he held on until 1964. His successor was Eisaku Sato who, in addition to being a disciple of Yoshida, was also Kishi's brother.[9] He was particularly adept at manipulating people, wooing or splitting anti-leadership cliques and playing his own assistants off against one another to maintain a stable administration. Remaining in office for eight years, he had ample time to groom an heir. During his term, both Takeo Fukuda and Kakuei Tanaka worked doggedly as his chief lieutenants and it was assumed that the former, being much the senior, would then take over. However, Tanaka was extremely ambitious and, after a bitter feud which became known as the "Kaku-Fuku War," he was elected the youngest LDP president and consequently prime minister in 1972.[10]

When he had to step down precipitously, in the midst of scandalous doings, it was not so easy to replace him. Both Fukuda and Ohira eyed the post, had relatively similar claims and equal backing. Dangerous friction would have arisen if either won the post. Thus, Etsusaburo Shiina, acting as kingmaker, proposed that neither be chosen but rather a lesser factional head, Takeo Miki, get the job. Seen by many as "Mr. Clean," he was the ideal person to improve the party's image. But he went at the task too energetically, calling for internal reform and allowing Tanaka to be arrested and jailed. Tanaka never forgave this and immediately plotted his revenge, joining Fukuda and Ohira to oust Miki, an action in which Shiina now cooperated.

Finally, it was Takeo Fukuda's turn and, with backing from Ohira (and even Tanaka), he became party president and prime minister. However, when he ran for a second term, in 1978, he was opposed in the "primaries" by Ohira, Nakasone and Komoto. Due to Tanaka's backing, Fukuda was roundly defeated and Ohira took over. But he bungled the next election by proposing a tax hike and was pressed by Fukuda to accept his "responsibility," which was an oblique way of suggesting he resign. Ohira was adamant about staying while Fukuda (backed by Miki and Nakasone) insisted that he should go. The two rivals therefore competed as candidates for prime minister, leav-

Unity (before the public) in diversity (offstage). The LDP concluding another convention.

Credit: Foreign Press Center/Kyodo

ing the choice to the Diet and not the LDP. Again Tanaka's influence was decisive in letting Ohira continue. But Fukuda kept pushing and was joined by Miki and Nakasone (who also wanted the post) in an anti-leadership plot. When many dissidents failed to show up for a non-confidence motion raised by the opposition, Ohira lost and was forced to call elections in 1980.

This caused serious disarray in the LDP, with the dissidents threatened with expulsion and responding that they intended to form a new party. But they soon reunited to fight the campaign in the midst of which Ohira died of a heart attack. This resulted in a landslide victory attributed to a "sympathy vote." It also simplified party business somewhat although there were still warring contenders for the party presidency. To avoid a confrontation at such a delicate moment, party elder Nobusuke Kishi maneuvered to have Fukuda and Tanaka accept Ohira's relatively tame and conciliatory successor Suzuki. After Zenko Suzuki decided not to stay a second term, it was again necessary to find an acceptable leader, which was attempted privately by top LDP executives and advisors. When they failed to impose their will, party elections were held to decide between Nakasone, Nakagawa, Komoto and Abe.

Nakasone, with a smaller faction, could never have won the 1982 primary without Tanaka's backing and also that of Suzuki, both of whom reaped numerous cabinet posts for their followers. Indeed, the deal was so evident that there was much talk of a "Tanakasone" regime. When Nakasone proved a more energetic leader than expected, there was some disappointment in the Tanaka camp that its advice was occasionally ignored and even more annoyance among Suzuki's entourage because of a "lack of gratitude" and slighting remarks made about the efforts of the former prime minister. Nakasone subsequently laid himself open to charges of failure when the LDP fared poorly in the national elections. Thus, when he had to run for reelection as party president, while relatively clear sailing had been predicted, there was a last minute effort by Suzuki and Fukuda to block—or at least humble—him by proposing that Tanaka's right-hand man Nikaido be chosen. Nakasone's success in the 1986 "landslide" election only angered the other faction leaders.

All this while, it was obvious that a man who was not even officially an LDP member was decisive in most choices of leadership and party policy. Kakuei Tanaka did not lose his clout, as so many had predicted. To the contrary, he·continued recruiting new members to his faction, often weaning them away from his rivals. His "Thursday Club" eventually included some 120 members or a third of the party's total Diet strength and others were supporting him more discreetly. Given the importance of numbers, this allowed his faction's members to hold crucial party and cabinet posts (including Construction and Justice). But it was not only a question of size. Far better organized than the others, the "Tanaka corps," as it was called, knew how to pull strings within the party and keep the government moving as well. Oddly enough, Tanaka and his chief lieutenants like Susumo Nikaido and Shin Kanemaru also had the closest links with the opposition and engaged in the essential wheeling and dealing to get legislation through the Diet. This made him the reputed "*shogun*-in the darkness" who could reward his friends, punish his enemies, and maintain a congenial balance in the party and throughout the political world.

These are just the main highlights of party history. There were innumerable other episodes which could not be included here and kept things constantly in turmoil. There were also, and this must not be forgotten, similar hassles and intrigues within most of the factions most of the time. Notable was the struggle between Kiichi Miyazawa and Rotusuke Tanaka to inherit the Suzuki (Ohira) faction, known as the "Ichiroku War," in which the former sought Tanaka's help and the latter turned to Nakasone. There was the stubborn tug-of-war between Fukuda, who refused to give up the top position, and younger faction members who wanted him replaced by Abe. Even more spectacular was the sudden suicide of Ichiro Nakagawa after losing the party election, reputedly due to heavy debts incurred in the campaign.

But the most crucial battle was for the Tanaka faction. For well over a decade Kaku-san had maintained control by playing his various assistants off against one another, Nikaido, Kanemaru, Takeshita, Yamashita and others. However, as he aged and the Lockheed case dragged on, preventing the faction from having one of its own elected party president and prime minister, dissatisfaction grew in the ranks. It was shown by Nikaido's willingness to unseat Nakasone, a man backed by his boss. It was aggravated by Noburo Takeshita's decision to set up a "study group," an idea disliked by Tanaka but ultimately permitted. After the don's heart attack in March 1985, the faction split between Nikaido and the loyalists and Takeshita, backed by Shin Kanemaru and many younger members. As it disintegrated, Takeshita grabbed the bulk while Nikaido got the rump, and the group ceased being the decisive element in party politics.

This is not quite as dignified as national history, which was not even that brilliant. In fact, it looks more like tales from Meiji days or, to be perfectly frank, the time of incessant warfare before Hideyoshi united the country. But what else can be expected of a party based on factions? There are bound to be shifting alliances and power plays, all the more so since there is so much stress on personal loyalty and so little concern for policy or principles. Yet, no matter how bitter the quarrels, and the periodic talk of splits, little likelihood exists that the LDP will collapse since together the various factions can monopolize political power and then share it amongst themselves. Individually, they would be weak and with only limited chances of success.

A Perennial Opposition

There is considerably less difficulty ascertaining the principles and program of the Japan Socialist Party (Nihon Shakaito) since so much of its effort has been directed toward formulating, and reformulating, them. Its initial program was adopted at the "reunification" convention in 1955, when the JSP was defined as a class and mass party. It was dedicated to bringing about a socialist society through a peaceful revolution. This platform, an acceptable compromise between a relatively balanced right and left wing, was periodically altered in favor of the more militant ideologues. The most important result was the "Road to Socialism," adopted in 1964.

The "Road" called for a "socialist revolution," one that would be carried out democratically and peacefully through the Diet. It also laid down the party's basic goals: socialist democracy; socialization of key industries, organization of small businesses and agriculture into cooperatives and planned production; land reform and improvement of the living environment; development of education, culture and science; construction of a society based on solidarity and cooperation; and a foreign policy that contributes to peace and prosperity.

These rather vague aims have been periodically stated more specifically and with regard to issues at hand. But the only ones which were vigorously promoted related to foreign policy and defense. They were expounded in

"Problems of the 1970s," adopted at the 1970 convention, and in various other documents. The most notable proposal was to abrogate the Japan-U.S. Security Treaty, conclude a mutual non-aggression treaty with the United States, Soviet Union and China, disband the Self-Defense Forces and adopt unarmed neutrality.

The JSP was considerably less explicit on its position regarding current economic and social problems. Obviously, it called for more social overhead, greater welfare and health benefits, more concern for the environment, less taxation, and a rejection of administrative reform. But it rarely went much further than a denunciation of LDP policies and failed to provide very precise or detailed insight into its own alternatives. Too many of its policies, in addition, were presented in painfully stilted and doctrinaire language rather than being easily comprehensible to the people and addressed to practical matters.

However, this seemed to be changing by the mid-1980s, by which time the "Road to Socialism" had little more than historical significance while actual policy was finally adapted to the prevailing circumstances (although this derived more from a desire to win votes than anything else). A turning point was grudgingly reached in January 1986, with the adoption of a "New Declaration." It endorsed a swing to the right which broke with Marxist-Leninist socialism and proclaimed that the JSP was not a "class party" but one based on various strata of society. Among the basic values were peaceful coexistence, liberalism and democracy, justice and equality, participation and humanism. This brought it closer into line with the Western socialist parties which had updated decades earlier.

Whatever the program, most actions were also directed primarily toward the interests of its clientele. The JSP was, more than others, a party of ideologues and intellectuals and an amazing amount of time was spent looking after their concerns which were frequently of a more philosophical nature. It was kept busy defining, and redefining, an ideal socialist society. It was deeply involved in the anti-nuclear and pacifist movement, this attracting a vast following right after the war if considerably less at present. When it intervened on more concrete issues, they often had some relevance to the fate of the public workers, since its strongest backer was the General Council of Trade Unions (Sohyo). In fact, Sohyo provided the biggest block of voters and largest share of financial resources. To some, it almost looked as if the relationship were the reverse, with the JSP disparagingly labeled "Sohyo's political department."

The JSP's history, even more than that of the LDP, was one of ceaseless internecine disputes. Some arose from the fact that it grew out of several different prewar parties, with different memberships and policies, and which had already been in conflict then. This was seriously exacerbated by the nature of postwar events, with the Socialists first welcoming the American intervention and then turning against it as the "reverse course" began. Difficulty in adopting common policies already created a brief rift in 1950 and a major split from 1951–55, which added new divergencies and resentments. After reunification, the left gradually gained the upper hand and tried to impose its policies on the right. One consequence of this was for some right-wing leaders to break away and form their own parties, namely the Democratic Socialist Party and Social Democratic Federation. This, in turn, further reinforced the left's control over party affairs.

Even after the departures, there were half-a-dozen factions within the party, thinly disguised as study groups. The most virulent was the ultraleftist Socialist Association (Shakaishugi Kyokai) which split the party into two warring camps, seen as pro-Kyokai or anti-Kyokai. There were inevitably other differences between pro-Soviet and pro-Chinese elements and also those who wished to keep out of the Sino-Soviet conflict. This created endless rounds of controversy, relatively little of which had to do with concrete issues. The worst confrontations were almost invariably ideological, often revolving around incredibly abstruse and abstract points of Marxist doctrine. Insisting on ideological purity and condemning opponents as "capitalist roaders" or "parasites" only made it harder to find any common ground. More often than not, it was the left which carried the day.

Be this as it may, it was still necessary for the party leadership to rally voters and win elections and it was impossible to do so on the basis of the left's interests and proposals. It was also necessary to consider the wishes of the trade unions. Thus, there was a tendency to swing to the left in internal debates and then tip back right somewhat when appearing in public.

Obviously, the continuous bickering and infighting did not help the Socialist cause. The JSP therefore suffered a sharp decline in its share of the votes and position in the Diet. After the 1958 elections, it held as many as 166 seats in the House of Representatives. But this fell as low as 90 in 1969, although recovering to 123 seats by 1976, and slipping to 86 in 1986. It has remained about this level since, making it the nation's second biggest formation and its number one opposition party, but still much weaker than the LDP. Moreover, it was increasingly a party of professional politicians, ideologues and intellectuals, and trade unionists. Its opening to the rest of society was very narrow and this was reflected by a rather mediocre membership of some 50,000.

Realizing that something had to be done to revitalize the party, there were interminable debates on its "reform" and "reconstruction," most of which only led to further dissension between right and left and rather little improvement. The principal responsibility here fell upon the Secretary General who was periodically mandated to create a new image and attract more members. However, no matter how hard he worked he usually either fell under the domination of the left or was blocked by the left in any attempt to seek greater balance. This was the sad fate of Ichio Asukata, former mayor of Yokohama, who was hailed as a "savior" when he took office in 1977 and scorned as a failure five years later. Still, he managed to get open election of the chairman and launched a campaign to recruit one million members, neither of which proved overly successful.

His successor since 1983 was Masashi Ishibashi, a party man who had been secretary-general and vice-chairman. He was also the first trade unionist after a series of lawyers, bureaucrats or proletarian party activists. Ishibashi initially looked rather unpromising as a specialist on defense and security affairs and author of *On Unarmed Neutrality*. Yet, he did make strenuous efforts to create a "new" JSP and open it to the public. He adopted a somewhat more pragmatic approach to the Japan-U.S. Security Treaty and SDF while playing down class struggle. And he organized contacts beyond the JSP's traditional clientele.

More important, he worked tirelessly to turn the party around. From a proud and combative organization which steadfastly fought the LDP on security and other issues, it had become a party with little vigor. In fact, it was generally felt that the JSP no longer had the will to win or would not know how to react if it did take over the reins of government. One sign of this was a less tenacious defense of its viewpoint and greater willingness to reach tacit agreements with the LDP that helped its interests, and those of Sohyo, even if the principles were neglected. Another was the decreasing number of candidates it fielded for Diet elections and the increasing number of mayoral and gubernatorial elections it did not even contest. After the JSP's electoral setback in 1986, he was replaced by Takako Doi whose chances of reversing the situation were slim.

The existence of breakaway parties was a definite handicap since they tended to attack the JSP's program and leaders and drew off some of its potential backers and voters. The Democratic Socialist Party (Minshu Shakaito), which came into existence in 1960, placed greater stress on "democratic" socialism and strongly criticized the Marxist tendencies of the JSP. It was open to people of any class and pledged to confront capitalism and totalitarianism of both right and left. The Social Democratic Federation (Shaminren), which was established in 1978, called for enhanced participation of citizens in politics and a "free" socialism. Both of them took a less stringent line against the American connection and Self-Defense Force. Both groups were supported by segments of the trade union movement, with the DSP relying heavily on the Japanese Confederation of Labor (Domei), the second largest center. They also attracted small businessmen and some middle-class people. While initially very optimistic about their prospects, the parties remained quite small, the DSP with some 30–40 seats in the lower house and Shaminren a mere 3.

Each of these formations grew out of factional conflicts. The DSP was founded by right-wing Socialists, driven by strong fears of Marxist and Communist influence. Originally, they fell out over the revision of the Japan-U.S. Security Treaty. But it was not only on the substance but also the form, condemning the leftists' approach of categoric rejection and insisting that concrete proposals and alternatives be offered. Shaminren resulted even more directly from virulent attacks on rightists launched by the Shakaishugi Kyokai. Yet, small as they were, they could not escape the bane of additional factionalism arising out of, for example, long-standing differences between DSP Chairman Ikko Kasuga and President Ryosaku Sasaki. This was eventually submerged in a revolt of the younger leaders who were tired of the old feuds and wanted a more up-to-date and realistic program. But their day did not come until 1985 when Saburo Tsukamoto was made chairman and Keigo Ouchi secretary-general while the elders were named "permanent advisors."[11]

No party has been more explicit about its programs and policies than the Japan Communist Party (Nihon Kyosanto). And no party has changed them more radically over the years either. When the Communists emerged after the war and held the fifth congress in 1946, they basically welcomed the Allied Occupation as paving the way for a peaceful and democratic revolution. But this approach was sharply criticized by the Cominform in 1950, which claimed it only served the "imperialist occupiers" of Japan, and called for active resistance. The party then switched to a theory of violent revolution and adopted confrontational tactics including the use of Molotov cocktails. This resulted in arrests and purges by SCAP and rejection by the electorate.

Realizing the mistake, in 1955, the militant line was dropped and, in 1961, the JCP returned to the theory of peaceful revolution against American imperialism and Japanese monopolistic capitalism, if necessary through a national, democratic united front. This new "soft" line was further amplified over the years in an effort to create a "lovable" Communist Party. The 1976 "Manifesto of Freedom and Democracy" even toned down the traditional jargon, replacing "dictatorship of the proletariat" with "power of the working class" and "Marxism-Leninism" with "scientific Socialism."

This was of little avail, however, as long as the party could be suspected of being "subservient" to external powers. Such charges were most notable, and clearly rang true, after the adoption of violent tactics at the behest of the international Communist movement, more exactly the Kremlin. This was countered by returning to a more peaceful approach and also dropping some of the leaders accused of having unwisely adopted "extreme leftist adventurism." But the JCP went even further in the mid-1960s, when it denounced the Soviet Union for the desire to maintain nuclear weapons and quarreled with Mao Zedong when he urged it to follow a "militaristic policy" in Japan. Both these ruptures lasted for over a decade and hardly were they healed than new differences arose. The JCP was embarrassed by the Soviet invasion of Afghanistan and intervention in Poland, among other things, and China's attack on Vietnam, to say nothing of pressure by both powers to take their side in the Sino-Soviet conflict.

That the Japan Communist Party was able to throw off foreign influence and also modify its policy so effectively can be traced to changes in the party leadership as much as any change of heart. The Cominform attack was directed specifically at an early leader Sanzo Nosaka, who lost out in a struggle with Kyuichi Tokuda, head of the mainstream faction. But the mainstreamers were either purged or fled to China while the moderates remained in Japan. Kenji Miyamoto, a committee member who stayed, was not only proven right as regards tactics, he could also consolidate his position. In 1958, he became secretary-general with Nosaka as chairman of the Central Committee. From then on, they weeded out the militant elements and dropped pro-Peking and pro-Moscow dissidents. Tetsuzo Fuwa, a relative newcomer and intellec-

The JCP's immovable trinity: Kaneko, Miyamoto and Fuwa.

Credit: Foreign Press Center/Kyodo

tual, was later appointed secretary-general. Long referred to as the "prince," it was not until 1982 that he became party chairman while Miyamoto graduated to Central Committee chairman and Mitsuhiro Kaneko was made the new secretary-general.

The JCP's turn to violent tactics drove away many of its earlier supporters and its electoral strength fell by two-thirds. Thus, it was necessary to rebuild the party, a task that Miyamoto tackled with great vigor. He placed less stress on ideological purity than practical matters such as cooperation with local groups, providing concrete benefits for people, and especially fighting electoral campaigns. From a mere 30,000 in 1958, the number of card-carrying members rose to nearly 500,000 and the readership of the party newspaper *Akahata (Red Flag)* reached above 3 million. This was a much better showing than its rivals and the organization was clearly more structured. Once the dissidents had been weeded out, there was no factionalism and little internal discord, a striking difference from the rest.

Yet, this "harmony" did not really appeal to the public which did not know how decisions were taken or whether they could be entirely trusted. The JCP's electoral strength rose remarkably during the first decade of the "soft" line and hovered around 10% of the popular vote and some 30 seats in the House of Representatives. While it was once expected to continue climbing, by the 1970s it stagnated, occasionally slumping and then recovering. Only in some heavily urban areas, Tokyo and especially Kyoto and Osaka, did it attain about 20%. But the party seemed to have reached its limits as concerned not only votes but membership. Despite repeated attempts, it was not possible to achieve the goals of 600,000 party members and 4 million *Akahata* readers.

What blocked the advance of both the Socialists and

Communists was not so much the LDP as the emergence of a new party somewhere in the middle. This is the Komeito or "Clean Government Party" which was officially established in 1964 but already ran candidates locally and in the upper house as of 1959. While initially founded by Soka Gakkai, an activist wing of the Nichiren Shoshu sect of Buddhism, it later turned into a more conventional party. Its history therefore reveals two very distinct phases. Originally, it clung to a unity of politics and religion and sought a loosely defined "Buddhist democracy." In 1970, however, it decided to end the formal relationship with Soka Gakkai and pursue a policy of "separation of politics and religion." The new platform stressed parliamentary democracy, protection of human rights, a peace-oriented diplomacy and "humanitarian socialism." It also pledged to work for the "welfare of all people on a middle-of-the-road *(chudo)* basis."

These changes were brought about under the leadership of Yoshikatsu Takeiri as chairman and Junya Yano as secretary-general. While personally designated by Soka Gakkai's president Daisaku Ikeda, they tried to steer a more independent course realizing that as long as the party was identified too closely with the sect its following would be limited. They were further encouraged to distance themselves from sect affairs by several events. One was an attempt by Soka Gakkai to prevent the publication of a critical book. Even more damaging was a secret ten-year "non-aggression" agreement with the JCP whereby the two should stop their mutual recrimination and cooperate on certain points. Then came charges of impropriety in the personal life of Daisaku Ikeda. This sapped what had once been an explosive increase in Komeito's strength and kept it to a level of about 40–60 seats in the lower house and the second-ranking opposition party. While this was appreciable, it had to be admitted that much of the vote and membership still came from Soka Gakkai.

Another party which started out with very high hopes was the New Liberal Club (Shinjiren), a group of former LDP Dietmen who aspired to form the nucleus of a second conservative party. The NLC broke away in 1976 because of the LDP's internal strife and plutocratic nature in general and the handling of the Lockheed scandal in particular. It promised instead a "new liberalism" and "gradual reform based on true conservatism." In its first attempt, there was actually an "NLC boom" and the Diet membership shot up from 6 to 17. But it soon slipped back toward the earlier level and occasionally looked as if it might disappear. The causes of this reverse were multiple. One was instability even within the small splinter group, with its founder Yohei Kono replaced and returned to the top post within only a few years. Another was that its policy was not attractive enough or, more detrimental yet, very likely to be put into practice. By 1986, the NLC conceded its failure and rejoined the LDP without having accomplished much.

Finally, while often overlooked, there are a number of minor parties and independents, most of them in the House of Councillors. Some are actually fictitious "independents," LDP adherents who do not obtain an official endorsement and run nevertheless, rejoining the party's ranks if they win. Others are genuine independents. The most famous was Fusae Ishikawa, a suffragist from pre-war days who symbolized women's rights for many of the older generation and was periodically returned with a huge vote. Among the smaller parties and movements, most represented special interests like the handicapped and salaried workers or propounded single issues like lower taxes or healthier lifestyles. There was also a smattering of far-right and far-left groups and some outright cranks. While not often elected and hardly influential, these people did provide a broader range of views and clearly met the needs of certain segments. But most of them were forced out or obliged to join existing parties or create their own by a change in the upper house's rules in 1983.

The proliferation of parties and the inability of any one of them to consolidate its position and become a serious rival to the Liberal Democratic Party meant that they could remain, individually and jointly, a no less "perpetual" opposition. The only real hope they had was to join forces in one way or another. This was so clear and compelling that, from the outset, there was cooperation at least on specific issues where agreement amongst them was sufficient. Most often, in the early days, it was the security treaty and defense matters that united them and, later on, taxes and welfare. In order to increase the chances of winning elections, smaller parties also pooled votes by selecting joint candidates. This was done repeatedly by the DSP and Komeito or JSP and Komeito with amazingly positive results. But the process of picking such candidates was long and tortuous and consequently not that many were fielded. By the 1970s, given their inability to come to power in any other manner, there was increasing talk of possible coalitions.

The first proposals came from the left. The JCP formally adopted a "Plan for a Democratic-Coalition Government" in 1973 based on a progressive united front with three basic objectives: neutralizing Japan by abolishing the Japan-U.S. military alliance; breaking down big-money politics and defending the people's livelihood; and establishing democracy in Japan with democratic management of the Diet. In 1980, the call was repeated and the conditions somewhat relaxed with less stress on immediate abandonment of the SDF and willingness to accept a self-reliant defense setup. But these offers only appealed to leftists in the JSP, especially those in the Socialist Association, which inevitably sparked more internal quarrels in which the anti-Kyokai forces united to prevent closer relations with the JCP. Since no other party wished to be drawn into a closer embrace, the Communists remained isolated.

All this while, the JSP had also been thinking of a coalition of which it would be the main element. The "Basic Program for National Unity," adopted in 1974, proposed a "national coalition government" that would blaze the path to a socialist Japan. The openings, however, were sought more to the right than the left and primarily among the smaller formations. It was periodically rumored that the DSP or Shaminren might return to the fold or at least become partners. But they were inveterately suspicious of the party's machinations and their policies brought them into closer relations with the centrists, Shaminren cooperating a bit with the NLC and the DSP concluding an agreement for cooperation with Komeito in 1979. Komeito then took a more active role in seeking partners for a "middle-of-the-road coalition." Instead, the following year it entered into an agreement with the JSP, albeit a looser one. This made Komeito the pivot in a somewhat unwieldy alliance between the JSP, itself and the DSP known as the Sha-Ko-Min concept. Since one major point was exclusion of the JCP, it provoked the ire of the Communists who had earlier tried to improve ties with Komeito and counted heavily on Socialist cooperation, accusing the latter of an unconscionable "swing to the right." But it need not have worried, for nothing came of this and, in the early 1980s, the JSP and Komeito were still vainly seeking compatible partners.

There was another form of coalition that the opposition occasionally toyed with and aroused lively discussions in the press. The theory was to bring some of the more liberal conservatives into an alliance, or even a new party, with right-wing Socialists and centrists to create a new stable majority. One proponent of this was Ikko Kasuga, former DSP chairman, who spoke of a "grand coalition." An even more striking backer was Takeo Miki, whose group had actually participated in the 1947 Socialist cabinet. He repeatedly stressed the need for a counterbalance to the LDP and was described as "the man closest to the opposition camp" by Yasuhiro Nakasone. But most often this exercise involved little more than fishing in troubled waters. In 1974, when there were rumors of a split between Fukuda and Ohira, it was thought that the Miki and Nakasone factions might tie up with centrists. Later, when Toshio Komoto challenged the mainstream, it was hoped that his smaller faction could be wooed away. More recently, when Komeito and the DSP mixed in the last minute attempt to have Susumu Nikaido take over from Nakasone, there was a vague idea that this could split the Tanaka corps and lead to a major realignment. None of these intrigues made much sense, especially since some of the potential rebels were hardly sympathetic. Moreover, they usually had much more to gain by sticking with the LDP.

Thus, coalition was more of a buzzword than a reality despite over a decade of plans and efforts. The final results were not only disappointing, they may have been counterproductive. For the Liberal Democratic Party realized that it could play the same game. And it could play from a position of strength since it was able to offer those who cooperated palpable returns immediately. This was not lost on the many politicians who gravitated to it for other than ideological reasons. A noteworthy case was Zenko Suzuki, who eventually became prime minister, and left the Socialists in the late 1940s because he wanted to offer the fishermen he represented more than words. The temptations were even greater at the local level since no mayor or governor could count on much state largesse without LDP support. More surprising, some of the opposition parties began to cooperate with the LDP on specific issues, requesting modifications of bills that interested them in exchange for their adoption. This became particularly noticeable as of 1979 and involved the NLC, DSP, Komeito and even JSP in what Ohira termed "partial coalitions."

A genuine coalition with other parties was not only feasible, it was greatly facilitated by the factional structure of the LDP which could be stretched to embrace other groups. The first to take this up was the NLC, which entered the Nakasone government in 1983 despite earlier criticism of his policies. More significant, both the DSP and Komeito began making broad hints that they could possibly join in a conservative-centrist coalition if some of their policies were accommodated and they received enough seats in the cabinet. The more probable outcome was thus an expanded LDP or the LDP in coalition with one or more of the middle-of-the-road parties in the event that it could not rule alone. And, even if such a formal arrangement never came about, it was already undermining or destroying the earlier hopes of leftist and centrist coalitions.

There was all the more reason to have doubts about the ultimate success of the opposition parties because, despite any differences, they had much in common with the LDP. Most of them were also parties of professionals with little direct contact with the people or popular membership, with the sole exception of the Communists. They suffered about as much from factionalism, when it was not ruthlessly suppressed, and a lack of diversity actually appeared more suspicious. There was hardly any internal democracy with decisions taken by a small circle of leaders, most of them rather old, and then imposed on the rank-and-file. Outsiders did not know how the chairman and party executives were chosen. There was scarcely more information about how party policy was determined or what was being negotiated in the Diet. Even major changes, like adopting or dropping basic programs and joining or leaving coalitions were arranged behind the scenes.

Moreover, it was apparent that the parties were more active in defending the interests of whatever their particular clientele was rather than those of ordinary citizens or the nation as a whole. It was impossible to deny trade union or Soka Gakkai influence or the more unrealistic concerns of certain ideological schools. With little internal financial support, the need to please backers was all the more urgent. The only concession made to the general public was probably the wrong one. Instead of creating their own alternatives to prevailing policy, most of the opposition parties simply moved closer to the middle in the political spectrum. They tried to fit in with what they thought was the emerging national consensus rather than direct it intelligently. In such a case, where their lines were no longer very different from those of the LDP, and their behavior not that much better, it was naturally the incumbent which gained. So, there was increasingly less point to voting for the opposition.

Who Are The Politicians?

Obviously, in a country where people (as opposed to policies) are so important, it is essential to take a closer look at the political personnel, who they are, where they come from, what their potential assets and liabilities may be.

Inevitably, many of those who surfaced after the war

had prior experience under the old regime. Some of them were actually nationalists or even militarists, briefly purged and then left free to reenter the political arena. In fact, there were probably more reactionaries of this stripe engaged in Japanese politics than in any other defeated enemy. Hatoyama and many early leaders were deeply involved in prewar politics and Kishi was a Class-A war criminal and member of General Tojo's wartime cabinet. There were also dozens of ex-bureaucrats, many from the notorious Home Ministry. This naturally precipitated nasty clashes with members of the former peasant and proletarian parties and especially Communists who were jailed, went underground or fled overseas and later emerged as Diet members in the opposition. While these types are gradually disappearing, given the longevity of Japanese politicians, a fair number are still around. As late as 1982, Nakasone appointed no less than four former Home Ministry officials to his cabinet.

Among the representatives of all parties, it is surprising how few are generally regarded as "politicians," namely people who entered politics of their own volition to pursue political goals or represent a given segment of the population. And this is particularly true of the postwar classes. Only about a quarter of the new Diet members gained their experience in local assemblies and the grassroots element has not fared very well in later assignments. One of the few well-known "politicians" is Miki and, in a way, Tanaka could also be regarded as belonging to this category. While the LDP showing is poor, it is as good or better than that of the other parties.

A somewhat smaller group consists of bureaucrats. This originally arose in the LDP when Yoshida packed the party's ranks with bureaucrats to replace the purged politicians and also to guard his flanks. Among these bureaucrats, some rose to the highest positions, including Kishi,

Sato, Fukuda and Ohira. This enabled them to recruit further classes of bureaucrats, many from Finance but others from Construction, Agriculture, Posts and Communications, etc. Voters apparently had a latent respect for officialdom and felt that their connections could be useful in winning public works projects and state subsidies. Most of the ex-bureaucrats were enrolled by the LDP. But some were also absorbed by middle-of-the-road parties, albeit in smaller numbers.

Their counterpart in the "progressive" camp has been party officials or trade union leaders. Nearly half of the JSP's Diet members have a trade union background, mainly from Sohyo-affiliated unions, and a smaller share of the DSP, these usually related to Domei. The biggest batch comes from public sector unions, especially the Japan Teachers' Union and National Railway Workers' Union. The Communists also field trade unionists in elections, although these are often dissidents from Sohyo and Domei, running without a union endorsement and often against the official union candidates. The Communists, and the Socialists to a lesser extent, also coopt their own party officials for political assignments in preference to other possible candidates. Similarly, Komeito recruits Soka Gakkai officials.

A fair number of Diet members come from a rather unusual background. They are what are locally called *talento* or celebrities, namely famous authors, actors, comedians, television commentators and the like. Relatively well known through their professional activities, they can succeed in politics because they are popular and attract votes. Most were invited to run by the LDP, although other parties, including the JCP, have used this gimmick. Some few went into politics because they were tired of the way the parties operate and wished to offer an alternative. *Talento* were quite numerous during the 1970s, especially in House of Councillors national constituency seats, since they were widely known. But, by eliminating those seats and forcing members to join parties, the pros squeezed many of them out.

There is one final source of political personnel whose significance has grown of late. This is due to the notable increase in the ranks of sons (and other relatives) of politicians with well over a hundred "second generation" Diet members at present. To this may be added a growing contingent of former secretaries or assistants who succeeded their boss when he retired. Such arrangements arose most often in rural and peripheral districts, but not only there. While these types are especially prolific in the LDP, they can be found in all parties. Obviously, with existing politicians picking their heirs there is less chance than ever of bringing in new blood.[12]

What is amazing is the modest number of those who enter politics from other trades and professions, including those which are frequently major sources abroad. Relatively few are former lawyers, accountants, academics, journalists or even company executives. This latter group has had some moderate success in recent years and one factional leader was particularly prominent in business circles, Toshio Komoto. Tanaka is also a businessman of sorts. And Shintaro Abe is an ex-journalist. If few such are recruited into the LDP, even fewer have found their way into the other parties. There are not many "proletarians" among the Socialists and Communists, although there are numerous Soka Gakkai laymen in Komeito. As for women, they have gotten short shrift and there are actually less in politics now than thirty years ago, with more on the left than the right.

There is another gap which is even more ominous. There are dreadfully few people who enter politics because they are moved by the plight of their fellow citizens

Background of candidates for election to the House of Representatives.

The age of cooptation.

	LDP	Komeito	JSP	DSP	JCP	Other	Total
Local Government	81	2	51	16	7	6	163
Second-generation	96	2	11	7	0	7	123
Diet member's secretaries	75	3	13	7	1	8	107
Organized labor	0	0	63	10	1	4	78
Central bureaucracy	60	1	1	2	0	4	68
Law	11	3	5	0	8	1	28

Source: Asahi Election Almanac.

Note: There is some double counting due to candidates with several backgrounds.

or think they can provide better solutions to the challenges Japan is facing. None of the parties are really open to persons with strong convictions or who plead a cause, even if it is their own cause. Rather, there is a definite tendency for the parties to go out and recruit new members from among those who obviously hold similar views but whose views are not very pronounced. As in other institutions, the party will provide the necessary training, whether through example and osmosis or formal education and indoctrination.

All this makes politicians a rather closed and inbred (perhaps even incestuous) band. They carefully control most forms of access to the profession and strive to coopt any newcomers. Moreover, there is a noteworthy tendency for politics to turn into a "second job" for bureaucrats and party officials or a "family trade" for sons and relatives. This alone makes it increasingly difficult for Japan to generate dedicated and principled leaders.

It would not be quite as bad if the politicians at least looked outward and mixed regularly with the rest of society. Alas, they are more set in their ways than many other segments of the population and tend to mix only with their own kind or those who can help them in their tasks. The relations between politicians and bureaucrats or businessmen are extremely close, perhaps too close. This applies mainly to the LDP which is the only party that has been in power and therefore has to consider the views of these sectors. The other parties associate largely with their own clientele, trade unions, party officials, laymen, small businessmen or whatever. But they tend to ignore or snub those outside these restricted circles to an incredible extent. It took until the 1980s for the LDP to bother consulting with trade unionists. And Ishibashi was the first JSP leader to invite businessmen to speak at party seminars. This was hardly a way of getting to know the needs of a broad cross-section of the population which might be regarded as a valid task of any politician.

There have also been amazingly few contacts between members of opposing parties and even between members of supposedly friendly parties thinking seriously of creating a coalition. Many of them, by the way, took place in secret and were only discovered when the news was leaked to the press. These meetings were usually held at a very high level and involved very few people, often just one or two representatives of each party. This was hardly a way of building bridges. As for the LDP's relations with its opponents, much of this was also done under cover and not very frequently. Not until parity came about was such a thing encouraged in the Diet since it was necessary to gain some outside support to adopt crucial legislation. And Fukuda was the first to meet officially with the heads of certain opposition parties, albeit rarely and briefly. This is indeed a strange situation for a country which prides itself on harmony and consensus.

Given the narrow range of views of LDP members, it might have been expected that the ruling party should create numerous advisory bodies or regularly consult think tanks to tap the knowhow and insight that could not be obtained from within. Yet, until Nakasone's term, this path was hardly ever taken. Now some such bodies finally exist. Alas, most of them consist of hand-picked members whose views are known to be sympathetic and who are unlikely to put forward suggestions without first clearing them with the prime minister. As for actually appointing ministers from outside the party, something that is quite common in other countries and is not prevented by the constitution, such an act was extremely rare. In fact, there have been only a handful of non-politicians in such posts including more recently Michio Nagai in Education and Saburo Okita in Foreign Affairs. The problem is not only dealing with outsiders, which is painful enough, but that the number of portfolios is limited and party members are intent on keeping them for themselves. Indeed, it proved difficult to reserve a ministerial post for the NLC when it joined a coalition.

Finally, what about relations with the people? Appearances of the prime minister or other ministers in public are very few and far between. They do attend high level meetings and make speeches at ceremonies, they are occasionally interviewed by the press, and one can catch a glimpse of them on television. But these are all carefully staged and not impromptu debates in which they might make spontaneous comments. The only exception was Tanaka who held periodic TV "chats" with the public at large, a practice he soon gave up. Other leaders have been more aloof or inaccessible. Moreover, even when they did appear in public, it was hardly to take the people into their confidence and explain what national policy was and why. Most statements were so vague and ambiguous that the listeners knew little more than before.

If politics is no longer a calling or a crusade, there must be some reason for people to enter the profession. To some extent, this doubtlessly derives from the prestige and status of politicians. While, for traditional reasons, they must bow to the lowliest, they are indeed a superior lot in that they decide how the town, prefecture or nation will be run. And they are accorded at least formal respect. In addition, it is clear that they enjoy a certain degree of power in performing their duties. They can decide how monies are spent, where public works are directed, or what economic, defense or foreign policies will be adopted. Power has always attracted people and in Japan, where it is so hard to attain, its attraction may be even greater.

There are also the salaries, emoluments and perquisites.

Diet members receive a handsome wage and bonuses, not a fortune mind you, but much more than the average person (¥ 16 million in 1985). Many local assemblymen do almost as well (¥ 10-13 million). They also have allowances for travel, some staff, postal expenses and necessary equipment. Perks include chauffeur-driven cars and railway passes. They enjoy lavish wining and dining, special "seminars" at hot springs and summer resorts, and periodic junkets abroad. And politics need not be the only thing they engage in. There seem to be few restrictions on running a business on the side or even working for pressure groups, lobbies and companies which are interested in better relations with the government. Then there is the odd bribe or kickback. However the money is obtained, it is perfectly evident that most politicians are faring quite well and some have become absolutely rich.

It would probably not matter quite as much whether Japanese politicians are paid more or less than their foreign counterparts or even paid more than they are worth if there were not so many of them. Alas, over the years, the race has been multiplying at a terrific pace. By now, there are 764 Diet members while the American Congress, serving a population twice as large, has only 535. The situation is far worse on the local level with Japanese cities having anywhere from five to fifty times more council members than their American sister cities. The reason why there are so many politicians is not chance or the will of the people. It was decided by the politicians themselves. They were the ones who created or expanded the various organs and determined how many members there should be. Doubtlessly thinking of themselves and their heirs, they made the seats as numerous as possible.

While getting into political circuits and winning elections may require some personal initiative and ability, the situation thereafter is considerably more structured and stable. As in most Japanese institutions, promotion is based on seniority. All freshmen Diet or other assembly members are regarded as being in the first grade. Each time they are returned, they move up one grade. Each grade brings them closer to choice assignments and political power as such. Losing an election, aside from the fact that one might not get back in, means an interruption in this rise, bumpier progress and a loss of face. While seniority applies in many other parliaments as well, it is particularly regimented in Japan and various customs and traditions make it harder to step out of line.

Naturally, the personal element does play a certain role. Some are too dull to be entrusted with important tasks and others a bit smarter than average. But it is rarely ability and even less often the policies one propounds which help in accelerating the normal ascension. Connections are considerably more useful. This can include the old school tie, with many graduates from Tokyo and Waseda Universities in the political world as well. Even more useful is a bureaucratic tie through the former ministry. And there are also family connections, given the number of sons, sons-in-law and other relatives around. The most notable case is the Kishi dynasty, since Prime Ministers Kishi and Sato were brothers and now elder stateman Kishi is busily helping his son-in-law Shintaro Abe to reach the prime ministership. Otherwise, ranking politicians tend to adopt younger ones who meet their fancy and use them as assistants or lieutenants, giving them major posts before their time. Examples of this are Sato's aides Tanaka and Fukuda or Miyamoto's "prince" and now JCP Chairman Fuwa.

Neither the slow rise nor the favoritism were especially suited to cultivating new classes of dynamic and conscientious leaders. Younger politicians were severely discouraged from taking initiatives or even showing personal interests and many found that the best way to get ahead was to act as yes-men and flunkies. But it is not as if the oldsters were much better off. For, since no one in their immediate entourage had the guts to contradict them or even bring obvious inadequacies to their notice, they continued making foolish mistakes and often talked utter rubbish, to which their supporters gravely nodded assent, but which upset outsiders and the general public. Worse, this kind of atmosphere further reduced the chances of dealing with problems objectively and rationally while increasing the risks of personal clashes and loss of face.

This would have been less tedious if not for the increasingly time-consuming process of rising to the top. Japanese politicians can stay on as long as they care and relatively few resign, this most often at a ripe old age. In fact, the average age of Diet members is about 55 and mayors and governors are no younger. Those who hold on tightest are in the highest positions as shown by the ages of the LDP's factional heads or prime ministers, among the oldest national leaders in the world with most of them coming to power in their sixties and early seventies. The only exception was Kakuei Tanaka, then a precocious 54. Things were similar in other parties, aside from Komeito which has a retirement age of 63, and the JCP's Miyamoto only moved upstairs at the age of 73.

This created what is known as the problem of "change of generation." While it appears most prominently in the LDP, since these men may ultimately become prime minister, it exists throughout the political system. Elders cling to power and fear that once taking their hands off the levers they will be sharply reduced in influence and status. Few accept a decent retirement and only Miki and Suzuki stepped down gracefully to let Komoto and Miyazawa take over their faction. Tanaka, still a young man by

Japanese standards, cleverly played his lieutenants off against one another, Nikaido, Kanemaru, Takeshita, and so on. Even Fukuda hoped to make a comeback and stubbornly kept Abe down. This meant that the so-called "new leaders" had to wait until they were in their sixties or seventies to take power. Of course, a revolt was conceivable and much talked about since the early 1970s. But it never came off and was about as improbable as the aging crown prince forcefully replacing the aged emperor.

Given the similarity of their recruitment and the slow process they follow in rising to the top, there is a substantial—and increasing—similarity in the style and characteristics of Japanese politicians. In order to win favor, either with the electorate or their seniors, it is necessary to please. This means adopting a very low posture, bowing and scraping, and then providing the desired services. It is not easy to grab something from the "pork barrel," and that requires guile more than push since a frontal approach rarely works. Rather, it is necessary to develop a very broad circle of contacts in government and business and, through an exchange of favors, obtain the support one wants when it is most needed. The formation of such links, and using them to pull strings surreptitiously, involves the fine art of *nemawashi*. Over the years, such acts, frequently repeated, create a vast web of personal relations and loyalties or *jimmyaku,* which is the politician's main stock in trade.

It is not surprising that freshmen or junior politicians should have to work their way up slowly, although limitations on their activities are much greater in Japan due to a distaste for excessive individualism. What is more unusual is that senior politicians and even party executives and government officials are expected to adopt a relatively timid and withdrawn attitude. There is much stress in contemporary society on a willingness to hear one's juniors out, to listen to all possible alternatives, to slip into the emerging consensus.

For this reason, the more circumspect politicians do their best not to rock the boat and lay much stress on things like "patience," "tolerance" and "harmony," to borrow the slogans of former Prime Ministers Ikeda, Sato and Suzuki. They are reputed to have patiently waited until having heard the various views in the party (or at least the views of those who counted) before putting forward their own. In addition, just to play it safe, they might hold off with a solution in case the problem should disappear of its own. If it were still around and bothersome, they would then adopt a policy in the mainstream whether it was wise or foolish. Of course, the alternative was to foist one's own policies and views on the benighted masses or have them reflected from below by one's assistants. In this way, a leader could look as if he were following the *vox populi* and still do what he had always intended. The ability to manipulate others was, and still remains, the difference between the clumsy amateur and the true master of Japanese politics.

But it could hardly be claimed that a cautious and consensus-based approach was the "traditional" Japanese way. As a matter of fact, most of the early leaders were men of a very different mold. Yoshida was often criticized for his "one-man rule" and Kishi repeatedly got into quarrels with the opposition and his own party. Their successors were, on the whole, more subdued personalities. But Tanaka came to power billed as the "computerized bulldozer" and someone who could finally get things done and Nakasone made it abundantly clear that he had views of his own and even a long cherished program. Still, this approach was not really appreciated and both ended up in considerable trouble, more for reasons of attitude than policy. Tanaka was disliked for throwing his weight around and later accused of running the country through "plutocracy." Nakasone rubbed many people the wrong way due to his smoothness and internationalism while irritating his colleagues even more by his smugness.

Whatever the explanation, it would appear that Japan will have no further superstars and instead a race of standardized and mass-produced leaders in the future. There is no one among the "new leaders" who came into politics on his own, clawed his way to the top despite adversity, or even put together his own faction. The same applies to the other parties as well. All rising politicians are the understudies and protégés of existing leaders, often chosen because they were well-mannered and willing to labor in the shadows. They have been shaped by a society which more than ever fears those who stand out for any reason. And, by the time they ever make it to the top, they will be old men anyway. Yet, there is some fear among the ordinary people that these new figures will be too intellectual, articulate or rational, charges which could be made of an Abe or Miyazawa. While generally approved in other countries, these could be serious drawbacks for Japanese leaders who are not really expected to know what they want or why but feel and grope their way along.

Finally, whatever a Japanese leader wants or does, he is bound by the conventions and practicalities of the language. While it did not have to be that way, Japanese usage has turned toward vague and ambiguous expressions and stating anything too clearly or precisely is seen as vulgar or pushy. Thus, to get where he wishes, a leader is expected to fumble and mutter, bring out half an idea while holding the other half in abeyance until he knows how it will be received. Policies are put through disjointedly as hints, a few words now, a few words later, words that can be understood in various ways and retracted if necessary. Then, if the reaction is not too adverse or it is necessary to go ahead, the words are repeated time and again (and perhaps denied immediately thereafter) in order to create a mood even on such concrete issues as the budget or defense. While this gets by, and is generally accepted within the country, it creates sticky problems when foreign affairs are involved and others are listening.

All this, and much more, has engendered an almost permanent leadership crisis in Japan. For "leaders" are not really expected to lead in the conventional sense of looking ahead, spotting difficulties before others, taking urgent measures to ward them off or the like. They are not even supposed to warn of coming problems and define them too clearly, lest the public become worried and panic. This means that problems often creep up on the Japanese and, by the time their existence is officially acknowledged, they have grown to monumental proportions. That makes them even more difficult to solve than before and requires decisive action . . . which is the worst sort to attempt in a nation built on consensus.

What Do They Do?

Even if it is not the most scientific approach, there is a distinction commonly made between "small-time" and "big-time" politics. The former is personal and concrete, the latter more general and sometimes impalpable. For the former, efforts are usually restricted to the direct electorate while the latter has to englobe the whole national, and conceivably even international, community. The former involves day-to-day needs and activities, the latter is geared to a much longer time frame.

In Japan, there is tremendous concern with small-time politics. Politicians *must* know how to satisfy the concrete needs of their constituency, or at least the portion thereof that votes for them or can be regarded as their clientele.

They *must* establish very close and personal relations with the people who count and spend an inordinate amount of time in finding out just what they want. They *must* then go to extreme lengths to fulfill many of these putative needs without much concern as to whether they are justified or not.

Some of them could normally be regarded as lying squarely within the political realm, such as requests for better water, sewage, schooling, police protection or the like. This can be obtained most often through a suitable allocation of local or national funds which they will try to influence. Given the importance of the central government, and the extent to which local expenditures are subsidized, this may force them to work at both ends. Their primary concern here is to get as much out of the "pork barrel" as possible and they will be judged by their success in doing so. While not the noblest form of political endeavor, it is certainy an indispensable one and in Japan it probably rates much higher than elsewhere.

But Japanese politicians are also tied down with any number of tasks that their foreign counterparts might reject as superfluous or demeaning. For, given the stress on human relations, they have to take care of all sorts of relatively personal requests. This includes not only finding jobs for their constituents' children but getting them into good high schools and colleges. They are regularly asked to settle traffic violations or deal with the tax authorities. They are also expected to help small businessmen find work and big businessmen to avoid bothersome formalities and regulations. It is wise to attend sundry funerals and weddings, leaving incense money at the former and a gift at the latter.

In order to handle such matters, it is essential for politicians to seize all possible opportunities to spread their circle of useful contacts who can help get things done. Foremost are bureaucrats at various levels who work in the ministries concerned with the assorted tasks they undertake, Construction, Posts and Communications, Education and so on. This starts at the top and works its way down to the local level since a wish could be granted above and yet intercepted or ignored below. They also have to know a fair number of businessmen who can help in their own way, by locating factories in their constituency, recruiting more personnel, and so on.

It is even more important to maintain good relations with other members of their own party and, in most cases, of whatever faction they belong to. Individually, they are most unlikely to accomplish much whereas, by joining with one another or, more likely, helping the others in return for help when they need it, they can impress their wishes on the government, bureaucracy and business community. Since their own strength depends very much on the relative strength of their faction, they will engage in the interminable factional rivalries and try to increase its ranks. They also have to pitch in to improve the position of their party.

Aside from this, there is the vital matter of getting elected and then reelected.[13] For, although there is no such obligation, Diet elections have been uncommonly frequent and members may have to campaign every two years or so. In Japan, this does not so much imply working out an appealing platform as going out and finding the voters. Since door-to-door canvassing and radio or television campaigning are restricted, it is a matter of driving around in a loudspeaker van, making brief appearances at crowded intersections or train stations and holding countless meetings and conferences. The message is usually quite simple: "vote for me, my name is such-and-so, I am with the such-and-such party." He may just add what he has gotten his constituency in the past and intends to bring home this time. Time constraints make it hard to do more and there does not seem to be overly much interest in policies anyway. Just how insipid electioneering can be is best illustrated by posters which show pretty girls or babies and stress image rather than concrete goals.[14]

Of course, it takes money to run. Lots of money. So, much of each party's energy goes into raising funds. While the JCP and Komeito have regular sources in the form of membership fees and sales of their publications, this has to be supplemented by political donations *(kifu),* which are the primary source for the LDP, NLC, DSP and JSP. The former obtain most of their funding from private companies; the latter from trade unions. From year to year, more political funds have been collected, breaking the ¥100 billion barrier in 1980 and exceeding ¥210 billion in 1984. Officially, the biggest income was obtained by the JCP, with the LDP in second place, followed by Komeito, JSP and DSP. But due to monies collected by its factions and other sources that were never reported, the LDP unquestionably did much better than any other party and probably all of the others put together.

Some of this money trickled down to ordinary politicians who usually received a sum of a million or more yen from their party and faction leaders. But it was impossible to run a campaign on that sort of money . . . or even ten times as much. The costs were truly astronomical. In relatively safe or small districts they might get by with ¥100 million or so. In larger constituencies or tighter races, the bill could rise to ¥500 million and even ¥1 billion for the Lower House. For the Upper House, it was estimated that ¥300 million was par for the course in the mid-1970s and perhaps ¥900 million a decade later.

Thus, politicians had to engage in endless fund-raising exercises of their own. They would include rallies, parties and other events to celebrate one occasion or another or more direct appeals for aid to local merchants or manufacturers. This was particularly effective for LDP members who had something to offer in return. The pickings were much leaner for the others who had to count on labor or civic organizations or donations from like-minded citizens or friends and relatives. Every possible stratagem was tried to fill the coffers, especially at election time. For the amount of money they could tap was often decisive in determining the outcome, all the more so since campaigns were based more on a soft sell than hard policies.

This explains why political success is usually traced to the "three *ban*:" *jiban* (electoral support), *kaban* (bag loaded with money) and *kanban* (reputation). The first thing a politician has to do is to win elections, usually by meeting the political or material demands of voters. This is not a simple matter and requires considerable organization, since an amazingly large share of it is done on an almost personal basis. Providing such assistance and, even more so, mounting election campaigns, is very expensive and cannot possibly be done without ample funds. By providing such services year in and year out, a politician can acquire a favorable reputation. In this way, many parliamentarians manage to be returned five, ten and more times. Mayors and governors are even harder to dislodge once they are elected.

Naturally, politicians have to mobilize the voters and, to this end, most have established a local *koenkai* or support organization.[15] Some of the membership consists of individuals who back the politician's program while others are really just "bosses" who can swing the votes of groups they control such as farm cooperatives, chambers of commerce, trade unions or cultural clubs. Unlike local party chapters in other countries, however, the *koenkai* is a direct emanation of the politician, mounted and often financed by him and used to enhance his popularity. It

Bowing low to the voters, shoppers and other passers-by during election season.

Credit: Foreign Press Center/Kyodo

may hold rallies, meetings and seminars in nearby luxury hotels or hot springs resorts. In exchange for listening to what he has to say, the participants often receive a gift on parting. This makes the organization a drain which has to be met, along with the other expenses, by soliciting funds from diverse sources.

Naturally, a major source of both funds and electoral support is the political party and, in most cases, also a faction. They usually distribute annual contributions and a special amount during electoral campaigns. They can be even more instrumental in helping to obtain public works or state subsidies to reward the local electorate and supporters. Thus, a party endorsement is precious and can be especially valuable in relatively safe fiefs. An independent has much more trouble acquiring the "three *ban*" and this explains why so few go it alone.

There is no doubt that most Japanese politicians are first

rate when it comes to small-time politics and catering to the specific interests of their constituency. They would not long remain in office otherwise. But these tasks are so demanding that there is relatively little energy left over for big-time politics. Constantly engaged in meeting people, exchanging favors, getting something from the "pork barrel," the politician of any party has little enough time to think of broader or higher things. Beset with the hopes and desires of his local backers, he can rarely devote himself to regional or national, let alone international, affairs. It is thus that most remain nothing more than professionals for the best, hacks and politicos for the less distinguished, while scarcely any ever rise to the heights of statesmen.

Politicians are therefore, on the whole, brokers for their electors and certain pressure groups or lobbies. That becomes the sum total of their political action and, when they are faced with more fundamental or loftier matters, they do not quite know how to react. This is most unfortunate since it is still essential to have these other aspects which provide the general framework for everything else. No amount of petty politics, no matter how fruitful or how much desired by the populace, can entirely replace the higher level of politics.

When trying to explain this lack, which already became apparent in discussing the programs of parties and activities of politicians, part of the blame can be placed on the intense concentration on small-time politics. But there is another reason, actually a more essential one. Most politicians do not really have much knowledge of policy issues or even much inclination for such things. As noted, a fair number have been recruited into the parties and simply absorb whatever the prevailing ideas are. Rather few have gone into politics with personal goals or ideals and these they have to keep pretty much a secret until they are finally in a position to act on them. Moreover, since there is strict party discipline in voting, there would be little room for variance. More serious, the public at large does not really seem that interested in what a politician's stand on broader issues is and rather holds him to routine tasks and responsibilities of direct and concrete benefit.

Naturally, policy can and is being worked out by the political parties all the time. But this is restricted to relatively small circles of party executives and bosses and what is decided is only made known to the rank-and-file when there is little that can be done to alter it. There is almost no open and frank debate on party policy at any level or at any time. This includes the party congresses and conferences which are carefully choreographed in advance. Even the questions that are raised have usually been prepared and are formulated so as not to pick fault but rather allow the dignitary to expound more fully on the excellence of his propositions.

More disconcerting, what generally passes for policy remains exceedingly shallow. It is little more than broad principles about the general direction the nation should take. It is frequently brief and goes into few details. Worse, there may be any number of inconsistencies and contradictions which are never resolved and whose existence almost goes unnoticed. In addition, most of the basic programs are already regarded as obsolete by those who proclaimed them. From this, it must be concluded that Japanese parties do not really regard fixed and durable policy that highly and do not want anything that can tie them down. They much prefer loose statements of philosophy that can be interpreted any which way as time passes and interests change.

While relatively sketchy and wishy-washy platforms are the norm in political circles and appear with great frequency around the world, legislation is quite another matter. The laws that govern the state must be laid down as carefully and precisely as possible if its machinery is to operate with any degree of smoothness. Nowadays, many of these laws must also be extremely detailed and take into account highly technical aspects. This requires a completely different approach and a good deal of competence and expertise. And that is where they get into serious trouble.

Those who are expected to take the leadership here are the politicians and the parties they belong to. So, it is worthwhile looking at the efforts which are made to this end, especially in the Liberal Democratic Party.

The LDP has an extensive committee system designed to deal with every possible issue. Most of it comes under the Policy Affairs Research Council (PARC) and its decision-making organ, the Policy Deliberation Commission, which has dozens of divisions and subgroups. However, they meet only once or twice a week even during Diet sessions and consist of anywhere from thirty to well over a hundred members, which makes it quite impossible for them to deliberate efficiently. It is equally impossible for the LDP to service so many bodies and handle its other political and administrative tasks with a staff of less than 300 officials.

Thus, most of the powers have been assumed by small groups or "cliques" (zoku) of influential politicians, usually those who previously held posts as minister, vice-minister or head of a Diet committee or council division. Essential budgetary decisions, the crucial point for most, are taken by the three top party executives, the secretary general, Executive Council chairman and PARC chairman. The many divisions and subgroups thereby become little more than forums where ordinary LDP Diet members can be notified of pending legislation by the party's leaders or bureaucrats. Yet, even the "cliques" or executives do not truly formulate legislation. They simply express general desires or issue broad guidelines and look after some particularly sensitive matters.

It could not really be otherwise since none of the LDP bodies have a sufficient research staff to gather the basic information or make concrete and detailed proposals. The individual Diet members, of all parties, are even worse off. They only receive allowances and permits for two or three regular assistants and a tiny office which could hardly accommodate more. This could be expanded only if they were to pay out of their own pockets, a step hardly anyone takes. This makes it absolutely impossible for them to get the expert assistance they need to do a proper job. And it can be concluded that, aside from some items of special importance to their constituency, they cannot really follow the Diet proceedings very intelligently or vote in full knowledge of what they are doing.[16]

It could not even be said that the situation is that much better for the ministers, although they are major participants. They also have to devote more time to routine political activities than broader policy, although they may be relieved of some of that load while they are in office. But they cannot be freed of the need to maintain good relations with their colleagues. Actually, their responsibilities make this more vital than ever, for factional strife and backbiting have usually been a greater threat than complaints from the opposition. Before making any proposals, they must engage in very extensive and delicate negotiations, not in large or formal bodies, but basically on a one-to-one basis in the traditional *nemawashi* form. They must avoid disturbing the many varied interests of prominent colleagues or stepping on the toes of their predecessors in the post.

When it comes to ability, it could scarcely be claimed that cabinet members are of a particularly high caliber. They were not, at least initially, chosen by their constituency for broad concern or in-depth knowledge and often look upon their ministerial activities as a means of fulfilling local needs. They most often lack expertise in the sector they are assigned to and this is further aggravated by the rather haphazard rotation from one post to another. The more varied a person's background, the easier it is to rise in national politics, but this makes for amateurism and incompetence. That is particularly true since the rotation is not only incessant but at short intervals. Since so many politicians have to be offered a portfolio, it is impossible to remain minister for long and therefore cabinet reshuffles occur almost every year. Even quick learners rarely have the time to properly understand the basic issues and get along with the ministry personnel, let alone impose the party's position on their underlings.

This has resulted in a motley array of ministers, most of them appearing for the first—and perhaps only—time. Few have shown any brilliance. In some cases, the person appointed was inappropriate because of insufficient talent, interest or ability in the given field. In others, he was the wrong man because he was personally involved in some of the pending legislation or was known to represent special interests. A previous bureaucratic career, by the way, was no proof that the person knew much about the basic issues or was free from bias. Only in more fortunate, and rare, cases could one speak of relatively competent or conscientious ministers, such as Fukuda and Ohira in Finance, Abe and Miyazawa in Foreign Affairs, or Komoto in EPA. And even then it was a bit much to bill them, as was frequently done, as "financial wizards" or "economic czars." Quite to the contrary, most ministers were not able to do more than go through the motions (if properly coached) and avoid the worst.[17]

Similar observations can be made about the defects of Japan's prime ministers. They were selected on the basis of factional balance. But the ability to raise a large following or negotiate alliances with other bosses is not necessarily a sign of competence in dealing with more concrete national issues. Few prime ministers had a personal program aside from Yoshida, Ikeda, Nakasone and perhaps Tanaka, so they tended to float with the tide and follow the crowd rather than lead. In addition, very few stayed in office long enough to carry out any program given the slowness of the Japanese decision-making process. With the number of terms as party president limited to two, it is now extremely difficult for anyone to be prime minister longer than four years, which is quite short. And most prime ministers in recent years only stayed an often tumultuous two years.

What is even more debilitating is that most prime ministers have not really controlled their own cabinets. Only a minority of the portfolios are held by members of their own faction who are their subordinates and on whom they can count. Most other ministers are drawn from factions which may be allies at the time of appointment but can easily become rivals a bit later. And some are even aspiring prime ministers who look forward to the demise of the existing government. Moreover, many of the cabinet members have personal interests, a clientele to promote and a strong desire to make a name for themselves which leads them to take all sorts of independent initiatives. With cabinets lasting only a year or two, the worst dissidents can be quickly dropped. But there is no time to turn this essential institution into a tool for strong or unified policy.

Lack of knowledge, lack of supervision, and lack of time of the individual politicians certainly hamper the work of the Diet and cabinet. But there are other problems which have arisen in the sheer mechanics of processing legislation. The Diet has to meet for a 150-day session which traditionally starts in December and almost immediately recesses for about a month due to the New Year's holiday and then later on for the "Golden Week." There are no debates on Mondays or Saturdays. And most committees meet only two or three times a week. Since they deal with many subjects, it can easily happen that even important bills are debated only once a week. The session can be extended, but that is strongly resisted by the opposition. At any rate, the limited time is poorly spent and much of it is wasted.[18]

Within this much truncated period, it is customary to spend some months debating the budget with little time left over for other bills. During this debate, the whole cabinet is required to be present, not only those whose allocations are being considered, and the prime minister is expected to be available for many other debates as well. This means that the government is often tied up in Diet proceedings and can spend much less time supervising the bureaucracy, traveling abroad or meeting important foreign visitors and, in general, engaging in considerably more useful tasks.

As for the debates, they hardly merit the name. They are formal and stilted, questions are placed by the ruling party to make its proposals look good or by the opposition to make the ministers look bad. Few are pertinent or even designed to bring about amendments. If the opposition objects, it is more likely to delay the proceedings in order to embarrass the prime minister and induce the LDP to accept private compromises. This can involve pointless interpellations, dragging out the voting procedure, or boycotting meetings. Such tactics obviously exist in every democratic assembly and are not exclusive to Japan. The real difference is that there is almost no substantive debate to clarify the purposes and likely effects of legislation.

Shortly after the war, when the conservatives had a

large majority and prime ministers were more vigorous in pursuing their aims, the Diet was often in a turmoil as an equally adamant opposition tried to prevent controversial legislation. The debates were downright acrimonious and, on occasion, members engaged in open quarrels and fist fights to block voting. The LDP would then ram through any desired legislation, heatedly accused of abusing the "dictatorship of the majority," but still getting what it wanted. Ever since parity was attained, the LDP has had to be more circumspect since it could not so easily railroad issues. Instead, it would moderate the initial bills and eventually accept minor amendments to make the opposition happy and bring about a smoother acceptance. This has indeed expedited the Diet's work somewhat. But it is still a rather inefficient body which approves only about a hundred bills a year while many essential ones have to be postponed another year or two.

This rather mediocre performance of the national leadership, by the way, was still immensely superior to the situation in the prefectures, cities, towns and villages. They also had local assemblies inhabited by local politicians who were empowered to legislate on local issues. Elected by even smaller units, where personal connections and special interests were even more prominent, the scope for wheeling and dealing was even broader and "pork barrel" politics became the name of the game. With even less knowhow, and less capable assistance, local representatives found it yet harder to adopt legislations and supervise the implementation thereof. The biggest drawback, however, was that at the local level political parties hardly functioned and policies or programs were even more conspicuous by their absence.

NOTES

1. Further background on these movements can be found in John Crump, *The Origins of Socialist Thought in Japan,* and Robert A. Scalapino, *The Early Japanese Labor Movement.*
2. For further details, see among others, Robert A. Scalapino and Junnosuke Masumi, *Parties and Politics in Contemporary Japan,* and Robert E. Ward, *Japan's Political System.*
3. The Ikeda and Sato periods are covered in Frank Langdon, *Politics in Japan.*
4. For a closer view of the "reverse course," see Maki, *op. cit.,* pp. 181–212.
5. See Kurt Stein et al. (eds.), *Political Opposition and Local Politics in Japan.*
6. For more on the LDP, see Haruhiro Fukui, *Party in Power: The Japanese Liberal Democrats and Policy-Making,* and Nathaniel B. Thayer, *How The Conservatives Rule Japan.*
7. Ezra Vogel vaunts the effectiveness of this arrangement. "By letting LDP leaders select the prime minister from among themselves, the Japanese do not risk the election of a top official who has charismatic appeal but is unable to work effectively in the central government." *(Japan as No. 1,* p. 64.) But, is it democratic?
8. It is rumored that as much as $400 million was spent on the 1972 election, about half of it by the Tanaka faction. *(No. 1 Shimbun,* Tokyo, December 1984.) Very large sums, even if not quite as astronomical, changed hands at most other elections as well.
9. The reason for such a smooth transition was apparently a secret deal between Kishi and Ikeda. It was therefore not quite a sign of the party's maturity.
10. Just how bitter relations could be was shown by the fact that feuding faction heads, although members of the same party, might not meet personally for years on end as occurred for Tanaka with Fukuda and Miki.
11. Even this was not a true break with the past since both men were protégés of Kasuga.
12. Among those who helped their relatives enter politics are Saburo Eda, Takeo Fukuda, Shigeru Hori, Yasuhiro Nakasone, Etsusaburo Shiina, Eisaku Sato, Shigeru Yoshida and dozens more.
13. This crucial aspect is dealt with by Ronald J. Hrebenar, *Japanese Political Parties and their Electoral Environment.*
14. The rigors of the campaign trail are described in Gerald L. Curtis, *Election Campaigning Japanese Style.*
15. For more about *koenkai,* see Curtis, *op. cit.,* pp. 126–52.
16. This compares with American Congressmen who have dozens of assistants and access to the Congressional Research Service, Government Accounting Office, etc.

17. See Yung H. Park, *Bureaucrats and Ministers in Contemporary Japanese Government.*

18. According to a *Yomiuri* survey of June 15, 1985, of the total respondents 35% felt that the Diet did not deliberate enough on important bills and another 12% that the deliberations were "totally insufficient." They also expressed a sentiment that the citizens' views were poorly reflected in the Diet.

3
The Bureaucrats

The Bureaucracy Carries On

If control of the government were left solely in the hands of the politicians, as the constitution decrees, it is unlikely that Japan would have become a modern state. There are simply too many gaps and inadequacies which would have to be compensated for by others. In the past, especially since Meiji days, this had been the role of the bureaucrats. Officials not only kept the administrative machinery running smoothly, in various ways they also determined the direction. After the war, SCAP recognized the bureaucracy's importance but tried to limit its prerogatives so that it might dutifully serve the elected leadership. This was to be done through a comprehensive "democratization" of the system, one it was assumed would be irreversible.

However, some significant changes were made. First was to reduce the power of the Home Ministry, which had been at the core of the nationalist regime and which not only suppressed the political parties, trade unions and media but also imposed its will on local bodies. Its successor was sharply diminished as regards its competences and size. On the other hand, the local authorities were given much broader functions and more authority than they ever possessed before in order to create a greater balance between the central government and local autonomies.

Other reforms were introduced to make the bureaucrats more responsive to the public, along the lines of the civil service in places like the United States. Their prerogatives were reduced and they were brought under more direct control of the nation's elected officials. Remedies were provided for private citizens who had complaints or grievances. The merit system was adopted for recruitment and promotion. And the old elite spirit was strongly discouraged so that public employees would regard themselves merely as "servants" of the people.

Nevertheless, since the reforms were rather limited and frequently circumvented, there was a definite continuity between the old and new.[1] The most decisive link was quite simply the personnel. Although nationalists were purged from the political parties, this was not done very thoroughly in the administration. SCAP needed people who could run the machinery and it was naively assumed that the bureaucrats were just executing orders from above. In actuality, they were very much a part of the nationalist system and some were intimately involved in drafting and applying the repressive measures or running the war economy. Yet, most of them stayed on or returned after the Occupation. Holding top posts, they could readily foist some of their views on younger colleagues.[2]

Thus, it would be even more difficult to speak of a fresh start for the bureaucracy than for the political parties. It did have some new and improved features. But it also had older traditions, some of which were highly undemocratic. Worse, it retained a larger share of old-style officials who were more reactionary than many politicians and, unlike politicians, did not face an opposition. That the Japanese public itself was not entirely convinced by the mutation is shown by the continuing reference to "bureaucrats" (kanryo) as opposed to "civil servants," a practice that will be followed here.

During most of the postwar period, the central government has been served by roughly twenty ministries and agencies. The former are, in alphabetical order, Ministry of Agriculture, Forestry and Fisheries (MAFF), Ministry of Construction (MOC), Ministry of Education (MOE), Ministry of Finance (MOF), Ministry of Health and Welfare (MHW), Ministry of Foreign Affairs (MFA), Ministry of Home Affairs (MHA), Ministry of International Trade and Industry (MITI), Ministry of Justice (MOJ), Ministry of Labor (MOL), Ministry of Posts and Telecommunications (MPT), and Ministry of Transport (MOT). The latter are presently the Defense Agency (DA), Economic Planning Agency (EPA), Environment Agency (EA), National Land Agency (NLA), Science and Technology Agency (STA), and a new Management and Coordination Agency (MCA) which replaces the earlier Prime Minister's Office and Administrative Management Agency.[3]

In addition to this, there are about a hundred special corporations or special juridical persons *(tokushu hojin)*, taking half-a-dozen different forms, usually referred to as "public corporations." They include major companies like the Japanese National Railways (JNR), Tobacco and Salt Public Corporation, Nippon Telegraph and Telephone (NTT) and Kokusai Denshin Denwa (KDD).[4] Others are smaller and sometimes more specialized, such as the Japan Housing Corporation (JHC), Japan Highway Corporation, Japan Railway Construction Corporation (JRCC) and assorted bodies to build expressways, bridges and airports or promote regional development and social uplift as well as one body to channel foreign aid, the Overseas Economic Cooperation Fund (OECF).

Then come the various local authorities. Japan consists of 47 prefectures, some of which are also leading cities like Tokyo, Kyoto and Osaka. Like the other major cities, they are all divided into districts known as wards. Then come several thousand towns and villages. This adds up to some 3,300 "local autonomies," a rather large number for a country as small as Japan. And each one of them has its own bureaucracy to handle the related administrative work and perhaps some public corporations as well. While concerned with the well-being of their own population, they also spend much time liaising with the central government from which essential subsidies are derived.[5]

While each of these many units is relatively independent, there are particularly close relations among some of them and they fall into an informal ranking. Ministries and agencies of the central government naturally take precedence over local bodies, no matter what the rules may say, due to time-honored traditions and also subsidies the local autonomies have become dependent on. In this way, the Ministry of Home Affairs has reasserted some of its earlier influence. The public corporations are directly or indirectly subject to some ministerial body in charge of their sector, as the JNR and JRCC to the MOT or the banks to MOF. Some of the newer agencies must pay homage to older bodies, as the EPA to MITI and MOF and EA to MITI. At the top of the pecking order is MOF, due to its inherited prestige and budgetary authority. Another leading body is MITI. But well-established ministries, with solid backing from specific sectors, like MOC or MAFF, are quite autonomous.

Such extensive machinery naturally requires extensive staffing. By the mid-1980s, the bureaucracy consisted of about a million employees of the central government, another million of the public corporations and 3.3 million of the local autonomies. There were a further quarter-of-a-million in the Self-Defense Forces. While a seemingly large number for a country the size of Japan, it was hardly excessive for an advanced country and could have been justified if properly distributed among the various sectors.

That this was not always the case was most evident for agriculture, a declining field with far too many staff, and education or welfare, without enough. There was also a plethora of local employees for what remained a fairly centralized state.

Recruitment to the administration is a very serious matter in Japan and strenuous efforts are made to ensure objectivity and impartiality. With a long Confucian tradition, it is not surprising that extremely strict examinations should form the basis. Every year such examinations are held and entry is open to graduates of every possible high school or university (depending on the level) and persons of every possible social or economic background. Indeed, two sets of examinations are held. One is to induct the higher civil servants and the other to recruit the much more numerous and more ordinary categories of civil servants and employees.

This would seem to be the fairest way. Everyone gets a crack at the same examinations and the best ones pass. However, since the tests follow a pattern, and certain schools adapt their curricula to that pattern, there has been an unmistakable tendency for the graduates of certain colleges to be disproportionately prevalent. Most prominent among them is the University of Tokyo (Todai), followed by other leading state universities, such as Kyoto (Kyodai) and Hitotsubashi. The share of private colleges, even the finest, is smaller, although Keio and Waseda do quite well. A large portion of the candidates at all schools comes from the law faculty. For the central government, there is little chance of connections or favoritism playing a role. On the local level, that is far from a hard-and-fast rule and there are many ways of landing a job even if one did not do so well on the exam (or had none).[6]

While the initial screening is rigorous, the same cannot be said of what happens thereafter. Promotion is on the basis of seniority to a large extent and most bureaucrats rise at about the same pace during the first ten or twenty years. But they are gradually sorted out and only one in ten or twenty will make it to top posts. The sorting is not based on tests nor is it particularly objective. True, ability plays some role and most, but not all, incompetents get weeded out. More crucial is the contacts one makes, the faction one joins, and whether this mutual aid group manages to elbow out the others or be discarded itself. While not decisive, it is during this latter phase that Todai or Kyodai credentials are especially valuable for they help in making the right connections.

Training of the bureaucracy is another important process. It is not only lengthy and comprehensive, it is indispensable since most of the new crop of bureaucrats do not possess any of the skills or knowhow they will need to perform their tasks competently. Japanese university education, even at the law faculty (which is not quite a law school), imparts little more than general knowledge. And, as is increasingly well documented, many university students do not work that hard, although those aiming for the higher civil service may be exceptions. Moreover, there is no specialized school for training officials, like France's Ecole Nationale d'Administration, and thus the initiates usually have not the slightest idea of what is expected of them.

Therefore, in a system distinctly reminiscent of both medieval apprenticeship and the method used in modern Japanese corporations, the newcomers will be rotated from job to job in order to get to know the ministry or agency. They may also be sent to external offices or subsidiaries. The best known routine occurs in the Ministry of Finance, whose recruits are turned into what is loosely called the "elite of the elite."

Junior bureaucrats spend their first year just helping out

older officials and adjusting to the atmosphere. In their second and third years, they study economics and finance or go abroad to learn some of the technical skills. In the fourth, they already get appointed as section chief *(kakaricho)* and in the fifth head a local district tax office. In the sixth year comes another promotion, this time to deputy director *(kacho hosa)*. Thereafter, they are shuffled around from bureau to bureau, spending one or two years at each, starting off as generalists and hopefully learning these multiple specializations fast. In their fifteenth year, the best will be promoted to director *(kacho)* and will then move from division to division. Finally, some few survivors will be appointed vice-minister at about the age of fifty while those who are not as lucky customarily retire.

This system, or something like it, is used in all ministries and agencies and even, with some modifications, at the local level. It is most varied and extensive for higher civil servants or "career" officials, whose ascendence is most rapid. But it applies to a fair extent to the rank-and-file. The purpose, more than accumulation of technical knowledge, is to meet the other people working there. With transfers every year or two, sometimes more often and occasionally less, it is possible to come into contact with an extraordinary number and feel a part of the new "family." This develops an exceptional *esprit de corps* within each bureaucracy.

Despite this, there is a lot of factionalism. Originally, cliques arose among people who had attended the same university *(gakubatsu)* or came from the same home town or prefecture *(kyodobatsu)*.[7] But most are now due to personal affinities and friendships with colleagues who have been encountered in the course of a career. Alone, one would feel isolated in a huge bureaucracy; together, one is more at ease. Even more important, there is little chance of rising to the top alone. The best way to get ahead, aside from any noteworthy ability, is to belong to an influential faction. This factionalism, however, is tightly contained within each administrative unit which itself forms a broader faction *(shobatsu)* in the overall bureaucracy.[8]

No less significant, this kind of recruitment and training makes the bureaucracy a very closed entity. The only entry point is the exam. It is almost impossible to be recruited at a later date, at least as far as the career officials are concerned. The number of civilians who have been admitted is minimal and they often proved hard to absorb. This means that it is almost easier to teach existing staff new skills than to bring in outsiders who already possess a necessary specialization. It is nearly as hard for one bureaucracy to assimiliate members of another. There is very little exchange between ministries and agencies. And what there is usually lasts only a few years, after which the person is quite relieved to return home.

Actually, the only concession to such needs and almost the only acknowledgement of an outside world from which something can be learned is the existence of increasingly numerous "deliberative councils" *(shingikai)*. There are several hundred of these and most ministries and agencies have a dozen or more, often related to the work of specific sections or divisions. Members consist largely of businessmen, academics and specialists and more rarely representatives of consumer, environmental, labor or other popular movements. Some of the more prominent are MOF's Tax System Research Council and MITI's Council on Industrial Structure.

But this is only a modest concession. For the members have been carefully selected by the ministry concerned and usually reflect its views. They are asked to study papers presented by the ministry, rather than to do their own spade work. And, in effect, they are primarily expected to endorse the ideas or drafts in order to lend them greater prestige. Of course, some members may not agree and there is a certain amount of free debate from which the bureaucrats could learn, if they would. However, the institutional machinery is so strong and the comments come at such a late date that the councils are not really advisory and serve more the purpose of adding a further seal of approval.[9]

Given their recruitment, training and internal cohesion, it is not surprising that the bureaucrats, and especially the higher officials, should come to regard themselves as an elite. They are far better educated than average, which makes a big difference in Japanese society, and they are entrusted with crucial functions. The only other groups they might look up to do not command much respect. The politicians are too crude and devious and the businessmen are too busy making money. The bureaucracy, by heritage and vocation, is expected to think more of the nation as a whole. Thus, it has a greater claim to patriotism than any other class. However, this is expressed more by an urge to lead than to serve the people and many bureaucrats would not hesitate to assume a somewhat more active role than was assigned to them. This scarcely complies with the rules of democracy or the new postwar ethos, but it is hard to avoid.

Superseding The Government

In liberal democracies, and according to Japan's postwar constitution, the bureaucracy or "civil service" is a body of state employees that is expected to help the executive branch accomplish its activities.[10] Its assistance may also be drawn on by the legislature. But there is no question as to its subordinate position. This is a dramatic reverse in the fortunes of a privileged elite which used to owe its allegiance solely to the emperor and was a prime mover from Meiji days on. Whether it was a permanent demotion remains to be seen.

While the Diet is entrusted with initiating and adopting legislation, it is abundantly evident that it could not do so on its own. The political parties do not have clearly defined programs which could be readily translated into laws and even their most detailed policies do not touch upon many essential matters. Moreover, even where they do have very specific views, Diet members and the government itself lack the necessary expertise to consider all the various factors. Nor do they possess the skills needed to draft, in proper legal terminology, what it is they actually want.

Since Diet members, and LDP committees, do not have adequate staffs, they are frequently forced to consult with the bureaucrats concerned to better understand the situation. More often, however, it is the ministry which is regularly dealing with certain issues that prepares papers or legislative drafts on its own and suggests to the government that they be enacted so that it can perform its tasks properly. Naturally, they will be looked at and considered by the politicians, who may not quite grasp all the implications or may disapprove of certain points. Alas, they have little choice but to request clarification of or propose modifications to the selfsame bureaucrats who presented the original ideas and have a second chance to influence the politicians' views.

Once a move has been approved by the ruling party, formal bills will be drawn up and presented. Again, due to lack of staff and knowledge, the ruling party will have to count on the bureaucrats not only to explain but to defend their viewpoints. Diet debates have been habitually reduced to a dull series of questions and answers and the opposition, rather than putting forth alternative proposals, is more likely to pick fault with the government's ideas. It will therefore look for weak points, even just minor or superficial ones, and demand an explanation, hoping to embarrass the minister.

The replies which are made have, in most cases, been drawn up by bureaucrats as opposed to the minister personally or his staff.[11] Almost no interpellations are responded to extemporaneously. Thus, bureaucrats regularly supply masses of answers to hypothetical questions they think may be asked. On occasion, to ensure a smoother passage, they also slip questions to LDP members so that the minister can make positive and even flattering comments about his work. More rarely, it would seem that opposition politicians leak their questions to the bureaucracy so that suitable answers can be prepared in advance.

The same thing happens for overall policy. The prime minister has almost no personal staff and is assisted instead by a large bureaucracy of his own. In addition, the leading ministries appoint special representatives to serve as his advisors. It is they who prepare his speeches, supply answers to possible interpellations and actually go through a dry run of cabinet meetings. Before the ministers gather, there is a conclave of ministry spokesmen who settle most outstanding questions so that little more remains for the politicians to do than give their approval. It is the rare prime minister who inserts more than a few personal remarks in his own speeches or would dare face questioners alone. And even those with special concerns or pet projects usually leave the bulk of the work to the bureaucracy.

Obviously, the bureaucrats cannot do a perfect job. In the course of debates, it may turn out that they did overlook something and it may be necessary to provide more intricate legal guarantees or mechanisms for the laws

"Really, it's very simple." Finance Minister Watanabe explaining the tax system.

Credit: Foreign Press Center/Kyodo

to work properly. While formally presented by the government, the vast majority of these technical amendments also come from the bureaucracy. Only a small number of sensitive issues are actually negotiated between the government and opposition and rather few amendments stem from the normal political process. In addition, only one or two bills are debated with much vigor during any session while a hundred more which are less controversial, affect fewer vested interests, or are simply more humdrum and technical go through pretty much as they are.

This makes Diet proceedings somewhat of a charade. The bureaucrats feed the prime minister, ministers and other Diet members their lines and hope to outguess the opposition. Any modifications in the bureaucratic script are usually minor and relatively tame. Almost without it being noticed, the basic roles are reversed. The bureaucrats become legislators and the politicians are reduced to brokers and lobbyists who plead the interests of their clients and occasionally win a point.[12]

But the political process is emptied even more of its vital essence by the fact that much of the "law of the land" does not even pass through this hollow machinery. Most formal legislation is so broad and vague that it can be implemented only after adding a full complement of regulations. In the realm of regulations, it is the bureaucracy which is master. There is hardly any observable concern in the Diet as to what is done to shape—and probably reshape—its writ in practice. This gives the bureaucracy a further opportunity to see that legislation is truly in keeping with its views of how things should be done. It is incredibly active here, for the amount of regulations it generates is monumental.

What is more, the bureaucracy has its own internal rules which are not part of the nation's official legislation, and in many cases are not even written down, yet have a decisive effect. Known as "administrative guidance" *(gyosei shido),* this consists essentially of opinions which are formally or informally expressed by the bureaucrats and are expected to be heeded by ordinary citizens.[13] There is hardly any debate on these rules, nor is there any effective way of overturning them, and yet they supplement and often enough actually contradict or overrule formal laws.

In some cases, this can be justified as filling the gaps in existing legislation or facilitating practical application. But often these gaps were intentionally left there by bureaucrats who refrained from proposing new laws and it is not rare for administrative guidance to go beyond anything that has been formally approved by the Diet. In other cases, it is used to moderate existing legislation or even waive application if that is regarded as in the best interest. Whatever the purpose, this is an extraordinary power for administrative personnel to possess. And the continued use of *gyosei shido* is all the more questionable since it clearly lacks all legal validity. Yet, anyone who should be tempted to ignore it knows that the bureaucracy has many ways of extracting compliance.

As for execution, a similar reversal of roles has taken place. Normally, the cabinet should be in charge. Obviously, given the tremendous number of things that must be accomplished, the actual implementation is customarily left to the bureaucracy even in liberal democracies and the executive branch merely controls and supervises what is done.

In Japan, with ministers who usually hold office for only a year or two and are often chosen with striking disregard to their competence, it is quite impossible to oversee things very carefully. Yet, even when ministers are competent and active, they rarely get much further. For one, they are kept busy in Diet debates. For another, they are burdened with numerous political chores. But, just in case, the bureaucracy exerts considerable efforts to keep the politicians from getting more than superficially involved in its activities. This applies to the formulation of ministry or agency policy and much more strongly as regards personnel matters.[14]

This is facilitated by the arrangement of having a minister and parliamentary vice-minister, both of them politicians, working in tandem with one or more administrative vice-ministers who serve as a link . . . and also a barrier. The politicians are expected to pass through these top bureaucrats to obtain any information and not go directly to lower-level employees. More generally, the bureaucracy closes itself to penetration by politicians. This can go to the extent of holding private policy meetings to which the parliamentary vice-minister is not invited. Bureaucrats can also chastise ministers they do not like by giving them inadequate information to do their job and make them look bad in Diet interpellations.

There have been some exceptions to this, but so few that they tend more to confirm the rule. Kakuei Tanaka, while in MITI, managed to impose his grandiose plans on the bureaucrats. Fukuda and Ohira, ex-MOF men themselves, had favorites among the bureaucrats whom they could sometimes promote a bit faster. Certain politicians tried to gain special advantages for bureaucrats who backed them. But, in the end, the bureaucracies usually closed ranks and circumvented bothersome measures or rearranged the hierarchy after the minister left, which was not long in coming.

So, it could hardly be claimed that it is the politicians who supervise the bureaucrats. Even this task has been taken over by the bureaucrats themselves. Much depends on self-policing by the unit concerned. Admittedly, there are several agencies which are empowered to investigate one aspect or another of the administrative machinery. The Board of Audit looks into the use of state funds and, in so doing, will report not only on illicit actions but also inefficiency and waste. The Prime Minister's Office (now absorbed in the Management and Coordination Agency) is expected to keep an eye on the various ministries and agencies to see that they are working purposefully in keeping with national policy. But the bureaucrats in these "watchdogs" do not want to tangle with their colleagues more than necessary and they rarely bite, although they do occasionally bark.

This leaves Japan with the classical question: who will guard the guardians? No matter how honest, sincere or patriotic the bureaucrats may be, it is impossible to ensure that they are moving in the right direction or behaving properly without outside control and supervision. Any other assumption would be naive and foolhardy.

But there are even graver problems. Given its tremendous influence on legislation and implementation, and the existence of internal rules and regulations, the bureaucracy quickly became an alternative power center. Anyone with special interests, businessmen, professionals, trade unionists, civic or religious associations, even the politicians themselves might be constrained to curry favor and solicit support.

It is frequently claimed that the bureaucracy is fundamentally neutral, that its favors cannot be bought. Alas, such a concept is barely conceivable. No group exists that does not have some biases. And Japan's bureaucracy is not immune to the temptations of power.

It is obvious that good relations must be maintained with the ruling party, especially one that has been in office without interruption for three decades. But there is little doubt that, beyond any justifiable concern for smooth working relations, the vast majority of the bureaucracy is politically conservative and prefers continued LDP rule. This much is announced in the media before and after elections and, given the recruitment, training and personal proclivities of the bureaucrats, could scarcely be otherwise. While few are more than passive supporters and most have some minor grudges, there are a number of top bureaucrats who openly backed LDP policies and later went into politics under its banner. True, few bureaucrats have gone on record as being dead against opposition policies or an opposition or coalition government. But the very fact that it would be harder to cooperate, something everyone realizes, is seen as a major strike against the opposition as opposed to a failing of the bureaucracy.

Like any other group, and especially one with a strong *esprit de corps,* the bureaucracy inevitably has vested interests with regard to its own position. Bureaucrats regularly propose and defend policies which are regarded as "rational," meaning reasonably logical and effective. But this usually implies easier to carry out because there is less concern for exceptions or the impact on less important members of society. Naturally, there is also a desire for measures which result in a further aggrandizement of the bureaucracy. This can take the form of additional personnel, larger budgets, greater authority, and so on.

So, while the bureaucracy may not flagrantly abuse its position or "sell out" to some pressure group, it is certainly very much aware of its prerogatives. According to one survey, which questioned both bureaucrats and politicians, the bureaucrats were rated just below the party leader and ahead of ministers, Diet members, mass media and interest groups as regards the degree of influence over policy formulation. They were also seen as considerably more influential than bureaucrats in Western democracies.[15] For what it is worth, Japanese bureaucrats are frequently more influential than bureaucrats in a dictatorship. With strong rule by one person or a clique, there is an official program or policies which are promoted and a leadership which is intent on having them executed.

That explains the Japanese aberration. The bureaucracy initially restored its influence in the postwar confusion and was aided by a rapid turnover of governments. It was reined in somewhat by Prime Ministers Yoshida, Sato and Kishi, men who knew what they wanted and also knew how to impose their will. Since then, there has been too much wavering or a preference for a gentler touch which left a vacuum that could be filled. Only Tanaka and Nakasone in recent years had enough of a program and determination to alter the situation somewhat. But they could not do much because their time in office was too short and the bureaucracy's authority was too firmly rooted. Moreover, while the politicians worked hard to gain greater control over budgetary allocations, they tended to ignore more general matters.

It is sometimes asserted that the presence of so many ex-bureaucrats in the LDP made it easier to manipulate the bureaucracy. That is hardly the case, for the bureaucrats-turned-politicians were more dependent on support of their erstwhile colleagues than the other way around. In fact, they often became their spokesmen in party circles. Those who eventually became ministers could certainly lead the staff better, but tended to select directions the ministry wanted anyway. And the ones who became prime minister occasionally paid too much heed to what the bureaucrats proposed and forgot that they had to accommodate popular wishes as well, a tick that gave them the air of "bureaucratic" politicians.

Thus, if the blame has to be apportioned for the reversal of positions, it is more the fault of the politicians for abdicating their role than the bureaucrats for usurping extraordinary powers. This applies not only to LDP members, especially in the government, who failed to exercise their prerogatives. It applies just as well to the opposition. It is perfectly clear that legislation is prepared and questions answered by the bureaucrats, pulling strings from offstage. And the massive use of administrative guidance is universally known. Yet, even opposition leaders do not dare challenge the bureaucracy for intervening or criticize the ministries (as opposed to the ministers) for inept measures. Nor does the general public say much. Perhaps, it is happy that things are left to more knowledgeable and reliable people.

Whatever the reasons, there is no question that the bureaucracy has seriously undermined the formal arrangements and upset the intended balance of powers. It is not the Diet which formulates legislation and the cabinet which executes it but the bureaucrats who, to a large extent, do both. More emphatically, it is not the politicians who supervise the bureaucrats but the bureaucrats who guide them. This does not quite make the bureaucrats a "shadow government," since they do not wish to rule and prefer avoiding the hurly-burly of the political process. They are more than willing to relinquish the appearances of power as long as they control some of the realities.

Can one still speak of democracy? Once again, if this is what the people want, or at least tolerate, then maybe it is permissible to tacitly change the rules and work in this manner. But it cannot be seen as democratic in any deeper sense because such infringements further reduce the degree to which ordinary citizens control the system.

Economic Encroachment

The bureaucracy has not only taken over many of the government's political tasks, it also usurped some of the normal functions of government as regards the economy. In so doing, it arrogated to itself certain rights and powers which should normally be held by private businessmen in a liberal economy. This goes against the basic economic tenets of Japan, which swears by free enterprise and likes to think of itself as one of the freest and most open economies in the world. That it is not, is already shown by the repeated references to an ominous, if somewhat nebulous "Japan, Inc."

This intervention is not really surprising given the long tradition of economic influence by the state, going back to Meiji (and even Tokugawa) days when the lords or Imperial advisors tried to promote agriculture or introduce new branches of industry. When many of the projects failed to flourish under bureaucratic management there was a greater willingness to trust in private entrepreneurs and eventually let the great combines *(zaibatsu)* take the lead. Colonial expansion and nationalism, however, reversed the trend and the economy was rigidly harnessed to wartime needs by the bureaucracy, often operating from the Munitions Ministry. SCAP not only released businessmen from government control, it was even more beneficial to smaller firms by disbanding the *zaibatsu* and imposing an Antimonopoly Law. Yet, it could not put an end to all interference nor slake the bureaucratic urge to recover some of the former prerogatives.

The reason for much of the uncertainty as to its scope is that relatively little of this control takes the usual forms encountered abroad. Most notably, there is only a very small public sector as compared to Meiji or wartime Japan or many European countries which have shifted to a mixed economy. In fact, the public sector just consisted of a few major public corporations and several minor ones. Those of note were Nippon Telegraph and Telephone and Kokusai Denshin Denwa, the domestic and international telecommunications monopolies, the Japanese National Railways and the tobacco and salt monopoly. Most of them, by the way, are heading for privatization of one sort or another.

There are also a number of financial institutions which played a substantial role just after the war and are still of significance today. The Japan Development Bank and Export-Import Bank of Japan are the largest. There are several others that are smaller or more specialized, like the Housing Loan Corporation, People's Finance Corporation, Small Business Finance Corporation, Agriculture, Forestry and Fisheries Finance Corporation and Medical Care Facilities Finance Corporation. And, of course, the national budget and monetary and fiscal policy can always be used to influence the economy.

But these are only the more evident manifestations and,

in some ways, the least impressive tools in the kit. Much more can be done in other ways to direct the economy. Most natural for the bureaucracy is to regulate specific branches of business and to license those who are entitled to operate there. Companies can then be promoted in various ways, either through financial aid and tax relief or by facilitating access to bank credit. Some ministries have gone much further by providing whole packages of incentives to specially designated industries to promote their rise. To this may be added protection from external competition. Finally, research and development can be encouraged by subsidies or fiscal means and crucial projects can be carried out for or with private companies.

Some of these activities are generally known and stem from ordinary legislation adopted for the purpose. But much more of the support—and control—arises out of the intricate web of regulations and informal advice known as "administrative guidance." *Gyosei shido,* which is applied very extensively in very concrete ways is probably the more essential element. Of course, it can be rejected by those who feel that the bureaucracy is intruding unduly. But the bureaucrats are usually wise enough to deal primarily with those who want help and, if they feel they must overcome resistance, they can very often provide a counterpart. In the worst cases, they can chasten those who do not cooperate by turning down requests for licenses, permits or loans.

Two bodies are especially prominent here. One is the Ministry of Finance whose activities affect the economy as a whole and several sectors more specifically. Its control of the banks, securities houses, insurance companies and other financial intermediaries is fairly comprehensive and it carefully defines what each category may do. Its ability to set interest rates for borrowing and lending naturally has a tremendous influence on the amount of commercial investment, construction and so on. Previously, it also regulated the quantity of funds flowing into or out of the country. Even more decisive is its say on fiscal policy, since it helps determine which groups will be taxed more heavily or benefit from special relief.

The most noticeable, and in some ways most politically sensitive, activity is to compile the budget. Obviously, the MOF does not do this alone and it is subject to government guidelines on which headings should be expanded (or cut back). Still, in general and regarding most aspects, it is able to draw up a budget whose overall size and sectoral allocations are roughly in keeping with its desiderata. This does not mean that it sovereignly decides and could arbitrarily make changes. Quite to the contrary, the pecking order between ministries and the proportion each receives is pretty well established by now. But, it can bully them into line in the interest of a more rational or balanced budget. Its real opponents, however, are the politicians who always want more spending but are much less willing to legislate new taxes.[16]

Less visible to outsiders, but no less instrumental in enhancing MOF's ability to determine events, is control over a special fund managed by a trust fund bureau which comes under its finance bureau. It collects monies from several government institutions including primarily postal savings and insurance and national and welfare pensions. Part of this is used to absorb national bonds and the larger portion is channeled into a Fiscal Investment and Loan Program which is so large as to be referred to as the "second budget." FILP's resources are then passed on to various state banks and financial institutions, public corporations and development agencies, and local governments which use them for infrastructure, public works or industrial investment. Most of the decisions taken on allocations of these funds bypass the existing political machinery and are determined first by the MOF and LDP leaders and then by the banks, corporations and local autonomies which receive them and politicians or bureaucrats who promote specific projects.

The Bank of Japan, theoretically independent but passably aligned on the MOF, also has important functions here. It decides on the discount rate, regulates monetary flows and permits overlending by commercial banks. It can relax or tighten up depending on circumstances. Although not usually regarded as a financial organ, the Ministry of Posts and Telecommunications has turned itself into one through the postal savings scheme which has ballooned in recent years. To attract savers, it has tended to pursue its own interest policy on occasion.

The second important body is the Ministry of International Trade and Industry. It carries out extensive activities in numerous industrial sectors in order to promote and protect domestic industries when possible, rationalize and help them survive if necessary. This is done by its specialized bureaus, each looking after its own clients and aiding them in whatever ways it can. A sub-agency is expected to look after smaller firms while the main machinery is more concerned with larger ones, those whose action can more readily propel the economy. MITI's ardor is curbed only somewhat by the Fair Trade Commission.

Judging by its name, the Economic Planning Agency might be regarded as the most significant economic body since it deals with all sectors of the economy, industrial and other, and all aspects of development, production, finance and other. In practice, however, the EPA is a smaller and lesser body and it lacks the essential tools to achieve its ends. It does not control the budget and it cannot channel much aid to companies. It must therefore cooperate with MOF and MITI which have the power and which, in addition, supply some of its key personnel. The result has therefore been that the EPA only produces plans, makes suggestions and collects statistics, useful but not truly decisive functions.

Several other ministries also have a notable economic impact in their own sectors. The Ministry of Agriculture, Forestry and Fisheries promotes certain crops through subsidies and protection from imports. It provides extension services, modernizes forestry and fishing operations and negotiates fishery agreements in foreign waters. The Ministry of Construction supervises many of the public works projects and can, through zoning, and rezoning, encourage or discourage building in certain places. The Ministry of Transport not only looks after the JNR, the country's largest railway network, it also regulates and licenses airlines, shipping lines and trucking firms. The Ministry of Health and Welfare fosters the domestic pharmaceutical industry.

The activities of the Science and Technology Agency are felt more diffusely. Its projects contribute to raising the overall technological level; they also tend to have practical spinoffs. Other crucial R&D is carried out under MITI, MOT, MPT (more particularly NTT), MHW and others. The role of the Ministry of Labor is the obverse, since it is expected to look after the needs of the working force and, if excessively zealous, could get in the way of economic programs. The same would apply to the Environment Agency.

While entrusting such matters to the bureaucracy may appear to simplify things, it must be remembered that not all economic issues come exclusively under the purview of any specific bureaucratic institution. Moreover, anything that is done in one sector is bound to have an effect on others and helping one can, under certain circumstances, hurt others even if there is a generally positive impact. It is therefore essential for bureaucrats in one sphere to think of what is being done elsewhere so as not to overlap or duplicate or, worse, work at cross purposes and conflict. That is increasingly important nowadays since many activities affect a broad range of sectors. This applies to more technical fields such as telecommunications, which would interest the MPT first of all, with regard to licensing, but also MITI, since it deals with equipment makers. And the STA might promote some useful R&D while MOF would have to decide how to tax any revenue generated. Whenever questions of a more political nature arise, the number of interested parties mushrooms. Trade policy, a constant concern, is not just the domain of the Ministry of Foreign Affairs and MITI, it also affects the EPA, MAFF, MHW, MOT, MPT and just about every ministry depending on what aspect comes up. Naturally, it also keeps the Prime Minister's Office busy.

Coordination, however, is not so easy since each one of these ministries and agencies has its own interests which could well clash with those of others. This is a rather frequent occurrence. For example, MOF tends to be conservative on budgetary, fiscal and monetary policy, and the BOJ even more so. MITI is always agitating for economic stimulation and aid to some client or other. And just about every administrative body is eager to get more funds. Such rivalries seriously disrupt the planning process since MOF often tries to hold back while MITI is pushing further and the EPA has to strike a balance. MITI is naturally at odds with the FTC and EA as well if their concerns interfere with its activities. Finally, as regards trade conflicts, while the MFA and perhaps prime minister are trying to mend fences with foreign partners, just about everyone else is too busy protecting its domestic clientele to care.

Such discord arises not only between ministries but also

within ministries. There is an inevitable competition between MITI's various bureaus to get more resources to aid the industries under their competence or to see that they lose less if trade concessions have to be made. There is incessant rivalry within MOF between those promoting the interests of banks or securities houses, since each wants to encroach on the territory of the other or repel such invasions. Some agencies are in a particularly tough spot because they have personnel that has been seconded from other ministries and carry their quarrels with them. This is the bane of the EPA which receives directors from both MOF and MITI or many of the public corporations which house ex-officials from sponsoring ministries.

Nevertheless, despite these inadequacies and drawbacks, it is perfectly clear that the bureaucrats play a crucial role in economic affairs. In fact, once again, they manifestly have a greater influence here than do the politicians. Thus, it is permissible to ask to what extent they express the national will and are therefore legitimate and "democratic." Also, given the very extensive and sometimes decisive nature of certain interventions, it is possible to wonder just how "liberal" the Japanese economy is.

An Almost Immaculate Elite

A bureaucracy which assumes these weighty and sensitive tasks, whether it has usurped them or just filled a vacuum, must be truly exceptional to fulfill such a role. It is often assumed that Japan's bureaucracy, more than any other in the world, fits this description. In fact, there have been countless allusions to it as supremely competent, able to run the whole political and economic show smoothly, and also extraordinarily incorruptible and patriotic in not benefiting unfairly from its position. While some of the flattery may be justified, it is hard to bear the more exaggerated comments out in practice.

In Japan's cultural tradition, recruitment from elite universities is all too often seen as guaranteeing an elite bureaucracy. Nevertheless, elite universities do not always offer the best education nor are all those who graduate necessarily very good. Even special examinations to enter the career civil service do not guarantee that only the best get in. The only thing that has really been proven is that those concerned were particularly adept at learning certain subjects which regularly appear on the tests and that they possess a good memory for rote learning. This does not seem to disturb those who design the tests because they got in on the basis of similar criteria and are more interested in compatible colleagues than competent ones.

Since so many enter from the law faculty, and so few with a technical background, it is obvious that these examinations test only general knowledge. This would not be so much of a problem if the training process imparted more specialized skills. To some extent, that is attempted. But, as a former top bureaucrat pointed out, "if your post is changed once or twice a year, you cannot show your ability." Nor can you get more than a superficial understanding of what your tasks are. Thus, most bureaucrats remain amateurs throughout their career and it is nearly impossible to come by the sort of expertise that is increasingly indispensable in every field, not only science or technology but agriculture, health, economics, foreign affairs and anything the government handles.

More important than any skill is the motivation, something that is extremely difficult to determine with a test. It was felt that during the Meiji era and at certain other times exceptionally sincere and patriotic individuals were attracted to the bureaucracy. The early postwar period may have seen a repeat of that. But all recent indications show that those looking for a government job are the least lively candidates who simply prefer a safe and secure position in government service to the rough-and-tumble of the private sector. In fact, every time things get difficult in the private sector, the enrollment for state exams shoots up. This is hardly the best atmosphere in which to recruit eager, conscientious or reliable civil servants.

The tendency to seek security would only reinforce the built-in pressures in the bureaucracy to tame the hardier personalities in the interest of cooperation and harmony. There is nothing like strict seniority and the need for multiple approvals before taking the slightest action to make newcomers conform to the existing pattern. Rather than try a fresh approach, a smart bureaucrat will resort to cherished precedents or follow standard procedures long after these stale practices have proven ineffective. Should they fail once again, that is safer than making innovative efforts for whose effects he will be personally responsible. Indeed, even if a brilliant idea succeeds, this is no guarantee of praise since the Japanese in general and bureaucrats in particular do not really like individuals who stand out from the others.

More and more, it is noted that bureaucrats who show imagination, like challenges or take initiative are unappreciated while those who follow the crowd and defer to their superiors rise more rapidly. Meanwhile, there are many notable cases where the former have been squeezed out. When such things happen in bodies which are already known for their caution and circumspection, it can only be assumed that sclerosis will set in and relatively little new can be expected. While that is not overly harmful in a system where the politicians provide the necessary leadership and bureaucratic inertia can be a useful counter-weight, it is seriously detrimental for a bureaucracy which has to take the lead.

A further handicap arises from the pronounced inclination to look inward toward the needs and positions of their specific group as opposed to others and which naturally makes bureaucrats regard themselves as separate from the masses. That is unfortunate since many lower level employees must deal regularly with the public and cater to its needs. Even the more remote officials come into contact with business or civic leaders as well as politicians of all sorts. It is necessary for them to know what is going on outside their walls and occasional opinion polls or statements from deliberative councils are not enough. When bureaucrats fail to mix with the people, and consider themselves as just another segment of the population, there is a tendency to become elitist in the worst sense. Admittedly, there is less of the prewar arrogance and today's bureaucrats can be excruciatingly civil if need be. But they clearly feel a notch above the rest.

Such feelings might be understandable for a group which really is superior. However, as already noted, neither the education nor the training of bureaucrats sets them out distinctly from other Japanese. And their performance, while somewhat better than certain other groups, is not truly exceptional.

In order to keep its employees honest and hardworking, the state provides them with an acceptable salary. Moreover, since public employees cannot strike, the government usually keeps their wages rising as fast as the national average. Still, remuneration is not always as high as in the private sector and some university graduates would doubtlessly be earning more if they had joined a prestigious company. In exchange, they have guaranteed tenure. It is almost impossible to get rid of a civil servant unless he commits grievous blunders or an actual crime. Moreover, in earlier years, there was no specific mandatory retirement age and employees could continue working well after their colleagues in private companies had been turned out. This has recently been rectified in most bodies with retirement at 60, which is quite acceptable. A further compensation is larger pensions and retirement allowances than are available for most private sector workers or self-employed. All in all, the bureaucrats have done reasonably well and are not making excessive material sacrifices for their careers.

What is odd in this context is that wages at the local level have often been higher than for employees of the national government. The gap was as much as 10%, although it is falling slowly, and represents an obvious aberration in the Japanese system since academic and other qualifications are much stricter to get into the national bureaucracy. The only explanations would seem to be that local legislators and elected officials were more lenient in their practices or that some had closer relations with the bureaucrats. This latter conclusion is very persuasive since it is in former "reformist" strongholds like Tokyo and Osaka that wages were most out-of-line. Many of these administrations also inflated their staff at an untoward rate, not only due to new services and activities but to keep on good terms with the public sector trade unions.

This makes feather-bedding a more prominent feature of local bodies. But its presence is visible throughout the bureaucratic machinery and can hardly be avoided since it is inherent in the recruitment method. The administration takes in a new class of employees each year and cannot really fill its ranks later on. Thus, it must be estimated how much personnel will be needed ten, twenty or thirty years hence. Employees, moreover, are not hired for specific jobs but to handle whatever work may arise on the basis of a very fluid division of labor. Under such conditions, there is bound to be much overlap and duplication and thereby excess staffing. This happens in the private sector as well. Only there, much stronger efforts are made to get rid of redundant workers in order to maintain profitability.

While security of tenure is essential to create a loyal bureaucracy, it is not always the best way of having hardworking personnel. This is particularly true in a seniority system where employees rise slowly but surely whether they work hard or not. This has resulted in a fair amount of inefficiency which, according to citizens' groups or any casual observer, involves coming late, leaving early and goofing off in between. It is perfectly obvious that many of the bureaucrats are not engaged in their official tasks but rather personal conversations, drinking tea or just reading newspapers to while the time away. They do not rush over to the counter or serve citizens with the same rapt attention as in most private establishments. Once again, since it is essential to maintain harmony (and the money comes from the state), little is done to correct this.

There is also a good deal of waste to judge by the annual reports of the Board of Audit. Some of this derives from mere sloppiness and poor selection of the goods and equipment that were purchased. Even larger sums were often lost due to ineffective planning and execution of projects which did not really meet needs. But often enough the losses were less excusable. Many agencies and public corporations claimed subsidies which were not due or falsified information to get more, as when declaring non-existent school children or teachers to collect bigger subsidies. The sums involved were often considerable, as much as ¥20 billion a year for the small fraction of the total number of offices that were inspected.

In addition, there was some outright theft of public properties and embezzlement of government monies. And it was not unknown for public employees to take bribes, especially at the local level, for procuring material or services from specific suppliers or awarding construction works to favored contractors.

One of the more frequent irregularities is almost typical of the bureaucracy. It consists of padding costs by billing for official trips that were not undertaken (including meals and accommodation), charging for fictitious purchases (substantiated by false vouchers), and collecting wages for unworked overtime (or to remunerate non-existent workers). This money is then used to illegally increase the earnings of the bureaucrats. This sort of cheating is rife and periodically one ministry or corporation or another gets caught, and meekly apologizes, while others continue and hope to get away with it.

Another practice is even more widespread. This is *amakudari* or "descent from heaven" whereby bureaucrats parachute into another job upon retiring. This usually occurs after early retirement, at the age of fifty or so, especially when stepping down to make way for younger careerists. It applies mainly to elite bureaucrats but is not restricted to them. How many are involved is hard to tell because only those moving into occupations closely related to their previous duties must ask permission (which is almost always granted) and this is only necessary in the first two years after retirement. Waiting a bit longer, going into an unrelated field or taking a job with a public corporation enables them to get around the formalities. So, while only a few hundred senior civil servants are formally authorized each year, thousands of ex-bureaucrats probably enter such jobs.

About a third of these bureaucrats are reemployed by public corporations or other state agencies and another third by private companies.[17] The remainder go to the diplomatic corps, academia, think tanks or local bodies while some try politics. The luckier ones get very attractive posts with handsome salaries, generous perks and fat retirement benefits. In many cases, it is clear that the jobs are a form of reward for having helped the corporation, company or LDP politicians while in the bureaucracy. And, for the most part, the jobs themselves consist of little more than maintaining good relations with one's former colleagues and associates. This means that it is essentially a form of collusion with those who are still in government service and should not be subject to special appeals. Yet, given the close personal relations, they are bound to repay favors to their seniors and some are willing to go even further because they, too, want a cushy *amakudari* job when they retire.

That the purposes are not entirely above board immediately becomes obvious when one considers which ministries have been most successful in placing former employees. Those which pull the most strings always do best, such as MOF, MITI, MOT, MOC and MAFF. Some of them have a direct pipeline to public corporations, especially MOF which can send its people anywhere and the MPT which has good access to NTT and KDD. The MOT passes its retirees on to the JNR and JRCC and the MOC to an array of construction and development agencies. This is not accidental since, in years past, these ministries deliberately created or fostered the agencies and corporations which became retirement homes. Others have done particularly well with private companies, most notably MITI, but also MOF, MOT and MOC. MITI has no trouble unloading people on numerous industrial sectors and MOF tries the banks, securities houses and insurance companies. MOT employees flock to private railways and airlines, MOC's to construction firms, and ex-MOE people go to private colleges. As for the Ministry of Home Affairs, it staffs a vast empire of local bodies.

There is no shortage of explanations and excuses for this practice. It is noted that the bureaucrats are still young and energetic at fifty, that they have to make enough money to retire properly, that they possess all sorts of useful knowledge. But they could have worked longer and then lived off a comfortable pension. And they are most definitely not hired for their technical skills which, as generalists, are rather meager. Anyway, the only thing they are seen doing is visiting their old colleagues and getting work for their new colleagues. Moreover, it is usually agreed some time before retirement that such an employee will get such a job and this agreement is not only tacit but, in some cases, written. It is seen not only as a favor to the employee but also to his bureaucracy, which often cooperates to make the arrangement fruitful. Under such conditions, *amakudari* is just another form of corruption. The only differences are to follow certain rules, preserve appearances and defer payments.

The more obvious defects have already been noted by the bureaucracy itself. There is certainly no approval of bribes, theft, embezzlement or gross waste. Those who misbehave in these ways can be dismissed and even criminally punished. Other practices are on the border line and the reaction has been strangely muted. Use of fake overtime and the rest to increase wages and allowances is so widespread that it is almost tacitly accepted. And the custom of *amakudari* is so deep-rooted that it is regarded as an unquestioned perk. When there is enough public outcry, the bureaucracy does take some action. There are occasional resignations of officials in charge, who are promptly given another job somewhere else, and some bureaucrats are docked a month's salary. Otherwise, there is a tendency to hand out warnings, admonitions and the like. But the punishment is very light and hardly an obstacle to future misbehavior. This is shown by the repetition of the same old abuses year after year.

Thus, the Japanese bureaucracy is neither supremely efficient nor spotlessly clean. It may be better than in most developing countries and perhaps some advanced ones, but it has its faults and weaknesses. This means that, if it is to do its work properly, it has to be controlled and supervised by some other body. It was impossible for the guardians to guard themselves. Not realizing this, and not doing something about it, was a disservice to the nation . . . and also to the bureaucracy.

Regrettable Limitations

While leaving policy formulation and implementation to the bureaucracy is better than simply going without, there are definite limitations to this approach. The most obvious is that the bureaucracy was not established for this purpose nor is it suitably equipped. The bureaucrats have their own duties which take up much of their time and they have relatively little contact with the public so they are in no position to sense what the emerging needs are. It is only when needs become overwhelming or events make it hard to keep the administrative machinery running smoothly that they become acutely aware of problems.

Yet, even when a problem is perfectly obvious, the bureaucrats do not necessarily want to tackle it. They have no wish to replace the politicians in sounding out different quarters as to views and proposals. Should the solution require a compromise, they do not want to hammer out the details. In addition, the bureaucratic personality and tradition is hardly suited to such activities. Most of the personnel is relatively cautious, having learned that the best way to get ahead is to move slowly and not make waves. While good at dealing with one another, they are poorly adapted to dealing with outsiders. And, by the time a problem has turned into a crisis, there is little chance that they would not attract the ire of some segment of the population no matter what solution they were to propose.

The bureaucrats are certainly no more eager to pick up hot irons than the politicians. But they may be obliged to when circumstances arise in which they cannot do their job otherwise. For example, if there is inadequate tax revenue, it is quite impossible for MOF to balance the budget and some items must be cut or new taxes raised. If schools are to function properly there must be adequate staff. If environmental pollution is not to blight the nation there must be some regulations and means of enforcement. If trading partners complain of dumping or developing countries appeal for aid, some action must be taken to preserve good relations.

In such cases, the bureaucrats will press the politicians to do something and, if they do not, try to arrange their own budgets and activities in such a way as to handle the matters. But time will elapse while waiting for the politicians to notice the problem and do something. More time will elapse in building up courage to replace them. And yet more time will elapse until the bureaucracy can find its own solutions.

This last element, however, is largely the fault of the bureaucrats and cannot be shifted to the politicians. Japan's decision-making process in every sector is extremely slow and time-consuming, but rarely more so than in the bureaucracy. The standard procedure, in theory, is regarded as bottom-up. In practice, it really consists of a decision taken at the top to deal with a problem and then giving instructions to those further down to prepare appropriate measures. These are not spontaneous ideas nor are they left entirely to the wisdom of those fashioning them,

MITI, the police and demonstrators debate the merits of
nuclear energy.

Credit: Foreign Press Center/Kyodo

for it is known that the only way to succeed is to come up
with proposals that will be accepted with little ado by
every single higher echelon.

Thus, those engaging in policy formulation will consult
with their seniors, engage in *nemawashi* with colleagues in
other bureaus who may be affected, and especially check
on the precedents. They will play it safe rather than try to
come up with spectacular initiatives. They may also use
vague wording and bureaucratic jargon that permit multiple interpretations. Once they have put their ideas in
writing, a memo *(ringi)* will be circulated to one office after
another to be read and approved. Unless every last seal is
duly affixed, the proposal cannot go forward from the
ministry. And it may require a dozen seals before this is
done and months for the whole process to be completed.[18]

Where things become particularly delicate, and real

obstacles arise, is when a decision requires the participation of more than one ministry or agency. The decision-making process is very well run in within any individual bureaucracy since it is regularly used. But there are relatively fewer occasions when cooperation is needed with outsiders and there are no supraministerial or even interministerial bodies entrusted with reconciling proposals or breaking log jams. That this is sorely lacking can be understood from the earlier reference to the many examples of issues which cross bureaucratic boundary lines and where coordination between two, three, four or more bodies may be needed.

When this occurs, the ministries will usually set up informal committees in which representatives of the various parties try to work out an acceptable solution. However, given their internal cohesion and rampant sectarianism, it is hard for them to consider the interests of others. It is even harder to reach a compromise since any change in internal policy has to be approved by the many officials concerned. This makes it necessary for the spokesmen to return repeatedly for fresh instructions. If one bureau or another refuses to budge, and no compensation can be found, the negotiations can drag on forever. It may be possible for a larger or more prestigious bureaucracy to prevail over a weaker one, but even this is far from certain and can take a lot of time.

Unwillingness of certain ministries, and of their specific bureaus, to make concessions can also be traced to a pronounced clientism which makes the whole game more complicated. By constantly working with specific, narrow segments of the population, and being judged by their ability to help, the bureaucrats go out of their way to promote special interests. If pressed to accept measures which could jeopardize such interests, they will tend to dig in their heels if asked to do so by their clients. This is particularly so since these are often well organized pressure groups which have considerable political clout and can make the life of a petty employee who might betray their cause awfully unpleasant. Until these far from extraneous matters have been settled it is hard for the bureaucracy to start working out a uniform approach, let alone a broader arrangement with others.

If a bureaucratic agreement cannot be reached, then it is necessary to appeal to another level. The most appropriate is obviously the political leadership. However, the politicians probably evaded the issue to begin with and may not be willing to take the onus for a clear-cut decision. In addition, divergent interests between political parties and also within the ruling party are such that often politicians take sides rather than pushing for a compromise. Every time a budgetary allocation or provision in a bill affects their own clientele, they will head for the ministry or agency concerned and make strong pleas. When several are involved, they will support one against the others. Thus, the tug-of-war may simply become more extensive and intractable than before.

One result has been a fair number of hopelessly awkward and unworkable compromises. Another is a tendency to leave issues in abeyance until a conclusion can finally be reached while busily making believe that everything has been settled and everyone is satisfied. Meanwhile, work continues behind-the-scenes on a formal decision and, until it intervenes, each ministry or agency continues doing what it wants. This kind of situation does not really upset the Japanese. But it can create considerable embarrassment and nasty reactions when dealing with foreign countries that want a quick and unequivocal response.

There has been one further outcome, namely an amazing dearth of legislation. For all its meticulousness and concern for detail, there are vast areas in which the legal system shows glaring gaps. These are the so-called grey zones in some of the ministries where one must go and seek a ruling from the person in charge since there is nothing set down in writing. There are also some darker nooks and crannies where the bureaucrats do not even bother laying down rules unless the confusion and abuses become too disturbing.

Some of the gaps arise in areas where one would expect no such occurrence. Supervision of the activities of real estate agents and action to prevent land speculation are incomplete. Even the operation of the stock market, which involves much insider trading, price manipulation and cornering of stocks, is poorly controlled. While the banks are overregulated, consumer finance companies and loan sharks *(sarakin)* can get away with murder. These assorted items come under MOF, which seems not to care. As for MITI, while it is constantly fostering the interests of large companies, it pays little attention to those of smaller firms. And the Ministry of Labor, which does not have to worry much about employees of large companies, somehow forgets to look out for part-timers, homeworkers and women workers in general although they are in desperate straits.

Even on more concrete and practical matters there is a tremendous lag unless something goes seriously awry. Japan was extremely late in adopting environmental legislation even though it was abundantly clear that many forms of pollution were becoming an enormous threat. It did not confirm the safety of drugs until after the side-effects of some had crippled or killed dozens of people. Regulation of health foods came a decade later. There were hundreds of unlicensed "baby hotels," with thousands of infants, before the Ministry of Health and Welfare got around to checking some and found them frightfully substandard. For a long time, it was possible to take out a life insurance policy in the name of a third person who was not notified thereof. Only after some of these third persons were killed to obtain insurance money was it finally concluded that the law should be tightened up. While supposedly ahead on technology, Japan was behind on the regulation of copyrights for software and data base and its legislation regarding genetic engineering and "value added networks" was hopelessly outdated.

In other cases, regulations exist only on paper, but there is inadequate machinery or concern to make them real. This is perfectly evident for prostitution, which is rampant and clearly visible to any policeman, yet where terribly few arrests take place. Drivers of mopeds and bicycles follow no rules whatsoever. And, according to a police report, over 90% of the cars in Tokyo are illegally parked. But no one bothers towing them away. Even more amazing, fire regulations are generally and criminally ignored. This was discovered when a fire in the Hotel New Japan killed 33 persons because the alarms had been turned off to save electricity. Even after a special "safety campaign" by the Fire Defense Agency one-third of Japan's hotels and inns still did not meet the fire code. Nevertheless, they were permitted to operate and some were even certified safe. A few of them burned down shortly thereafter.[19] Meanwhile, propane gas explosions kill or maim hundreds of people year in and year out due to faulty installation and operation.

Frequently, while the machinery exists, it may not be very well used and there can be mind-boggling inefficiency. This was most startling in the more commercial operations. The Japanese National Railways has been making deficits for decades because its running costs are higher than its competitors and it charges more for the same distance traveled. This has lost it many commuters where there are rival lines. Its freight business has been stricken by competition from more efficient truckers. Now the post office is losing most of its parcel service because private companies have set up nationwide networks to move packages faster and sometimes cheaper. Meanwhile, the cost of postage remains higher than in many foreign countries despite the great population density. And long distance calls within Japan as well as overseas calls are exceptionally expensive. But the worst example of bureaucratic bungling and stubbornness is the ill-fated nuclear-powered ship *Mutsu* which, although a failure from the day it was launched, could not be scrapped for over a decade.[20]

On the other hand, there are sometimes regulations and machinery, but it is hard to figure out the purpose except to give the bureaucrats more work. Noteworthy aberrations include a MITI form containing forty questions about the specifications of every single boiler operated by large companies. Another required each car rental office to report the date every vehicle was rented, to whom, the destination and the time and place of return. And one set of regulations spawned a whole industry. The Ministry of Transport required inspection of every car every two years and, as of the tenth year, annually. This *shaken* was very costly and time-consuming for the car owners and yet not very effective. For the cars could be specially adjusted to pass the tests. Meanwhile, local authorities apparently spent nearly half of their time processing paper work related to subsidies from the national government.

So, leaving legislation, implementation and supervision to the bureaucrats is not really the ideal solution. No matter how honest or efficient a bureaucracy, there are simply some things it cannot do on its own and which must be accomplished by a more responsive and popular leadership.

NOTES

1. According to Nobutaka Ike, "it appears that the bureaucracy proved more than a match for the Occupation and that civil service reforms were one of the least successful." *(Japanese Politics,* p. 159).
2. This continuity in the bureaucracy is described with regard to the Ministry of Labor in Sheldon M. Garon, "The Imperial Bureaucracy and Labor Policy in Postwar Japan," *Journal of Asian Studies,* May 1984, pp. 44–57.
3. Of considerably less importance are the Hokkaido Development Agency and Okinawa Developent Agency.
4. The Tobacco and Salt Public Corporation and Nippon Telegraph and Telephone have since been privatized, perhaps followed by Japanese National Railways.
5. How the localities operate and relate with the central government is studied in Richard J. Samuels, *The Politics of Regional Policy in Japan.*
6. Just how hard it is to suppress elitism appears from Akira Kubota, *Higher Civil Servants and Postwar Japan.*
7. Among the largest cliques are those of University of Tokyo and Waseda University old-boys. Another consists of ex-officers of the defunct Imperial Navy.
8. For a blow-by-blow description of administrative factionalism, see Chalmers Johnson, *MITI and the Japanese Miracle.*
9. Miyohei Shinohara and Toru Yanagihara, *The Japanese and Korean Experiences in Managing Development,* p. 22.
10. For a description of the bureaucracy, its organization and functions, see Kiyoaki Tsuji (ed.), *Public Administration in Japan.*
11. This interface is studied in Park, *op. cit.*
12. Ezra Vogel describes the process in not very different terms. But, for some inexplicable reason, he assumes the process is positive and democratic. "The public may have no particular respect for the politician who enunciates the conclusion in a policy speech, but it knows that the conclusion has been carefully prepared by the best minds of the country. For most of the public, the outcome appears not as something a narrow group of bureaucrats decided but something 'we Japanese' decided." *(Japan as No. 1,* p. 90.)
13. For a definition of administrative guidance and its applications, see Hiroshi Shiono, "Administrative Guidance," in Tsuji, *op. cit.,* pp. 203–16.
14. Ezra Vogel does not deny this, he just thinks it is good. "Although not immune from political pressures, bureaucrats do not hesitate to unite against politicians who obstruct their perceived mission." *(op. cit.,* p. 56.)
15. See Akira Kubota, "Political Influence of Japanese Higher Civil Servants," *Look Japan,* December 10, 1980.

16. For who does what in shaping the budget, see John Creighton Campbell, *Contemporary Japanese Budget Politics*.
17. Many public corporations serve regularly as rest homes for ex-bureaucrats who make up the vast majority of their top officials.
18. To see how complicated, slow and often futile the process can be, try another book edited by Ezra Vogel, *Modern Japanese Organization and Decision-Making*.
19. *Japan Times*, November 1, 1982.
20. See Dane Lee Miller, "Drifting Ship, Drifting Government: The *Mutsu* Affair," *The Japan Interpreter*, Spring 1978, pp. 202–22.

4
The Business Community

Who Represents Business?

Business, the third major pillar in the power structure, is usually a rather amorphous group given the vast number of companies in a multitude of sectors. However, businessmen do have many common interests and, in order to attain whatever goals they may set, they tend to establish formal associations or looser clubs. In Japan, this has gone exceptionally far because of a long tradition of business activism and the existence of what is called the *zaikai*. Often translated loosely as "financial circles" or the "business world," it is something more and can best be understood by its principal personalities and typical actions.[1]

In leading (and lesser) Japanese companies, as the founders and professional managers grow older, they gradually relinquish control over day-to-day operations to their subordinates while maintaining some say on personnel matters, this to ensure that they continue exercising real power. Meanwhile, they are willing to accept a post as chairman and perhaps later on, to make way for a new chairman, as honorary chairman or counsellor. In such positions, they become *zaikai-jin (zaikai* people) and devote much of their time to more exalted matters such as the health and prosperity of their line of business and more general economic, social, and political issues. This activity is known as "lobbying through the *zaikai*" *(zaikai kat-*

sudo), an effort few companies would be foolish enough to neglect.[2]

On the basis of their experience and maturity, these former executives are expected to transcend the petty concerns and egoisms of their own companies and attain a broader view of things that could even vie with those of the politicians and bureaucrats. Some expound their views amongst the employees or more widely through lectures, interviews and television appearances. A few have actually concocted worldviews or philosophies which they proselytize for the good of Japan. In addition to any individual efforts, they frequently join together to boost the standing and effectiveness of the business community in national affairs.

The present organizations were founded shortly after the war when the business community was at its lowest ebb. Whatever their personal opinions, most businessmen had accepted the prewar and wartime regimes and some ardently supported the militarists. Although others disliked the stifling controls or feared the war would end badly, they also played along. This attitude was enough to bring down retribution on the *zaibatsu,* which were to be disbanded, and many older executives from firms which collaborated and who were later purged. Already weakened by such measures, the new managers feared an incipient threat of chaos or Communist takeover.

To meet these challenges, businessmen began to reorganize. Foremost among the new bodies was the Japan Federation of Economic Organizations (Keidanren) which was founded in 1946 and now groups well over 800 major corporations and 120 trade associations. While the corporations are all among the largest, it does have an input from smaller firms which belong to the trade associations. Still, it is regarded as the bastion of big business because most of its leaders are drawn from such circles and its corporate members occupy a disproportionate position in the whole. While less than 1% of the companies in Japan, they possess 13% of total employees, 40% of total sales and 50% of total capital.

Keidanren has the most extensive range of interests and most intensive activities. It is concerned with numerous domestic issues, not only economic but also social and political, as well as international problems and foreign affairs. It has a huge budget, a staff of nearly 200, and some fifty standing committees. Beyond this, it can rely on financial support and technical or other knowhow from members. Year in and year out, it takes a stand on essential issues as they emerge and emphatically expresses the business view in resolutions and publications. Its meetings, conferences, receptions and other events are attended by ministers and prime ministers and it appoints members to the many advisory and deliberating councils or provides information and advice more discreetly to leading politicians and bureaucrats.

Keidanren's president, who is sometimes referred to as the "prime minister" of the *zaikai,* can be an extremely influential person. This was not always so, since the first decade was a formative period during which most businessmen were too occupied with reviving their companies to bother about much else. Under Taizo Ishizaka (1956–68), its activities multiplied as the business community itself prospered in an age of high growth and mounting respect from the people at large. Ishizaka himself preferred free enterprise and decried government entanglements, but the move was for stronger support of industry. This was further intensified by his successor Kogoro Uemura, a former career bureaucrat who encouraged closer cooperation with the government and LDP. This trend was sharply reversed under Toshio Doko, elected in

1974, and somewhat attenuated under Yoshihiro Inayama, as of 1980, and Eishiro Sato, who took over in 1986.

While Keidanren deals with the government (namely the ruling party and bureaucracy), it does not have much to do with labor-management relations. That is left to the Japan Federation of Employers Associations (Nikkeiren), which was founded back in 1948 to resist and eventually halt the labor agitation of the time. It backed a number of companies racked with bitter disputes and helped them undermine aggressive unions, for which it was nicknamed the "fighting Nikkeiren."[3] Since then, it has regularly coordinated management's response to the wage and bonus demands expressed in the spring and autumn labor offensives. While its rather tight-fisted guidelines were not always obeyed by its own members during the high growth era, they have closed ranks since the recession. Under its first chairman, Takeshi Sakurada, and its present one, Bumpei Otsuki, it has been highly effective in its special sector.

The Japan Committee for Economic Development (Keizai Doyukai), also founded during the period of turmoil in 1946, took a rather different tack. It was a more informal group, bringing together relatively progressive middle managers from somewhat less ponderous companies. Rather than fight labor or try to impose its will on government, it wanted to develop a new and more enlightened approach. It therefore emphasized harmony between labor and management and played down crass capitalism. Its members were more favorable to cooperation with the government and one went so far as to propound the concept of "amended capitalism." More recently, it has been concerned with improving relations with developing countries or exploring the new frontiers of technological progress. While it has not recovered its initial dynamism,

Keizai Doyukai still contributes its ideas, many of which have since been absorbed as part of basic *zaikai* philosophy, albeit frequently more preached than practiced. And, under its present chairman, Tadashi Ishihara, it is becoming more active politically.

Unlike the three others, the Japan Chamber of Commerce and Industry (Nissho) was only reestablished in 1953 and is not as fiercely independent or assertive. It was created under a national law, receives some state support, and cooperates more directly with the bureaucracy. But it is extremely influential due to the fact that its membership is by far the largest, including tens of thousands of companies big and small which belong to nearly 500 local chambers spread throughout the nation. Oddly enough, its most active period came under Shigeo Nagano (1970–84) who, although chairman of Nippon Steel, made exceptional efforts to organize small firms in order to obtain greater government backing. Since then another big businessman, Noboru Gotoh of the Tokyu Group, took the lead in preparing for the 21st century.

In addition to these four umbrella organizations, there are literally hundreds of trade associations in every branch and often sub-branch of manufacturing, services, commerce and finance. Most of them arose spontaneously and merely perpetuated earlier prewar associations. They, too, usually operate under national laws and cooperate very closely with the corresponding bureaucracy. They naturally wish to promote the interests of their membership in any and every way and, along with more formal activities, do not hesitate to engage in murkier activities like control over entry, sharing markets, and adjusting prices. Within their own precincts, they are exceedingly important.

There are also dozens of bilateral and multilateral committees, commissions, conferences and clubs between Japan and other countries, whether East or West, North or South. Some seek closer economic cooperation and exchanges while others focus on relations between businessmen. Most of them, whatever their name or supposed sponsor, actually stem from Keidanren, Nissho or Keizai Doyukai and contribute to improving Japan's international situation. Aside from this, Keidanren and the others receive foreign dignitaries, including heads of state, and send numerous high powered delegations abroad.

Such formal organizations, however, are not the only guise under which businessmen can deal with politicians. All up-and-coming LDP leaders, especially those looked upon as potential prime ministers, have attracted personal advisors who can inform them of trends in business circles and help them obtain necessary funds. In some cases, they actually formed broader groups of ten, twenty or thirty such advisors including leading *zaikai-jin* like Doko, Inayama, Otsuki and Nagano, regional business figures and heads of top companies to serve this purpose. This could even be institutionalized with regular meetings and an official name. It was not as if the businessmen imposed themselves on the politicians, they were avidly courted, especially by those who initially had few business connections like Suzuki and Nakasone.

Finally, the individual companies are frequently active in promoting the general interests of the business community as well as the more specific ones they may have. They do so in countless ways, such as by maintaining warm relations with appropriate bureaucrats or politicians and, in addition to mere commercial advertising, engage in public relations or produce publications to enhance the overall image of business. Alas, at this level, it is hard to keep the narrower and broader interests separate and there has been a tendency to go too far. This is probably most applicable to the construction industry which lives from state contracts and is vitally interested in certain political decisions. This has led it to become more influential in certain spheres than more prestigious big business.

What is most striking about these organizations, the individual companies and Japanese businessmen in general is that they have not hesitated to express their views on key national issues and to take steps to ensure that business opinions should be duly considered. This could take the more commonplace form of proposing or endorsing appropriate economic or social legislation and criticizing other alternatives. But it could go much further by supporting the ruling Liberal Democratic Party against the opposition parties. And it might result in blatant string-pulling within the LDP.

Naturally, the business community could not speak with one voice or adopt positions that were always uniform. There was too much diversity among the companies by size and sector as well as variations between what different groups or generations of business leaders sought. Most notable were the divergencies between Keidanren, strongly oriented toward the concerns of big business, and Nissho, which paid more attention to the problems of smaller firms. There could also be conflicts between different branches, banking versus securities, power companies versus power consumers, or rising versus declining sectors. But many of these points could be settled amongst them and there were always overriding issues where just about all companies had common concerns, the most obvious being taxation and promotion of business.

It was all the easier for the four leading federations which epitomize the *zaikai,* namely Keidanren, Nikkeiren, Keizai Doyakai and Nissho, to coordinate and cooperate in that there was a notable cumulation of posts. The same people were on the board of several organizations and major companies, or their representatives, belonged to all four. They also had many joint committees and held joint seminars or press conferences. The *zaikai-jin,* relieved of most corporate duties, had more than enough time to attend meetings and get to know what their peers thought. Since many kept this up for a decade or more, they could become a reasonbly homogeneous and cohesive group, at least when it came to relations with outsiders like politicians, bureaucrats or foreigners.

What is more, the *zaikai* was often one up on the politicians and bureaucrats. Its spokesmen had the research staff and access to information which politicians lacked and could therefore make more cogent and persuasive presentations on crucial issues. Expertise here could even exceed that of the bureaucracy's generalists. Since business leaders stayed in place longer than ministers or high officials, they had more experience than their counterparts who, as juniors, also owed them deference. They also had access to funds which the politicians dearly needed and those in the LDP, in particular, could not survive without. And they could offer suitable rewards to bureaucrats who cooperated.

Their principal drawback is that, having spent their whole careers within specific companies and defending their interests, the *zaikai-jin* did not always have a very keen understanding of what the interests of other people were or, indeed, how other people lived. They naturally cared little enough about the more personal worries of the working class, with whom they had to contend, or the broader ranks of ordinary citizens, whom they had dealt with mainly as consumers. More serious, most business leaders were getting on in age by the time they first entered the *zaikai* in their fifties and many stayed into their sixties and seventies. That made it very difficult for them to fathom the concerns of younger generations or feel the changing times.

Yet, none of this keeps the *zaikai* from being a tremendous force in the nation. It is not just the reflection of a nebulous or poorly articulated agglomeration of views but a phalanx of organizations and associations with abundant funds, personnel and other resources. Its activities are continuous and extensive. And it is borne by men who enjoy considerable authority in their companies and prestige more widely. In fact, there is no equally potent business community anywhere else in the world. It would therefore be quite impossible to grasp the operation of the political system without carefully considering what is done here.

Paying The Piper

When business circles speak, political and bureaucratic circles listen very respectfully and usually do something about whatever the subject may be. This is so self-evident that even casual observers notice. What they may fail to do adequately is ponder why the *zaikai*'s voice is so clearly heard and patently effective amidst the general cacophony of political life.

In this case, it is not because there are many direct business representatives in the Diet or local assemblies, as occurs for the bureaucrats. Actually, not many businessmen go into politics and few of them have done particularly well. Toshio Komoto, founder of a major shipping line, is a rare example whose tenacity eventually brought him one of the smaller factions. Tokusaburo Kosaka, former head of a chemical company, was briefly seen as a "new leader." The only businessman who made it to the top was Kakuei Tanaka, a contractor by profession but a politician by taste, and he was hardly typical of the category whose input has been only modest.[4]

Rather, it is because of financial backing of the ruling

party that business gained an ascendency. Year after year, corporations have been contributing to its finances and the amounts have tended to grow with time. In 1984, according to the Ministry of Home Affairs, the Liberal Democratic Party collected some ¥26 billion. Its factions received another ¥8 billion, with Prime Minister Nakasone's group on top followed by the Komoto, Fukuda, Suzuki and Tanaka factions. But Tanaka's poor showing was misleading since he intentionally kept a low profile and allowed half-a-dozen of his lieutenants to collect funds as well.

Where this money came from was also indicated in the MHA's report. Over half of the funds were political donations *(kifu)* from companies and organizations. The rest consisted of membership fees and purchase of tickets for fund-raising events. Since much of this also came directly or indirectly from the business community, it accounted for the bulk of the LDP's revenue. The industries which were most generous were also known and did not vary much over time: banking, construction and real estate, electronics and telecommunications, automobiles, steel and machinery.

How the money got there was pretty well known, at least for the funds that were reported. The principal mechanism was a National Political Association (Kokumin Seiji Kyokai) which replaced a discredited National Association (Kokumin Kyokai) in 1975. Basically, it served as a pipeline from Keidanren to the LDP. Each year the Association would tap its corporate and organization members for political donations as well as monthly dues and "special assessments" for elections. The amount they paid was not a spontaneous expression of solicitude but, in many cases, the result of detailed allocations worked out by Keidanren, taking into account company

"Thank you for your further support." Nakasone entertained by top business leaders.

Credit: Foreign Press Center/Kyodo

size, financial strength, business situation and other factors. No sooner deposited than this money emerged in the LDP's bank account.

Hefty as these sums are, there is no reason to believe that they represent anything like the total. For one, they include only the monies paid to the national and prefectural headquarters, factions and individual politicians. Missing are sums paid to local chapters and the numerous support organizations. Also missing are contributions which were purposely kept off the record. Just how much this amounted to nobody knew. But it was obviously a lot to judge from the annual reports of the National Tax Administration Agency which showed ¥46 billion in "unaccounted-for expenditures" in 1985, a portion of this known to be political funds and kickbacks. Since this figure applied only to the fifth of the major corporations that were inspected, the total sum would be vastly larger.

Moreover, ever since the 1974 elections, when Keidanren's financial role became too prominent, it has tried to show only moderate contributions. Meanwhile, corporations which have special requests or get special treatment naturally have to make special donations as well. Some of this is reported. Much of it is not. That is why most authorities feel the official figure should be multiplied by a factor of three or more. This would put the LDP's actual intake at something like ￥75–￥100 billion which would appear more realistic.

There are two other forms of financial support which should be noted. One is loans from commercial banks, since the LDP has been heavily in debt for many years. Another is remuneration of politicians who work as advisors or board members of companies and trade associations and are paid exceedingly well for this activity. What they actually do is uncertain. But there is rarely any way of mistaking the intentions. One notorious case was a justice minister who was hired by the consumer loan association as an advisor just at the time this sector came under criticism. Such a practice is forbidden by most liberal democracies, but Japan is particularly liberal on this point.

While the amount of money is important, since money counts so much in getting elected, even more significant is the share which comes from any given source. If the LDP could raise substantial funds itself through membership dues, sales of its publications or ordinary fund-raising events, it could remain reasonably independent. Yet, despite some recent efforts, the share of contributions from the business community has revolved around 90% or more of its funding. It is hardly possible to be more dependent and thus the very threat of a reduction is enough to make it kowtow to business interests.

Money is not the only thing the *zaikai* can supply.

Companies have been uncommonly active in getting out the vote. Smaller firms especially, where personal relations are particularly close, do not hesitate to instruct their workers on how to vote. Larger ones tend to do this more discreetly. But there is never any question about how the companies want the elections to turn out. While they may not be heeded, executives do have considerable influence over their employees. In rural constituencies, where many factories are located, it is easy enough to tell if the workers followed instructions or not.

When one considers that the big companies associated with Keidanren employ over a tenth of the labor force, and the many small and medium-sized enterprises related to Nissho bring it to about half, this makes a tremendous number of voters who can be approached. Electoral mathematics also explain the exceptional clout of construction firms since there are well over five million employees in the building trades. With their livelihood so directly bound up with government decisions, they would not hesitate to vote the right way. More recently, in order to further their industry, life insurance salesmen have been promoting the LDP as well.

During most electoral campaigns, business circles have preferred working behind-the-scenes. However, in decisive elections such as the one which first brought the LDP to power and others which ensured its staying there, they could be considerably more assertive. A good example was the 1974 upper house election when, under the direction of Keidanren, each major corporation "sponsored" a specific LDP candidate, financed him and openly campaigned for him. The outcome was a minor backlash for the LDP and major criticism of business leaders. This sort of commitment was quickly played down when Toshio Doko became Keidanren's new president. But it cannot be excluded that something similar might occur in a future election if the LDP were threatened with losing power.

Still, on the whole, business leaders leave political campaigning to politicians and concentrate on more general and diffuse action which may be no less effective. One is part of the ongoing public relations activities in which the major business federations express their views. No matter how much they may occasionally chide the LDP, they never leave any doubt that they feel it is the only acceptable party. More insidiously, they hint that it is the only party which can maintain a sound and productive economy and thereby deliver the consumer goods most ordinary citizens want. At election time, the appeals become more precise and pressing.

On the other hand, the business community has never hidden its repulsion for the Japan Communist Party and, somewhat less belligerently, the Japan Socialist Party. No matter how attenuated their programs or how eager the efforts to be "lovable," the leftists and Marxists are thoroughly distrusted. They are therefore criticized for foolhardy policies or duplicity in presenting more reasonable policies they do not really believe in. This is not restricted purely to verbal abuse. Most companies have done their best to keep any suspicious elements off their payroll and turned away the radical students when they sought work (a practice permitted by the courts). They also undermined more aggressive unions, splitting them if need be, and usually wound up with moderate and cooperative house unions affiliated with Domei rather than Sohyo.

The approach to the middle-of-the-road parties has been subtler. Businessmen have not been entirely adverse to Komeito, which propounds no loathsome socialist doctrine and has the advantage of absorbing part of the JSP clientele. The Democratic Socialist Party, which divided the Socialist camp, has been even more welcome for that very reason. While disapproving of the NLC's split from the LDP, this was still a conservative and pro-business party and did eventually rejoin the LDP's ranks. So, these three parties have been praised for making suitable adjustments in their programs and have benefited from political donations and other support.

The most interesting wrinkle, however, arises in connection with the DSP. The biggest threat to continued conservative rule is either a coalition of leftist or centrist forces, in both of which DSP participation is crucial. But the DSP is one of the weaker parties and could be squeezed out if not adroitly aided. Thus, for some time already, major companies have been making substantial contributions to its funding. Even more intriguing, in many elections they also suggest that their workers vote DSP, especially if they can vote for more than one candidate or the LDP-man is unpalatable. This keeps the DSP viable and also increases the *zaikai*'s influence over it. This could prove decisive if one day the LDP had to opt for a coalition.

Relations with the bureaucrats are also quite cozy, although the manipulation takes different forms. While public employees are paid reasonably well and can expect a decent retirement, and therefore have less acute needs for money than politicians, they are not immune to certain temptations. As noted, they do enjoy fine wining and dining, especially when their own wages or pocket money exclude this. It is nice to have an occasional round of golf, at the expense of some big company, and especially if they bet on the game and win a lot of money when their host turns out to be a poor golfer. Then there are the real bribes (winning at golf is mere sport).

Nothing tops the lure of a cushy *amakudari* post. To

show that there is no mystery about who is chosen or how this comes about, a few examples will be given. There is the former director of the MOF's banking bureau who was recruited by a major securities house that wishes to diversify into banking. Or the former director of MITI's machinery industries bureau who negotiated the automobile agreement with the United States and was subsequently picked up by Japan's leading automobile manufacturer. Or the former MOC vice-minister who joined an architectural consultant's office. Or the top military brass who routinely become advisors for the leading defense contractor. And many, many more.

But that is only one side of the picture. The primary task of most bureaucrats is to satisfy the needs of their clientele, these needs being more palpable and pressing than the more diffuse interests of the public. The bureau or ministry for which they work has been doing this for decades already. So, no young bureaucrat would think of doing anything else. If he did, companies have warm relations with many classes of seniors who have served them well and whose influence can be used to move a recalcitrant junior.

Moreover, through their contacts with the politicians, which are much more extensive and forceful than those of most bureaucrats, they can bring pressure to bear. Admittedly, ministers, vice-ministers and other politicians do not ordinarily try to dictate the general policy of a bureaucracy. But they do not hesitate to make specific demands if this is in the interest of their clientele or constituency. Then they can be very hard-nosed and tenacious overseers and often obtain what they want from junior bureaucrats. Senior ones might, in theory, stand pat. But they are just the ones who are on the point of retiring and are tempted by the many advantages of cooperation.

This explains the incredible clout of business circles in

their relationship with political and bureaucratic circles. It cannot be regarded as absolute in the sense that every politician or bureaucrat can be influenced or, more crudely, "bought" or that the *zaikai* can always foist its views on the ruling party and administration. There are some who reject this interference and certain points which are not readily negotiable. Such limitations, however, do not invalidate the conclusion that the business community is indeed immensely powerful and effective.

Calling The Tune

Japan's businessmen have always been perfectly clear on the basic principles of what they want and which can be summed up as a pristine form of capitalism with as little government interference as possible. They have repeatedly spoken in favor of private initiative, free enterprise and free trade. In fact, in the early postwar period they did so with an almost crusading zeal since they had lost this freedom for some decades and did not want a repeat. Even today, the principles are ritually uttered and, despite some talk of an "amended" capitalism, most *zaikai-jin* prefer a highly unadulterated form, at least as they see it. This is not altered by the pious references to business' social responsibility and concern for the well-being of the nation and mankind.

However, in the course of economic development, both in Meiji days and since the war, they have adopted any number of practical policies and short-term tactics which are grossly different. Rising from the ashes of defeat, businessmen insistently clamored for financial aid and even a certain amount of direction from the state to get things going. Then, as the economy swung upward, they pointed to the benefits of promoting strategic industries with loans, tax incentives and government procurement.

Moreover, to protect industries until they could stand alone, there was an irrepressible urge for quotas and tariffs. To repel the awaited foreign onslaught, it was felt that closer regulation of markets by the companies concerned, and even cartels, should be permitted.

Naturally, none of this had much in common with *laissez-faire* and there probably never was a period in Japanese economic history in which anything resembling a classical "free" economy existed. This did not seriously disturb the businessmen for what they wanted, when the frills were removed, was really to control their own destiny and even impose their will on others on the assumption that what was good for business was good for Japan. This they have been attempting, with remarkable success, from start to finish. There was barely any deviation from this rule through the many twists and turns of formal policy and whatever the lofty principles inherently meant.

Economically, what was sought—and eventually obtained—was an extraordinarily comprehensive array of measures to support business in general and emerging sectors in particular. This ranged from tax relief and rebates to specially low customs duties for necessary raw materials and intermediate goods, from easy access to low-interest loans to outright subsidies. Companies were firmly encouraged to induce advanced technologies and special efforts were made to promote research and development. Protection from imports was very thorough and amazingly long-lasting. It consisted of tariffs, quotas and sometimes outright bans. There were also any number of administrative complications and nontariff barriers. This left time for domestic companies to organize markets in such a way that foreign competitors could scarcely penetrate later on. Meanwhile, to keep them from working within the system, foreign investment was also restricted.[5]

There were other things the government could do. By

regulating the banks and other financial institutions, it was possible to influence the allocation of domestic savings and to keep them within the country. To allow companies to concentrate more on overseas expansion than local rivalries, the antitrust machinery could be toned down. By not pressing social concerns like better wages, working conditions and shorter hours for labor and by neglecting environmental hazards, a single-minded pursuit of production was facilitated. And, by going slow on social overhead and welfare, more investment could be pumped into productive machinery. Meanwhile, vast programs of public works could be undertaken to stimulate domestic demand and keep contractors and suppliers busy.

This was a generally acceptable program for all companies and especially big business which benefited most. Naturally, there was less to be gained by smaller firms and, in fact, some inconveniences and drawbacks. But it was usually possible to provide a sop for just about everyone and small-scale enterprises also got special funds, state support and their own agency. Most of the conflicts and divergencies could readily be overcome, at least in the earlier period, by simply offering something to everybody. After all, it was the public at large, as workers, consumers, taxpayers and ordinary citizens who had to foot the bill. Only more recently, when the *zaikai*'s policies switched from increased spending to reduced taxation was it hard to meet everybody's needs.

The business community had a big advantage in pushing such a program because the scope was sufficiently narrow for it to concentrate its efforts on a relatively small number of issues and also a restricted circle of politicians and bureaucrats. Yet, while it did not have much of a social policy, it clearly affected that domain. By containing wages and fringe benefits, discouraging social overhead and welfare, and ignoring environmental and consumer needs, it lowered their priority. Some progress was made during the high growth period, when there was enough money for everything. However, after the tax revolt, it was these items which were not just neglected but actively rejected and attacked for foisting an unwanted burden on the economy.

Foreign policy was also affected by this concerted thrust of the *zaikai*. Businessmen never thought much of development aid of a general or idealistic nature and obstinately claimed that facilitating imports (usually of raw materials) and making investments (to help sell Japanese goods abroad), was already a signal contribution. They grudgingly agreed to offer more projects and improve relations with foreign partners when faced with unpleasantness and retaliation and played a significant role in structuring contacts with foreign business circles, but that was regarded as quite enough. They did not want Japan to undertake major foreign policy initiatives since that would be risky and costly. And, for much the same reasons, they did not want to overdo defense spending.

Given its philosophy, program and policy options, it was obvious that the *zaikai* had to back the conservative parties and, while so doing, enhance its own position within the establishment. Businessmen never made any secret of their unstinting support of the Liberal Democratic Party although, on occasion, they criticized its policies or leadership. And this support has often been decisive in determining Japan's political fate.

The original merger of the Democratic and Liberal Parties was largely instigated by business circles which had been financing both and feared that a resurgent Socialist Party could take power. By switching their allegiance, and directing their funds to a single party, they did much to keep it from falling apart again. That is why they criticized factionalism so harshly and made it abundantly clear that they did not want any division in the ranks. They also notified the LDP, in many and varied ways, as to what policies the *zaikai* wished to see adopted in return for its aid. These policies, which were briefly outlined above, were by and large the ones which predominated over the past few decades.

In order to maintain good relations with the LDP, the business community as a whole tried not to interfere in the complex and embittered personal intrigues. Admittedly, some businessmen backed one faction more than the others. But, since there was bound to be a rotation, they did not want to get on bad terms with someone who might suddenly come out on top. If anything, they were very good at switching to whoever the new leader was. Still, and this was clearly perceived by the press and public, *zaikai-jin* favored certain leaders. They rallied behind Yoshida, and then Ikeda and Sato, and preferred Fukuda to Tanaka, whom they briefly supported and then helped dump. Miki they patently disliked. There were no strong preferences among recent leaders aside from Nakasone, a man who initially inspired considerable suspicion but won massive support for personally backing administrative reform.

Where they did intervene, promptly and sharply, is when LDP actions tarnished the *zaikai*'s reputation. There was near outrage when businessmen were summoned to the Diet after the oil shock and accused of contributing to inflation or blamed for participating too vigorously in the 1974 election. At that time, Toshio Doko distanced himself from the LDP and objected to the trend toward "money power." Businessmen also complained loudly about the excessive demands for funding and urged the party to call fewer elections or keep campaign costs down. Whenever it got caught up in factional quarrels, hurting its own image and becoming unable to accomplish its parliamentary tasks, the LDP was criticized. Yoshihiro Inayama went so far as to call the intraparty strife "a form of political degeneration" stemming from the politicians' "selfish lust for power and money."[6] But the business community never withheld funds long enough to impose a reform which, had it been successful, would have reduced its leverage.

While proper relations with the ruling party were extremely useful, a suitable relationship with the bureaucracy could be even more essential on occasion. This time the links were terribly convoluted since the bureaucrats were widely dispersed and their actions were more discreet and veiled. But the individual companies and leading organizations quickly established contacts with every last cog in the machinery and often personally with any bureaucrat who could possibly help (or harm) their cause. This resulted from regular visits, some because it was otherwise impossible to know what the essential regulations and administrative guidance actually implied. The rest were to obtain a bit more than usual. And, to consolidate good relations, bureaucrats were wined and dined, received handsome gifts, and might eventually find a job after retirement.

These intimate relations, however, underwent appreciable changes depending on the tack taken by business leaders at any given time. Shortly after the war, most businessmen were desperate to revive their companies and relied heavily on government assistance. They called on the LDP to adopt measures to help industry and urged the bureaucrats to implement them vigorously. Somewhat later, they became worried about the invasive nature of this aid with bureaucrats taking initiatives that breached the sanctity of free enterprise as they saw it. Nothing was disliked more than MITI's pretension to rationalize industry, which involved deciding on capacity, output and even mergers, vital prerogatives of any entrepreneur. Such excessive intervention was solidly opposed by business circles, including Keidanren's then president Ishizaka. As of the early 1960s, the need for government support and scope for bureaucratic influence began receding. Most companies were sufficiently consolidated to meet their own needs. They possessed considerably more capital, had a steady cash flow and could easily borrow more from domestic or foreign banks. Any government subsidies or R&D, while welcome, were just a modest supplement. Moreover, as the economy was liberalized and trade barriers came down, there was ever less to be grateful for. If anything, after the oil crisis, businessmen were critical of the administration for not adjusting to harder times by cutting its own staff and rationalizing activities.

By the late 1970s, the relationship was being reversed. There was much less need of bureaucratic aid and the government could afford to offer less. This relieved the *zaikai* of its dependence on both to a large extent. At the same time, the bureaucrats collectively and individually were increasingly dependent on business good will to maintain their jobs and find new ones after retirement. The LDP, which had periodically lost its majority and needed more campaign funds than ever, counted more on business largesse than ever. Ultimately, the business community turned on them by demanding small government and administrative reform. While not actually dominating, the businessmen had become the more influential partner.

At this point, one can return to the concept of "Japan, Inc." which had been imputed by some and categorically repudiated by others. There is no question but that the interests of government (both the ruling party and bureaucracy) and business were tightly intertwined in Japan, much more so than in any contemporary liberal economy. In fact, the Japanese themselves speak of "the government hand-in-hand with the private sector" *(kanmin-ittai)*. Formal legislation and regulations were adopted to promote domestic companies, and coincidentally undercut foreign ones, and then further reinforced by apparently arbitrary bureaucratic action. But there was really nothing arbitrary or mysterious about it, all three were simply doing their bit for Japan. This collusion is what has been regarded as the essence of the special relationship and it can hardly be denied, even if not all of the fanciful claims are true.

The big difference with most versions of "Japan, Inc." is that foreign and domestic observers frequently get the direction of the influence wrong. They assume the vital impulse must come from the government.[7] Seeing that business circles are increasingly less dependent on aid from the politicians and bureaucrats it is argued that such relations no longer exist, if they ever did, and that the whole thing is a myth. But, why can't these relations emanate just as well from the business side? Moreover, if business is calling most of the shots, does this not make the whole arrangement more effective? If these rather obvious conclusions can be conceded, then there is—and for many decades has been—exceptional collaboration between the politicians, bureaucrats and businessmen in the economic scene.

This collaboration naturally goes much further than economic activities. It affects, either by action or omission, just about every conceivable form of policy in the nation. In other sectors, business circles may not be quite as noticeable as for matters of direct concern. But they certainly intervene to an amazing extent in nearly every aspect of governance. In some ways, they actually usurp the role of the politicians in proposing or initiating policies. As for the bureaucracy, it no longer deals with businessmen in such a high-handed manner and has to knuckle under when the *zaikai* pursues a goal collectively and resolutely. In this way, both the formal government and the shadow government come under the partial sway of another power whose existence is not even mentioned in the constitution and unwittingly overlooked in most political analyses.[8]

NOTES

1. For information on the origins and background of this group, see Hiroshi Mannari, *The Japanese Business Leaders*.
2. How the *zaikai* influences politics is traced in Chitoshi Yanaga, *Big Business in Japanese Politics*.
3. This crucial period is extensively described in Joe Moore, *Japanese Workers and the Struggle for Power*.
4. It might be mentioned that such businessmen did not always give up their commercial activities and that their political connections were often used to enhance the position of related companies. Two of the best examples are Tanaka and his construction companies and Komoto and Sanko Steamship Co.
5. See Michael R. Czinkota and Jon Woronoff, *Japan's Distribution System*.
6. *Japan Times,* August 27, 1974, and May 24, 1980.
7. The preeminent role of the *zaikai* is no secret to the Japanese people who put it ahead of the political parties, cabinet and Diet in a poll on "who controls politics?" (*Yomiuri Shimbun,* June 15, 1985.)
8. It should be noted that business interests often dominate local politics even more effectively, especially where a large company is the primary employer and source of revenue. For Toyota's role in local government, see Gary D. Allinson, *Japanese Urbanism: Industry and Politics in Kariya*.

5
Lesser Figures

A Workaday Emperor

Under the postwar regime, no state organ was downgraded more than the emperor. The Meiji Constitution had created a system of Imperial absolutism where most acts and measures had to be approved, and often initiated, by the emperor or—in reality—those who advised and manipulated him. None of this was retained in the new constitution and the emperor merely became the "symbol" of the state.

He did maintain certain functions, but most of them were formal or ceremonial. He was to appoint the prime minister and chief judge of the Supreme Court. He had to convene and dissolve the Diet, proclaim elections, grant amnesties, award honors, receive foreign ambassadors, and so on. But all of this was undertaken with the approval and at the initiative of the cabinet, which decided what should be done.

Yet, even this drastic reduction in formal power was exceeded by Emperor Hirohito, who led a relatively quiet and retired life. He appeared rarely enough in public and barely established a dialogue with the people, even such as exists in many other countries where kings or princes maintain little real authority. Many of the social acts which are typical of European or Thai nobility were eschewed as the sovereign spent much of his time studying sea life.

And, what little desire he may have had to surface more often or actively was stifled by the court ritual and rules, over which he seemed to have scant control either.

There were, of course, periodic and endearing glimpses of the Imperial Family on special occasions. The emperor and empress waved to well-wishers on their birthday or national holidays and "informal" scenes were carried on television. There was a flurry of excitement when the crown prince decided to marry a commoner. Since then, while not taking over official functions, the prince and princess have appeared here and there to open conferences or grace other events. There are gossipy articles in some weekly magazines regarding the studies and marriages of members of the Imperial Family. But that is about it.

When the war drew to a close, it was feared that if the

Greeting the Imperial family on New Year's. Not masses, but many.
Credit: Foreign Press Center/Kyodo

emperor had been arrested or dismissed, the Japanese population would have risen up against the enemy and the conquest and occupation would have been much more arduous. That is probably true, so strong was the indoctrination and emperor cult. Yet, today, there is hardly a sign of support for the Imperial cause. Those who are particularly nostalgic are already old and a dwindling minority. Their only token gain was to maintain the Imperial date system *(gengo)* with the accession of each new emperor marking the start of an era. At the same time, those who vehemently oppose the Imperial House as a symbol of the detested wartime system have also diminished. Most people care little one way or the other and, as usual in such cases, cling to the *status quo*.

This makes the Imperial Family about as inconsequential as it had almost always been aside from the Meiji and nationalist eras, which were basically exceptions to the rule. The emperor has rarely ruled, governed or even been a notable presence in most of Japan's long history, leading a controlled and secluded life. He has lapsed back into that role again. Still, he occasionally adds a bright and hopeful note to the otherwise grimy and depressing political routine.

The Subdued Military

Far more essential was to bring the military into line. Throughout much of its history, Japan had been ruled by military cliques or dynasties and the *samurai* were on top of the social hierarchy until Meiji days, when they had to hand over their swords and were supplanted in the army and navy by commoners. But the new military quickly absorbed many of the old traditions and repeatedly came into conflict with the civilian authorities. Sometimes it was brought to heel; more often, it got what it wanted. After winning military control over the internal organization, generals and admirals gradually imposed their will on the nation.

While the military played a prominent role in other enemy nations, it was most conspicuous in Japan. Still, it was probably more a quirk of fate that General MacArthur and Prime Minister Shidehara agreed to insert a special Article 9 in the constitution which not only reduced its power but actually outlawed it. After providing that "the Japanese people forever renounce war as a sovereign right of the nation and the threat or use of force as means of settling international disputes," it added: "land, sea and air forces, as well as other war potential, will never be maintained."

Nevertheless, the three arms did emerge in the guise of the Self-Defense Forces. In spite of any constitutional impediments and political objections, the SDF has already grown to over a quarter-of-a-million persons equipped with powerful modern weapons. This resurgence caused serious misgivings in Japan and abroad since it was feared that the flame of militarism might be rekindled and the military could again take control.

For the moment, that seems most unlikely. The SDF is firmly under the control of a civilian Defense Agency and the ministers appointed, on the whole, have been reasonably moderate. They defend the interests of their bureaucracy and fight for every additional yen in the budget, but they have never tried to alter the principle of civilian control. Moreover, various governments have taken measures which imposed tight restrictions on the military's actual potential, such as the refusal to acquire offensive weapons, the 1% of GNP ceiling on defense expenditures and the "three non-nuclear principles."

A much bigger hindrance to its effectiveness, however, is that the military no longer enjoys much prestige in the nation. Its status is very low and many Japanese wonder whether it is worth the money it costs. There are relatively few who would support any increase in its powers or want to augment its budget. Worse, it is rather difficult to recruit able officers or enlisted men since a career in business or the bureaucracy is rated much higher. Those who do join think of it as a job and grumble about the lack of respect. Indeed, the situation is such that the SDF often has trouble holding on to its effectives. This popular rejection, more than any formal measures, is probably the strongest constraint.

Of far more concern to the average citizen is the police force. Numbering some 250,000, it is surprisingly large for a reputedly law-abiding society. Located throughout the country in small stations *(koban)* in the midst of the population, they have an unusually good idea of what is

Fukuda reviewing the Self-Defense Forces while others review the constitution.

Credit: Foreign Press Center/Kyodo

going on. While their primary concern is crime prevention, they do keep an eye peeled for extremists on both sides, if somewhat more notably leftists and radicals. Politically, they are most significant due to the special riot squads *(kidotai)* with some 10,000 members, enough not only to regulate the ongoing demonstrations *(demo)* but to contain and almost smother them in masses of burly men with helmets, shields and staves.[1]

A Judicious Judiciary

There is no state organ whose position was enhanced more under the new order than the judiciary. It was brought into the fundamental separation of powers as a counterbalance to the executive and legislative branches, a drastic change in a system where the courts played quite a minor role and were subject to the state's wishes. This time, the Supreme Court was not only at the head of a broad network of inferior courts, it was empowered, under Article 81, to determine the constitutionality of any law, order, regulation or official act.

While such provisions could be placed in the constitution, it naturally took more than that to make them operative. It required an independent judiciary which was not easy to attain since the lower judges rose out of a relatively conservative infrastructure and Supreme Court justices are political appointees. More important, and hardly the sort of thing that can be legislated, the judges had to be bold and farsighted individuals. Such people were few and far between and least likely to be found in the judicial system Japan possessed.

Thus, the Supreme Court was not a final arbiter in any real sense and it refused to tackle sensitive issues time and again. In cases with a strong political flavor, it most often decided that the question was beyond its jurisdiction as a political matter or dismissed it for some subsidiary reason, such as that it could only rule on concrete and not theoretical points which many questions of constitutionality ultimately were. In so doing, it frequently reversed more audacious lower courts.[2] Yet, even then, the courts went much further than their prewar predecessors and adopted a number of rulings which were quite interesting and had a definite influence on the course of events.

On the few occasions when the courts went too far, taking decisions that interfered with or merely embarrassed the other organs, the result was not a conflict such as might have arisen elsewhere. The executive and legislative branches simply ignored what had been done by a very junior partner in the de facto establishment.

The Common Folk

An even more exalted position was reserved for the "people" in whose will sovereignty resided, as per Article 1. This was indeed a spectacular promotion for what had been relatively downtrodden masses, long subject to the whims of the Emperor, *shogun, daimyo, samurai, genro,* politicians, bureaucrats, big businessmen and military. This populace, while normally docile, had nonetheless shown an undeniable will for progress ever since Meiji days. People formed associations and political parties, created trade unions and peasants' associations, and frequently engaged in perilous—and perhaps also subversive—political activities. Many braved the dangers of imprisonment and torture and some perished before their voice was silenced by the nationalist regime.[3]

Now, by the grace of a foreign commander, the people were at the pinnacle of the power structure and expected to run things. To say that the preparation was inadequate would be a gross understatement. That is one reason why the reality of power gradually slipped out of its hands to be confiscated by the ruling party, bureaucracy and business community as well as certain pressure groups. But the people did not give up entirely without a fight. Alas, as in bygone days, most of the struggles were sporadic, poorly organized and futile. They were followed by a number of waves of popular sentiment, which turned into wavelets, and were absorbed by the sands of time.

The first major struggle, perhaps the decisive one, came just after the defeat when resentment against the military and nationalists was strongest and the conservative politicians and businessmen had not yet reorganized. Amidst misery, hunger and disorder, thousands of mine workers and others went on strike and angry employees took over their companies. This was backed by the Communists, and more cautiously the Socialists, and to some it looked as if a massive upheaval were in the making. It was then that SCAP, previously willing to let events take their own course, intervened decisively by banning the Japan Communist Party and arresting its militants and also helping to break the strikes. But it could not really be credited with halting the turmoil. This was more a result of action by indigenous leaders who already ran the government, controlled the police and had the backing of business circles.[4]

During the 1950s, there were still a number of violent demonstrations, many of them directed against the Japan-U.S. Security Treaty (Ampo). From friends, the Americans had turned into enemies for many leftists who also disapproved of their role in the Korean War, which indirectly involved Japan. Even more anger was aroused by the rollback undertaken by Yoshida and Kishi. There were strikes and demonstrations in the streets and fights in the Diet regarding the revision of the police law, the education bill and other legislation. In 1960, things came to a head when Prime Minister Kishi rammed through the revised security treaty. This time, the anti-Ampo campaigns swelled prodigiously, attracting not only Communists, Socialists and trade unionists but also students and ordinary citizens. During the riots, one person died, and it was feared that more bloodshed might result if President Eisenhower visited Japan as scheduled. Thus, the presidential visit was cancelled and Kishi stepped down. But that was it. The treaty existed, close American relations continued, and yet the disturbances petered out. This was only partly due to smarter police tactics and the arrival of a conciliatory Ikeda. The Japanese "middle" class may have been frightened by these excesses.

The anti-treaty campaigns were not entirely without bearing fruit since, in the late 1960s, a radical student movement emerged in high schools and universities throughout the nation, including the most prestigious ones like Todai and Keio.[5] Launched by the National Federation of Students' Self-Governing Councils (Zengakuren), it was initially directed against the American bases and the war in Vietnam. It quickly turned against the Sato government for backing of the United States and adopting other reactionary policies. Later it condemned the educational system and authorities. While increasingly violent, the clashes could be largely contained on the campuses, although occasionally spilling over, and the often boisterous events rarely involved other than students or former students. In the end, it was probably less the police than the activists themselves who crippled the movement, splitting into rival factions and sects, some backed by political parties, others independent, and spending their fury on one another.[6] While some groups still exist, student radicalism gradually faded away without accomplishing its aims.

During the 1960s and 1970s, a welter of smaller campaigns sprang up, this time among quite ordinary people in towns, villages and city neighborhoods. Known as "citizen's movements" *(shimin undo)*, they organized for a variety of causes, most of which were related to their particular situation.[7] Many of them had an ecological basis, as they reacted to one source of pollution or another or tried to prevent the construction of objectionable public works that could destroy the existing environment. Some of the more prominent were directed against nuclear power plants, the *shinkansen* or airports and the most famous rallied against Narita.[8] But few went further than their initial cause to attack broader problems, even such issues as overall environmental degradation or nuclear energy. And, aside from some informal links with one another, they remained very parochial. Worst of all, most eventually ended up negotiating for compensation and completely forgetting any deeper concerns.

There were any number of other movements which arose, attracted popular attention, were deemed the wave of the future, and then subsided. As noted, there was a budding interest in ecological problems and this sometimes spread to broader manifestations such as overall control of pollution or condemnation of nuclear power plants. Consumerism emerged, often as an offshoot of traditional housewives' associations but also in more modern forms. And there were promising initiatives to promote grass-roots democracy, especially at the local and regional level. Citizens' groups emerged to counter certain government plans, remove untrustworthy politicians or combat bureaucratic inefficiency and excesses. But they rarely enrolled large numbers of people or reached the intensity felt abroad. In fact, some typical movements like minorities' rights, womens' lib (or gay lib), grey power, ecologists, the Greens or much of the artistic and cultural experimentation (including alternative lifestyles) hardly existed. Most of the movements remained very fragmented, revolving around some concrete case or a given person and even the nationwide federations were usually just loose coalitions of like-minded groups.

Only one rallying call proved lasting and had widespread backing, that was economic growth. Prime Minister Ikeda showed keen insight when he directed people's energy away from divisive political issues, like defense and foreign affairs, and toward development. Moreover, his appeal was not of a vague or general nature as in more idealistic regimes but very concrete and palpable. Japanese were urged to work for more consumer goods, better housing, some leisure and welfare, goals that few could reject. And the urge to contest them was weakest at a time when the economy was just coming out of the postwar slump and expanding at an unprecedented pace. The only moment this striving was relaxed came in the early 1970s, when people tired of GNPism. But the oil crisis and worldwide recession put an end to that as it became necessary to work ever harder to attain the good life.

In the end, it was the economic goals which won out over the more political goals of earlier days. In fact, it would seem that the Japanese had great difficulty in pursuing abstract principles or ideals. Material objectives were much easier to grasp. A television set, automobile, their own home, even GNP, were much more compelling. This proclivity partially explains why the political causes quickly petered out. Most Japanese revolted against the capitalists because they could not provide, not out of principle, and once the business community was able to deliver the goods, it was tolerated and even emulated. The Americans were envied more than hated. And the best way to exorcise that was to become as prosperous as they. Meanwhile, students gave up their ideals for a good job and citizens shelved their complaints for the right counterpart.

Moreover, as the Japanese became more affluent, they also became more conservative. The more they had, the less they were willing to risk. This was strongly accentuated in a society where it took only a few mistakes to gain a bad reputation and lose one's social standing or, worse, job. At the same time, they became more homogeneous. More and more lived in the cities and even those in the countryside had, or sought, a similar lifestyle. These two trends explain the odd, but constantly reaffirmed, results of a national survey which shows some 90% of the population claiming to be in the middle class, with the largest portion smack in the middle of the middle class. Very few will admit to being rich or poor any more than they would concede to having deviant—or even slightly different—ideas on most things.

Such a situation is naturally ideal for the ruling party. The Liberal Democratic Party is the supposed handmaiden of economic prosperity and, in the past at least, it delivered on many of its promises. It has done more poorly of late, but it can still claim to manage the economy better and this claim is not even contested by an opposition that is lost in the forsaken causes of yesteryear. The LDP is conservative, just like the bulk of the population, and it is somewhat more acceptable as the older reactionaries pass away. While it is none too clear on the specifics of its program, it is generally felt that with the LDP one can count on more of the same with few unexpected surprises whereas, by electing the opposition, there could be drastic changes and perhaps chaos. This is anathema for a population that prefers even a painful *status quo* to risky adventures.

Still, despite this support, it could hardly be said that the Japanese public holds the ruling party in very high esteem. This has been shown by one opinion poll after another recording only lukewarm approval of the nation's leaders. The best rating any postwar prime minister got was Tanaka, with 61% when he took office. Within six months that had slipped to 26%. Most other prime ministers started with 30–40% in their first year and dropped to 20–30% in their second. Ohira's government marked a low of 17% at the end of its term. The only one whose popularity actually rose was Nakasone. The other parties did not fare any better and most got a lower rating than their share of the vote. Meanwhile, about a third of the population indicated that it did not endorse any political formation.[9]

Other surveys revealed that many Japanese were not particularly happy about the bureaucracy, criticizing inefficient service, excessive paperwork and arrogant manners. Considering their present situation, more Japanese than not felt that things had been getting worse and would continue doing so. An increasing number were worried about old age. And there were many who objected to specific government policies such as administrative reform, curtailing welfare, defense and foreign policy, and so on.[10]

Yet, they did precious little about it. One poll showed that, despite annoyance with the bureaucracy, only 13% of the respondents ever complained to the public grievance offices or consulted politicians. Another noted that, while feeling something must be done to clean up their neighborhood, most did nothing. A further poll indicated that only 7% of the Japanese engaged in voluntary welfare activities and most of these were only done rarely and on a very small scale.[11] This behavior applied to old and young, with it being most notable in the rising generation. According to an international survey, only 40% of the Japanese youths were happy with their social environment, a much lower share than in the United States, France, Britain and

Germany. But, when asked what action they would take to rectify aspects of their society that frustrated them, the Japanese showed the least willingness to do anything.[12] This frame of mind is clearly manifested in the people's political comportment. Admittedly, a large proportion (70–75%) of the electorate turns out to vote. But this is the most passive form of participation and it is noteworthy that exceedingly few are members, supporters or contributors of any political party. In fact, there is a general feeling that party politics is "dirty" and that wholesome, upstanding citizens should keep out.[13] That is perhaps why the many abuses and irregularities continue, since politics is left in the hands of those who are more interested in their own betterment than that of the nation. If more Japanese were to join in the political fray they might be able to improve the situation somewhat.

Even if they do not have the time, energy or taste, certainly the Japanese electorate could go to the trouble of becoming more critical and enlightened voters. They could read about the issues, form their own opinions, and then encourage the politicians to take these views into account. But that is not done to any great extent either. Most individuals pay little attention to political issues, they do not discuss politics with their family, friends or business associates. Indeed, this is one of the most insignificant parts of their daily lives. That much becomes obvious when considering the large numbers which take no position on vital political issues or are unaware that they exist. For example, in a poll on administrative reform held just after the recommendations were presented to the government, 31% of the respondents admitted that they did not know them well and another 30% did not know them at all.[14]

Thus, when it comes times to vote, they all too readily let themselves be swayed by others, be it company executives, local dignitaries, political bosses or influential friends. Or they follow the hints given in the press. Or they simply vote the way they always voted, without thinking too much about it. Or perhaps they actually succumb to the pretty girls in the posters and the whole electioneering soft-sell. Or, since they have no strong views, they may ask themselves which party will deliver the most goods.

Still, to be fair, it must be added that even if the Japanese wanted to be intelligent and sincere voters, it would not be easy. Candidates do not bother explaining what program they intend to follow or how it is better than that of their opponents. It is hard to vote for a prime minister on the basis of his merits since, whatever they may be, he may be switched without warning due to factional realignments. The political parties provide little information on their plans and tend to change policies at short notice. Indeed, some were busy negotiating agreements with their rivals while quarreling with their allies. Meanwhile, the most important deals were made in private, behind closed doors, and sometimes never made public. No matter how public-spirited a citizen is, this makes it extremely difficult to follow the political scene and nearly impossible to influence it effectively. And this may have been exactly what the politicians wanted!

Whatever the causes, the outcome has been a stultifying undercurrent of apathy, one of Japan's oldest and dreariest traditions. No matter how strong a gripe or desire, the people tend to resist it and avoid taking action. They shrug things off with a *"shikata ga nai. . . ."* "It is inevitable. It cannot be helped." Naturally, they do not regard this as a shortcoming but rather pride themselves on being model citizens, for minding their own business, for keeping their personal and family life in order and for not creating a disturbance for others. These are all very fine and admirable qualities in their own way and they make it easier to live together in a crowded country. In Tokugawa or Meiji days, they were perhaps quite suitable. However, in the present context, they can best be interpreted as indifference and condemned not only as a failing but the root of many of the evils the Japanese suffer from.

That Japan is not producing model citizens, and the trends have only been getting worse over the years, is clearly demonstrated by the annual public opinion poll on society and state. Whereas paying attention to country and society once prevailed over placing stress on the improvement of individual life, the latter has since caught up. There are already more people who want to take advantage of society than be of use to it. When it comes to serving the state, or being served by it, the latter outnumber the former almost four-to-one. Fair numbers of respondents felt that people's views were not reflected in national policies and that public morality was not well observed. But rather few discussed politics frequently and, it can be assumed, even less did anything about it.[15]

Individualism, which has spread with amazing speed, only compounds this. More and more Japanese are primarily interested in their own lives or, at most, the well-being of their family and perhaps company. Exceedingly few engage in community activities, and most of these in the countryside rather than the larger cities. At the same time, each category of citizen thinks of its specific needs and forgets those of others. There is extremely little solidarity between different classes, sexes, racial or social groups, and so on. Very few men bother with the cause of women's rights, the majority does not care much about what happens to Koreans, Chinese, Ainu or *burakumin,* and the more affluent are indifferent to the fate of the poor. Even those who entered popular movements fail to establish close contacts with non-members.

This is partly the result of Western influences, which are

duly criticized. But it can be traced even more directly to the obsession with material improvement which has undermined so many social links and made people think too much of work and money. A further element, however, is perfectly indigenous. Japanese society is highly structured and age-old customs make it hard for men and women, juniors and seniors, insiders and outsiders to deal with one another comfortably or even to regard one another as part of the same group. This is already fixed in the language, which makes sharp distinctions between different categories with some paying deference to others. Since those who have to pay deference are more likely to be the ones who are agitating for change, they are immediately stifled and chances of open and frank cooperation are small. The opportunities for factionalism, fragmentation and petty quarrels, on the other hand, are greatly enhanced.

On the basis of such findings, it is easier to understand why so much of Japanese politics takes place as it does. This helps explain the stress on personal relations, selection of candidates based on personality and prestige rather than policies, and willingness to be influenced by others, especially those with higher status in one's group. It makes the urge for material rewards and prevalence of pork barrel politics more natural. And it somewhat justifies the distrust and indifference of the general public. It has long been argued that these are traditional characteristics, bound up with old and disreputable practices that would doubtlessly be shed by new generations of voters. They, it was claimed, would be more rational in their actions and demanding in their choices and thereby transform the whole system. Still, while there have been changes, they were far from decisive and not all were positive.

Polls show that the older generations more actively support political parties and those in the countryside are

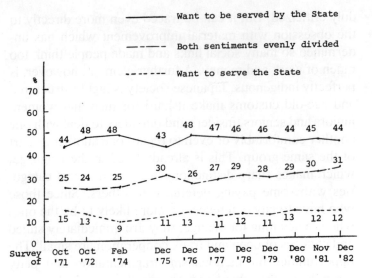

The acid test. Do you want to serve the state or be served by the state?

Source: Public Opinion Survey on State and Society, Prime Minister's Office, July 1983.

more committed than the city-dwellers. Meanwhile, the rising middle classes of educated salarymen and professional have failed to make an impact. Many who militated in their youth became disaffected later on or accepted a marginal role, sometimes manifested by a protest vote for the left or no vote at all, as a symbolic rejection of the system. The bulk, however, especially the huge segment of salarymen, simply had no time for politics. They had no time for anything but their career and company. Admittedly, they did not vote purely for material benefits and would have been scandalized if rewarded for their patronage with a can of cooking oil. But they still pay much closer attention to narrow, concrete and egoistic benefits than any broader concept of how the country should be run in the interest of all citizens.

The younger generations appear even less promising. All the polls, including those mentioned, indicate that they will not be as tough or assertive as their predecessors. Nor do they show much interest in higher goals and principles, this clearly demonstrated by a notable lack of political or intellectual ferment in the campuses and instead mere relaxation from the past rigors of examination hell and future exactions of working life. They are more individualistic and more self-centered. And they are more cut off than ever from their elders. The generation gap is already huge between many youths and their parents. The distance from them to the cantankerous old men who run the political parties, bureaucracies and business organizations, and determine their fate, is completely unbridgeable. Since there is so little they can do to change the situation within the foreseeable future, there are few who will make a try.

This does not mean that everyone accepts everything. But those who strike out against the system are a minority. It takes a tremendous amount of courage to do so and one may have to accept ostracism from the small group for aiding the broader society. So much has been discovered by those who "blow the whistle" and reveal the dirty doings in politics, bureaucracy or business from the inside—the only possible way of knowing. Rather than rebel or fight back, most tend to get around the rules or work under the surface, creating their own private arrangements with little thought to what is going on elsewhere. This is a shade better than resignation, for they are improving their own lot. Alas, it is again done with minimal concern for others and instead of bringing about a general improvement more often undermines the foundations of society.

Consequently, if the political situation is bad, it must be traced to the people as much as their leaders. After all, it is they who tolerate those leaders and who, if they were sufficiently resolute, could easily influence their behavior or drive them from office. And that is the bitter irony. For, in theory *and* practice, the ordinary Japanese possess the supreme power for the first time in their history. There is nothing that can prevent them from exercising that power if they so decide. Instead, they have swallowed their doubts and misgivings and allowed those who should be their servants to become their masters.[16] It is the public which has abdicated its role much more than the politicians, bureaucrats and businessmen who have taken it away.

High-Pressure Groups

While the population as a whole remained relatively amorphous, fragmented and indifferent, certain specific interests organized along social, professional, religious, ideological and other lines. By combining their numbers, and engaging in suitable activities, they were able to display an impressive pull in some cases and, in all, were more able to articulate their demands. Naturally, their demands varied tremendously. But they always had one thing in common—they were practical and narrow.

Normally, one would list business, especially big business, as the top pressure group. But its influence so patently exceeds that of any other lobby in Japan, and what is normally regarded as a lobby elsewhere, that it had to be dealt with as part of the power structure. It is simply recalled here because, no matter how great its clout, its basic motives and actions are those of just another lobby representing a group of people who, as individuals, are quite a small minority of the population.

Before the war, the strongest pressure group outside of big business, and in some ways even more influential, were the big landlords and landed gentry of the countryside. Many lords and other nobility retained large holdings under the Meiji and following regimes. Meanwhile, economic developments in the rural sector led to an ever greater concentration of land as impoverished peasants migrated to the cities. This land was often acquired by local merchants or businessmen and then cultivated by tenants who paid exorbitant rents. Naturally, the landlords were worried about unrest among the tenants and strongly supported the leading conservative parties while smaller agrarian ones were backed by tenants and poor farmers or farm laborers.

After the war, the Occupation authorities regarded the landlords as among the more reactionary elements of society and tried to suppress them. They also regarded the misery of the ordinary farmers as a reason for turning to nationalism. To solve both problems, it was decided to introduce a sweeping land reform. This idea did not really appeal to the postwar conservative parties which were asked to enact it, since it spelled the doom of some of their most ardent supporters. Thus, the reform had to be pushed through by SCAP and was effectuated in stages from 1946 to 1949. It eventually brought the number of tenants down to a mere 10% of all farmers and limited holdings basically to three hectares.

The result was a more equal and also very prolific class of owner-cultivators. Most of them were appreciably better off now that they owned their land. But they were dreadfully short of cash, equipment and knowhow, much of which had earlier been supplied by the landlords. That lack was only partly filled by the government, which directed more of its energy to restoring industry. Thus, many farmers, fishermen and others turned to the agrarian or leftist parties they had always supported.

However, by the 1960s, when the Liberal Democratic Party had to consolidate its position after gradually losing seats to the opposition, it turned more and more to agricultural circles. There was no reason it could not help ordinary farmers since, with the gentry gone, there was no conflict of interest. Moreover, since it disposed of public funds, it was in an extremely good position to spread some of the largesse to the countryside now that industry had revived. It would perhaps not have done so, or at any rate, not with such alacrity, if the farmers had not proven that they could organize as well as any other socio-economic category and eventually much more effectively.

The primary form of organization was already quite old and conventional, namely farm or fishery cooperatives (Nokyo) which sprang up in every village and whose members numbered over six million. They were even more imposing when organized on a regional and then national scale through the Central Union of Agricultural Cooperatives (Zenchu), National Federation of Agricultural Cooperative Associations (Zenno) and other bodies. While the cooperatives and associations were originally interested in normal professional problems, they soon became deeply involved in politics which turned out to be more decisive in raising farm income and living standards. Their principal advantage was that they could readily deliver the vote. The co-ops had very solid and continuous ties with the local farmers, who depended on them for specific assistance, and they could parley this into equally strong links with local politicians.

Once the LDP accepted to support the farmers, and channeled subsidies, loans, and other benefits in that direction, they obtained the bulk of the votes. The LDP's commission on agriculture was by far its largest with some 170 members. But the farmers also voted for a smattering of other parties and could expect support across the political spectrum. In fact, there were over two hundred

Agriculture Dietmen *(norin giin)* which made the farm lobby the second biggest after that of business.

This result may seem exaggerated when one considers that the farm population was only a dwindling minority by the 1980s. Not more than 600,000 households were engaged in full-time farming. But there were as many as four million which farmed part-time and still had an interest in the benefits of LDP policy. This added up to over 21 million people or nearly a fifth of the population (and a larger share of the voters). Moreover, most farmers (and fishermen) lived in relatively underpopulated regions which were disproportionately represented in the Diet. This gave their votes an extra value, one which they might eventually lose if the districts were redrawn. However, to prevent or delay this, the LDP staunchly resisted reapportionment and usually got away with it.

There was no professional category that could begin to compare with the farmers. And few enough tried. Two rather special ones were actually tools of the government. This was the post office masters and JNR officials who were either political appointees or bureaucrats. In rural districts especially, they had considerable influence and their suggestions might well be followed. With post office banks competing against commercial banks and the national railways dependent on subsidies, they had very good reasons to counsel an LDP vote.

A more genuine lobby was formed by the physicians in the form of a Political Alliance of Japanese Doctors, a subsidiary of the Japan Medical Association. Doctors were also very prominent members of their community and, if they so wished, could certainly move some of their patients to vote one way or the other. Initially, they were not overly interested in politics. However, once the government created national health schemes and the Ministry of Health determined many of their working conditions and terms of remuneration, they had to get involved. Under Taro Takemi, an extremely clever organizer who remained the JMA's president from 1957 to 1982, the medical profession alternatively cooperated with and railed against the government. To get its message across, the JMA contributed to the kitties of over a hundred, mainly LDP, politicians. Just in case, it also had a number of doctors elected to the Diet.

Seemingly more natural allies of the conservatives were the many nationalistic associations and clubs. Some of these were relatively colorless politically while others could be classified as right-wing and even extremist. The largest groupings were the veterans and bereaved families of the war dead, whose number was legion after the Pacific War. But their demands were quite limited, aside from some indemnities and a fitting memorial for their loved ones. Other associations engaged in active proselytizing for rightist causes and a small number resorted to violence. How many there were is uncertain. According to the National Police Agency, there were 460 active organizations with a membership of 140,000 and perhaps a total of three million sympathizers back in 1970.[17] Prior to that, they were much more numerous and influential. Since then, they have continued to decline as older members died without being replaced by new ones.

Despite these numbers, there has not been much activity since the early 1960s when nationalists as well as gangsters and hoodlums fought those who demonstrated against the Japan-U.S. Security Treaty and other conservative policies. Some nationalists, however, adopted a modern facade and acted as middle-men and fixers, such as Yoshio Kodama and Kenji Osano. Others financed clubs and leagues whose members dressed in uniform, waved flags and spouted propaganda from ubiquitous loudspeaker vans. They also turned out to heckle or harass leftist trade unions or political parties. But their foes were not only to the left. Like prewar nationalists, they disapproved of "corrupt" politicians and "greedy" businessmen, who were increasingly plentiful and conspicuous. While an extremist assassinated Socialist leader Inejiro Asanuma, attacks were also made against LDP leaders including Kishi, Ikeda, Tanaka, Miki, Ohira and Suzuki while Keidanren's headquarters were briefly occupied and ransacked.

There is not too much concern with politics among the nation's more traditional religions. Buddhist groups have tended to keep out of such activities. Shinto priests have been somewhat more active, but only cautiously so because of the stigma of collaboration during the prewar and wartime periods. Christians are very outgoing for their own causes, although not that much of a leaven since they only account for 1% of the population. More muscle has been flexed by some of the "new religions." The most noticeable is obviously Soka Gakkai which, under the direction of Daisaku Ikeda, formed and continues to support Komeito. In reaction, some of its rivals like Seicho-No-Ie or Rissho Koseikai supported other parties, ranging from the LDP to DSP. Due to its ability to help, and a professed belief in the value of religious commitment, most have gravitated toward the LDP, whose Diet members are very grateful for their financial aid and electoral support.

The only major pressure group located on the left of the spectrum is labor. The trade unions can hardly be overlooked since they have about 12.5 million members which accounts for some 30% of the labor force. Although the unionization rate dropped notably from 40% just after the war, this is the largest organized force in Japan. Moreover, workers as a whole are considerably more numerous than the nation's farmers and quasi-farmers. But they are much weaker. Among other things, workers are more dispersed. In addition, most are located in the cities where it is harder to mobilize voters and where the value of each vote is smaller. But that is not labor's main problem. While strong in numbers, it is weakened by tensions and disagreements that have racked it for decades. First of all, most workers are not unionized. Those who are usually belong to company or "house" unions which means that they only unite limited groups of employees with rather restricted interests and relatively little concern for broader issues. There are only a few true industrial unions, as for seamen, and then the public sector unions which are quite vast. A further source of division is that these many unions have opted for different national centers. The largest at present is the General Council of Trade Unions (Sohyo) with about 36%, followed by the Japanese Confederation of Labor (Domei) with 18%, the Federation of Independent Unions (Choritsuroren) with 12%, and other groups or unaffiliated unions for the rest. Periodic attempts were made at unifying the national centers or creating joint organizations, but they only papered over gaping cracks in the movement.

But it is not only a question of different centers. Sohyo groups mainly public sector and some private sector unions while Domei has most of the factory workers. Sohyo is affiliated with the Japan Socialist Party while Domei supports the Democratic Socialist Party. And there are also unions, or factions, which back the Japan Communist Party. This not only split the labor movement, it occasionally divides specific unions into warring camps that are aligned more with the JSP, DSP or JCP. So, the almost hundred trade unionists in the Diet cannot speak with a common voice since they were elected by different parties and often defend conflicting policies.

① 『5項目』方針を堅持し、共同行動
をＸ♭重ね全的統一を達成し♭よう
② 民間大示の統一は、団体間♭意を♭
本部役員

"Down with . . ." Sohyo boldly denouncing the government once again.
Credit: Foreign Press Center/Kyodo

While Sohyo is still the larger center, this may eventually change as the NTT and tobacco monopoly unions, conceivably followed by the JNR unions, leave the public sector body and move to Domei. This is extremely significant politically. For Sohyo has always been more blunt and aggressive in its political stands and supports the more radical JSP. If these unions were to revise their position, and strengthen the more moderate DSP, the labor movement will move yet further right. This is particularly fateful at a time when the DSP is actually thinking of a possible coalition with the LDP and, at any rate, toning down its criticism.

Another pressure group of a sort, this time regarding Japan's defense and foreign policy, consists of various pacifist and anti-nuclear groups which are mobilized for special events. Naturally, as the only country to have suffered from the atomic bomb, there is strong sentiment for some action to do away with nuclear weapons and this is centered on the survivors or, more often, bereaved families of those who were afflicated in Hiroshima and Nagasaki. There are other groups which demonstrate to prevent nuclear weapons from being located in American bases (or against these bases in principle) or brought in on American ships (or against such carriers in principle). While once apolitical, or only mildly leftist, the movement has tended to be captured and manipulated by the Socialists and Communists who, in return, provide most of the organization, funds and manpower. This resulted in a split between the JSP-affiliated Japan Congress Against Atomic and Hydrogen Bombs (Gensuikin) and the JCP-affiliated Japan Council Against Atomic and Hydrogen Bombs (Gensuikyo).

Beyond labor, there is a left wing consisting of many small organizations which are irreconcilably opposed to the LDP and sometimes antagonistic to the whole Japanese system. Many of these groups grew out of the earlier campaigns against the Japan-U.S. Security Treaty, others trace their origin to student radicalism and a few come from more recent popular movements. While the parent bodies were often massive, membership declined and most of these groups and sects are presently quite small and altogether can count on only about 15,000 activists and somewhat larger clusters of sympathizers. But they occasionally carry out sensational actions against the establishment, including periodic bombings and attacks on police boxes or the LDP headquarters. In addition, their presence can be felt in other, more variegated coalitions. Their impact, however, is greatly diminished by doctrinal strife and bloody infighting *(uchigeba)* that undermines any fragile unity and tarnishes their reputation with the general public.

While not organized as a pressure group or, indeed, organized at all, it is generally felt that academics and "intellectuals" like writers and artists should have considerable influence in a country marked by its traditional respect for the *sensei*. During the mass demonstrations of the 1950s and, even more so, the campus unrest of the 1960s, some professors and lecturers did have a rousing effect on their students, although not that many participated actively. There is still a latent preference for "leftist" causes in some circles. But just as many have become essentially apolitical or too deeply engaged in academic politics to do anything else and some found greater scope and status by counselling the LDP and government. Still, as a highly educated segment with a tiny slice of power, "intellectuals" do offer alternatives and as such occasionally appear to rock an otherwise firmly moored boat.

Finally, there are certain "citizen's movements" that carry on activities of a more general nature which, in their way, have a political impact. Normally, it would be assumed that most of them are anti-establishment and would therefore be aligned with the Socialists and Communists. In fact, that is how things originally stood. However, since it was easier to have their concrete needs met by the LDP, which controlled the funds to provide compensation or build public works, many of them have switched. The LDP now counts numerous consumer, environmental and other associations among its own supporters.

The fate of the "citizen's movements" is most instructive in considering the whole range of special interest groups. With most demands directed toward material satisfactions as opposed to fundamental changes or higher principles, it was possible for the LDP to draw many of them into its orbit. In the same way, it attracted the farmers, shopkeepers and some professionals. Only labor (and the far left) refused. And labor stays out partly because too much has to be done for management to grant it more than crumbs. Even then, there has been a noticeable slide throughout from left, to center, to right. Little remains to provide a counterpoise.

In many ways, Japanese lobbies, pressure groups and more unruly dissidents used much the same methods as in other countries. They contributed to political parties, got out the vote or demonstrated in the streets. What was different was the lack of ethical constraints on how far they would go and what methods they would use to convert politicians to their cause. And, the reciprocal, there were almost no bounds to the lengths to which politicians would go to win their support. Nor were there many legal constraints on how the exchange of favors took place, whether in formal donations or under-the-table. But the biggest—and most decisive—differences were not to be found in these groups so much as the general public which was so poorly organized to withstand their maneuvers and obtain a better hearing for those without special interests.

Media Power

Everywhere in the world, the mass media are extremely important in shaping public opinion. But they rarely assume as vital a role as in Japan. That is because the society is so compartmentalized by numerous relatively self-enclosed, inward-looking groups with little knowledge of what is going on outside and even less willingness to let outsiders know what is going on inside. The only way the general public can find out what is happening in political, bureaucratic or business circles, aside from brief and vague announcements, is through the media. And the only way the leadership can have an idea of what the public may be thinking is by following the media.[18]

No matter how essential this duty may be, it has been rather hard for the media to fulfill it because they suffer from many of the same ailments. There is substantial concentration, with the three major national dailies *(Yomiuri, Asahi* and *Mainichi)* controlling well over half of the total newspaper circulation, and most newspapers counting heavily for information on one news agency, Kyodo. The newspapers are affiliated with television and radio networks and sometimes run magazine and book publishing operations as well. Only the state-run radio and television company Nippon Hoso Kyoku (NHK) provides a conservative alternative. More liberal or radical alternatives are limited to some weekly magazines, books or the Communist daily *Akahata*.

The lack of alternatives would not be as serious if not for the fact that these few newspapers and television networks, like other institutions, tend to behave much alike even when it is not necessary. They will cover the same stories, in much the same way, and often come to the same conclusions. Their style is uniformly flat and grey and they are regularly criticized by their readers for being "stereotyped." Most of them make a point of proclaiming their independence and neutrality, but this usually means simply sticking to the general consensus and avoiding any comments or conclusions that go too far off the beaten path. In fact, the urge to maintain circulation has caused some of them to be exceedingly leery of saying anything that could displease any segment of their readership.

Even within this framework, there is definite room for a variety which would contribute greatly to the principal task of providing information. The media could engage in more in-depth analysis rather than the superficial treatment most items get. They could invite more comments from outsiders, including some who are far out, just to show a broader range of views. They could hold spontaneous debates on television or run opinion pages. By having a fairly rounded group of participants, they could still remain neutral and they would not have to endorse any viewpoint. Instead, the dominant organs tend to chew the information they receive first, rejecting some, and making a dull pap of the rest.

If one wants alternative views and a little spice, it is necessary to consult the weekly and monthly magazines, something more and more Japanese are doing. They provide more insight into the workings, and misdoings, of the politicians, bureaucrats and businessmen. They show, perhaps with too much verve, the underside of Japanese life. And some avidly portray the sensational and scandalous. A few, however, have been both courageous and reliable and have won a hearing, such as *Bungei Shunju*. And the economic and business weeklies, while not revealing much new, certainly provide deeper understanding. The most popular sources of analysis are the books written by well-known "critics." They are churned out at a prodigious rate and cover every topical issue as it emerges. While not always on the mark, they do at least add to the debate.

The second weakness of the media, this one in some ways more fatal, is that they are also compartmentalized. Most of the newspapers and networks are huge companies with a highly bureaucratic organization. Each year, new recruits are absorbed from the university, people looking for a job as opposed to people who love to write or present ideas. They rise through the hierarchy slowly and steadily, shifting from one section to another, covering domestic or international news, economics or politics, or taking a turn at advertising or personnel. Such rotation makes it quite impossible to develop much expertise in any area and this is reflected in the shallowness of much writing and, even more so, television news programs and documentaries. Since newsgathering is part of their trade, they have done their best to organize it to an extent unheard of in the free world. Just about every major central, prefectural and municipal government office, police headquarters or court has a "press club." There are about four hundred such *kisha* clubs throughout the nation. These clubs are reserved exclusively for correspondents from leading newspapers, networks and agencies, who must be accredited by them and attend the same interviews or conferences. Later, in a private session, the reporters often work out a common understanding of what has been said and all duly report much the same thing. There is no possibility of taking a different stance, or coming up with a scoop, without losing one's standing in the club.

Some journalists are even luckier. They make contact with prominent politicians, who either take a liking to them or want more coverage from their newspaper, and become part of an intimate group that meets the prime minister, minister, or faction boss at odd times, for breakfast, late at night, or a quick briefing in between. While not practiced as strictly in the business world, there are reporters who develop very close ties with certain companies and are rewarded by earlier notice of breaking news or other inside information which may be of use. This sort of relationship also exists with the trade organizations, cooperatives, labor unions and so on.

One drawback to this system, as far as the public is concerned, is that outsiders do not have entry. Colleagues from lesser newspapers and magazines, or foreign correspondents, are basically excluded from this primary source of news and can get it only second-hand. This also applies to the representatives of the Socialist and Communist media. It is even more questionable that the club members should coordinate views and treatment rather than present the facts and let the readers draw their own conclusions. The worst drawback, however, is that reporters become so dependent on the club or individual source that they no longer dare make critical statements for fear of losing access to the news which is their livelihood.

Relations with the general public, on the other hand, are rather sparse. Journalists, who are part of the nation's elite by education and training, do not go out of their way to study popular movements or causes and they do not even have a very rounded circle of personal acquaintances. Admittedly, efforts are made to take polls or publish letters to the editor, most of them quite innocuous or merely amusing. There may also be a women's column and special series on the problems of youth or old age, in which individuals are interviewed. But the press evidently thinks that its primary duty is to inform the people rather than find out what they think. Television and radio networks do not even set much store in informing and regard their primary objective as entertaining.

Both the bureaucratization of the staff and the effect of press clubs and special relations explain many of the quirks of the Japanese media which were already mentioned. They also have a pervasive effect on what news is presented and how. This is particularly important because the media, as noted, is so instrumental in shaping opinion on how the country is governed or the economy managed.

It is sometimes claimed that the press (but not television) is "leftist" in the sense of being anti-establishment, taking a strong stand on certain political issues and occasionally criticizing big business. This concept is perhaps a hangover from the early postwar period when there were indeed many radical newspapermen and one of the papers was briefly taken over by its staff. It is also true that, during the clamor over the Japan-U.S. Security Treaty, all major dailies came out against Kishi's handling of the matter and precipitated his fall. The press gleefully criticized Tanaka's "money politics," although only after the crucial step was taken by the weekly *Bungei Shunju*. And there are still nasty comments about "hawkish" moves in the government as concerns defense, foreign policy or nuclear armament.

But much of this criticism is ritualistic and subdued. The conclusions drawn are rarely that the Liberal Democratic Party should abandon its position but rather that it should reflect and consider the good of the nation. Meanwhile, even more scathing criticism is heaped on the Communists, Socialists and sometimes centrists. The worst swipe, however, is simply to write the opposition off as incapable of coming to power or running the country effectively. Equally negative comments are printed about the trade unions and leftist organizations.

Moreover, since the country is run by a triumvirate of politicians, bureaucrats and businessmen, it is not enough to situate the media only as regards the political parties. It is necessary to consider how they treat the other two. As far as the bureaucracy is concerned, there is relatively little general criticism, and that quite mild, of its programs. If anything, they are magnified and praised lavishly even before they are launched. Senior officials usually fare well, certainly much better than politicians, and are often congratulated for their elite nature. Admittedly, on occasion, there is criticism of abuses at lower levels, but hardly anything resembling a campaign for reform.

When it comes to the business community, there is precious little criticism and reams of laudatory articles on its economic achievements. The bigger a company, the more it is lauded. Even on political issues, the media go out of their way to interview business leaders and enhance the image of the *zaikai*. Oddly enough, when major companies do get caught in serious scandals or tax evasion, they are let off light while smaller ones are excoriated. There is also a tendency to keep off consumer or pollution cases which could put certain companies in a bad light. With advertising revenue so crucial, it would seem that the only sacred cow is business.

Thus, the media are clearly part of the establishment as opposed to anti-establishment, at least as far as the major dailies and networks are concerned. Journalists often like to think of themselves as a "press government" which is instrumental in forming opinion. Doubtlessly, given the circumstances, they are. But they are clearly shaping it in their own interests and those of the establishment. They pick up ideas, toss them around, make some critical comments, and then let the nation's leaders go ahead. In so doing, they hope their own views will be incorporated. These views, of course, are presented as the *vox popoli,* although the press rarely goes out of its way to find out what the people want. But the government tends to accept that idea and, since the views are merely variations on its own themes, it is happy to keep up the phony dialogue.

Foreign Pressure

Japan has a long and, it is maintained, honorable tradition of absorbing the "civilizing influence" of other countries. The first currents came from China and Korea and, while interrupted periodically, lasted for centuries during which they extensively reshaped the relatively primitive and rustic culture. Most later influences came from the West, first Europe and then, ever stronger, the United States. There was a brief Christian interlude in the sixteenth century, followed by the more pervasive Westernization after Japan's "opening" in 1853 and then the vast and intensive impact since the end of the Pacific War. Despite the amount of borrowing, it should always be remembered that the Japanese only copied "superior" nations and pointedly ignored the rest and even rejected its favorite models when they proved fallible.

From such "superior" societies the Japanese might absorb almost anything, assuming it was a cause of superiority. Their choices were not always those of the foreigners who tried to influence them or even, in some cases, of their own rulers who tried to channel these currents. Moreover, their taste was amazingly eclectic. They were quite willing to pick up things that were positive or negative or fundamentally contradictory to one another. Thus, it would be pointless to look for much rhyme or reason and outright silly to claim, as so many have done, that Japan borrowed systematically, borrowed only the best, and then fashioned its borrowings into some uniform and admirable whole.

Among its borrowings, and this just scratches the surface, were a bewildering maze of Western philosophies, including those of Kant, Hegel, Marx, Smiles, and Dr. Spock. Next to Buddhism and Confucianism, it found room for Christianity and now even Islam. While it took to capitalism, and imported later improvements like Keynesianism and Reaganism, it also dabbled in planning and many thought of socialism or even Marxism as a far better system. Twice set on the democratic path, it deviated into fascism of a sort in between. Less earthshaking this time, its people took up just about every Western sport, dance, and musical form, knew all the popular tunes, wore all the latest Paris (and other) fashions and rebuilt their cities in a mock-Western style.

Most of these fashions and fads, as well as some of the deeper and more durable acquisitions, looked very much like the original on the outside. However, in virtually all cases, they had been thoroughly revamped and reformed by those who adopted them. Since many of the borrowings were transmitted by written works rather than by Japanese who had experienced them in practice elsewhere, it was quite simple to drop some aspects which did not appeal to the translator-author and insert others he felt would improve them. Then, his readers would make further modifications, discarding and adding again.[19] Meanwhile, older customs and practices were absorbed to replace the original content or facilitate indigenization. The result was therefore something quite different, even if it had the same name, and something which was always more than half Japanese.

It often proved difficult to absorb so many cultural imports and consequently some of them had only a brief moment of popularity before being crowded out by the next. This next might be completely different and erase their memory or similar enough to build on them. Whatever the case, precious few were really strong enough to have an abiding influence on the country and were instead attached to this or that social category and/or generation, which quickly dated them in the eyes of those who adopted something even more modern. Thus, most of the fads which once moved the people and aroused enthusiasm or dismay just slipped into oblivion.

Some of these impulses, however, were of a considerably more serious nature. Present leaders, like their predecessors in Meiji days, felt that it was necessary to keep abreast of what was going on in the Western world, or among the more "advanced" countries in general. There were many useful pointers that could be adopted to solve problems Japan was likely to encounter as it progressed to the same stage. And, to show it was as "enlightened" as the next, some things might be adopted even if they were not really necessary. Right after the war, there was a tremendous burst of activity in virtually all fields and the process still goes on today, if more restrained and limited to those areas which are really new or where Japan has discovered notable lacks.

This copying has been undertaken by the politicians who liked to follow the latest trends in contemporary policy. They were keen to introduce planning when that was in fashion and rely on the private sector when it was concluded that this was a more dynamic force. They introduced welfare like everyone else, although a bit later, and then compressed it, like everyone else, although it had not gotten quite as far. They followed the American lead in freezing relations with the Kremlin, then thawing, and freezing, and thawing again. When it was deemed appropriate to help developing countries, they did their bit, and when it was necessary to accept Vietnamese refugees, they took some, albeit after considerable nudging. The impact on the bureaucrats was less marked, but quite significant since like their Meiji predecessors, they often merely copied foreign legislation, revised and adapted to Japanese circumstances. As for the businessmen, they were most aware of what was going on abroad since their livelihood depended on it. But, along with "dos," they were more acutely attuned to "don'ts," like don't spoil workers with short hours and high wages, don't let the trade unions get out of hand and don't permit the government to spend too much or overregulate business activities.

Under a benevolent foreign influence, the Japanese eventually made many brave and praiseworthy attempts at legislating social and economic uplift. For example, democratic governance, equalitarianism and human rights were enshrined in the constitution. There were also numerous social improvements like prohibition of prostitution, protection of minorities or banning of night work for women. There were economic gains like social security and children's allowances. To this may be added frills like the right to information, recall of municipal leaders, urban planning and zoning or protection of endangered species (aside from whales). Alas, while the intentions were good, if the mood changed, the laws might well remain on the books . . . without being applied.

This proclivity to borrow was only reinforced and, to some extent, institutionalized by membership in numerous international organizations. Despite its difficulties with the prewar League of Nations, Japan was eager to regain a place of honor in the international community. It therefore accepted the conditions of the United Nations and soon after entered its specialized agencies, including the International Labour Organisation. Somewhat later, it attained "developed country" status by joining the Organisation for Economic Cooperation and Development and General Agreement on Tariffs and Trade. Meanwhile, it proclaimed its support of the "free world" and even its backing of the "Western alliance," although it was not interested in adhering to any existing or new military organization.

Membership in these organizations, however, was somewhat different from merely assimilating Western and other influences. This time it was necessary to sign and ratify conventions which included countless stipulations defining proper international behavior. Japan was bound by them, had to comply with them and, if it did not, could sometimes be prodded to mend its ways by other members or the organization's governing body. Often new and more demanding conventions were adopted which Japan either had to accept or reject, in which case it might lose face. Or, it might be bound by treaties and agreements calling for reciprocal concessions by the various parties. Violating, or simply ignoring them, could again have unpleasant consequences.

This meant that Japan was hemmed in by an intricate web of obligations rather than just picking fads and fashions that appealed to it. For example, its labor conditions were subject to scrutiny by the ILO, its trading practices were examined by GATT, its defensive arrangements came to the notice of its ally, the United States. It was expected to increase its development aid by the OECD, including other donors, pushy organizations of beneficiaries, and the UN which included both. It was also necessary, if it did not wish to be regarded as backward, to partake in every last campaign of the United Nations, which dedicated years and decades to innumerable good causes, from care of the handicapped to equality of women.

While much of this pressure was not entirely effective or constraining, since most organizations had rather weak machinery for implementation, the bilateral and multilateral arrangements and closer ties with other parties could have a sting. This was most noticeable in the only sector which concerned the Japanese much, trade. If its partners felt that Japan were taking excessive advantage of their market, they had many ways of closing it off. If, in return, they felt that Japan had not opened its market as much as promised, they could find more than enough forms of retaliation. It was primarily, but not only, here that Japan had to fear foreign pressure (*gaiatsu*). For, since relations were broader, it could expect nudges if it were not holding up its end militarily or left too much of the burden of foreign aid to others.

Not surprisingly, Japan went through successive phases in its borrowing and complying. Just after the war, it was wide open to foreign influences since its earlier ideals and customs had proven erroneous, or at least ineffective. It was eager to learn the many things that made the West stronger than had been expected, and this included both its technology and philosophy. The younger generations, in particular, were tired of the more restrictive mores of their elders and keen to seek new, more exciting alternatives. This lasted for decades and has not entirely ceased today. But it has slowed down and, after so much borrowing, any additional increment is less noticeable.

More significant is a mounting counter-tendency to feel that it is no longer as necessary to borrow as in the past and that foreign standards should not really be accepted as suitable without further investigation. This arose from the emergence of Japan as a major economic power which managed to crush its competitors around the world and quickly passed all Western economies aside from America's. Since economics in the only field in which Japan is seriously interested, it did not bother checking whether it had caught up in other ways. Meanwhile, thanks to the media, people were fed with a heavy diet of exposés of other societies which showed their weaknesses in full and tended to ignore any strengths. This only confirmed the Japanese in their renascent feelings of superiority.

What convinced them most, of course, was the startling influx of foreigners coming to Japan to admire its achievements. The initial part was instigated by the authorities, who staged national extravaganzas in the form of international exhibitions and the like, starting with the Osaka Expo in 1970 and culminating in the Tsukuba Expo of 1985. Meanwhile, humble foreigners were craving Japan's benevolence, be it leaders of poorer developing countries seeking aid or representatives of advanced ones which wanted more investment. Then came swarms of individuals who wished to see what Japan had to offer in terms of culture, religion, or management techniques. This gave way to outrageous flattery by renowned academics and other sycophants who praised Japan as No. 1.

By the 1980s, the Japanese evidently felt that they did

not have much more to learn, although they admittedly were behind on some technologies. When it came to social institutions, however, they had nothing to envy a quarrelsome, divisive mass of lesser peoples. The time had come, many were convinced, for the world to "learn from Japan." This made the whole population more self-contented and inward-looking than before. While conceding some failings and problems, it was easier to regard them as bearable since everyone else seemed to be doing so much worse.

NOTES

1. For a slightly rosy view of the role of the police, see George De Vos (ed.), *Institutions for Change in Japanese Society*, pp. 174–244.
2. As T.J. Pempel noted, "the Supreme Court has been far more active in reversing anti-governmental decisions made by lower courts than in challenging any important government actions." *(Policy and Politics in Japan*, p. 19.)
3. Background information on earlier popular movements can be found in Tetsuo Najita and J. Victor Koschmann (eds.), *Conflict in Modern Japanese History*, and Harry Wray and Hilary Conroy (eds.), *Japan Examined*.
4. See Joe Moore, *Japanese Workers and the Struggle for Power*.
5. An excellent study of this movement is Ellis S. Krauss, *Japanese Radicals Revisited*.
6. A further weakness of the youth movements, noted by Krauss, Apter and others is that political protest is strongly age-related. Conversion or just indifference marked the passage to adulthood for all too many.
7. For examples of these movements and their activities, see Margaret A. McKean, *Environmental Protest and Citizen Politics in Japan*, and Kurt Steiner et al., *Political Opposition and Local Politics in Japan*, pp. 187–316.
8. See David E. Apter and Nagayo Sawa, *Against the State*.
9. Interesting material on the indecision and indifference of the Japanese electorate can be found in Bradley M. Richardson, *The Political Culture of Japan*.
10. *Japan Times*, March 10, 1980, October 17, 1983, and April 8, 1983.
11. Public Opinion Survey on Social Welfare, Prime Minister's Office, March 1983.

12. *Japan Times,* March 10, 1980, November 12, 1984, January 6, 1984 and December 12, 1984.
13. See Richardson, *op. cit.*
14. *Daily Yomiuri,* September 21, 1981.
15. Public Opinion Survey on Society and State, Prime Minister's Office, annual.
16. That may be why, according to Takabatake Michitoshi, "Japan's postwar democracy has form and fabric but no heart." (Koschmann, *Authority and the Individual in Japan,* p. 192.)
17. Albert Axelbank, *Black Star Over Japan,* p. 89.
18. Partial glimpses of the press in action are provided by Michael R. Reich, "Crisis and Routine: Pollution Reporting by the Japanese Press," in De Vos (ed.), *op. cit.,* pp. 148–65, and Nathaniel B. Thayer, "Competition and Conformity: An Enquiry into the Structure of Japanese Newspapers," in Vogel (ed.), *Modern Japanese Organization and Decision-Making,* pp. 284–303.
19. See Kinmonth, *The Self-Made Man in Meiji Japanese Thought.*

PART THREE

SOME ENCOUNTERS

6

Economic Issues

Manipulating The Economy

Ever since the spectacular upswing of the 1950s, observers have been tremendously impressed by Japan's economic prowess and have vainly sought the authors of policies which seemed to work admirably while everyone else was floundering. The place most of them eventually selected was the government, which was credited by Norman Macrae of the London *Economist* with running "the most intelligently dirigiste system in the world." According to him, "the ultimate responsibility for industrial planning, for deciding in which new directions Japan's burgeoning industrial effort should go, and for fostering and protecting business as it moves in those directions, lies with the government."[1]

Pinpointing the government as the center of operations is not an unexpected conclusion since it generates much of the action and most of the readily available news. In Japan, it was even more convincing as the prime mover of the economy in that it regularly issued plans and programs. In fact, it issued ten such as of 1956 and the early ones at least seemed to do extremely well. However, to anyone acquainted with planning, it would appear odd to have ten plans for periods ranging from five to ten years in a span of less than thirty years. This means that none of them ever reached its term and most were interrupted and often discarded in the middle.[2]

Thus, the concept of government direction has to be taken with a big grain of salt. This applies especially to the presumed role played by the man at the top, as in the case of the Ikeda "income-doubling" plan or the Tanaka "re-modelling the archipelago" plan. It was almost customary for every new prime minister, and even every aspiring candidate, to come up with his own brilliant scheme and insist it be adopted. This inevitably deprived planning of the very factors it needed most, stability and continuity. It was also unlikely that the prime minister had enough knowhow to inject particularly intelligent ideas into the process, even if he spent some time at the head of the Ministry of Finance, the Ministry of International Trade and Industry or Economic Planning Agency. After all, prime ministers were never chosen on the basis of their knowledge of economics, or their knowledge of any concrete subject, but for their connections and often longevity.

It makes somewhat more sense to look for the economic architects in the place they should normally inhabit, namely the Economic Planning Agency. Alas, while it was in charge of planning at least nominally, there were and still are precious few professional planners or economists about and most of the staff is hardly distinguishable from any other ministry. The more disturbing point is that, for a long time, half came from MITI and half from MOF, which created more of a clash than combination of talents. For, whenever a plan had to be adopted, MITI tried to make it as ambitious as possible while MOF tried to tone it down.

This would have created horrible complications if not for the fact that, for all practical purposes, much of the EPA's activities bordered more on public relations than economic manipulation. The plans, all the plans, were purely indicative as far as private companies were concerned. They could be followed, or not, as desired. In most cases, it would seem that businessmen did take a passing interest in what the plans said and then proceeded to do what they thought was right. Even the other ministries did not pay much attention to the plans and there was amazingly little real—as opposed to verbal—integration of major public works or other projects.[3] For no self-respecting ministry was willing to accept the dictation of a fledgling agency like the EPA.

On the whole, more effective action stemmed from the Ministry of International Trade and Industry. Unlike the politicians and planners, it was dealing with practical matters in trying to restore and then expand industry. It was the inspiration of the industrial policy and targeting for which Japan has become famous. During its early period, it really was directing the economy and helping companies pull out of the postwar chaos. Its prime achievement was to link the coal and steel industries so they could enable one another to resume production. It then proceeded to adopt special laws to promote the shipbuilding, machinery, petrochemical, electronics and other industries.[4]

More than just advice and guidance, it provided companies with very tangible support. It offered access to low-interest loans, advanced technology or essential raw materials, aid in selling the new products locally and especially protection from imports. No matter how extravagantly it is dressed up, Japanese industrial policy was simply a more thorough and refined version of the standard "infant industry" strategies that have been around for decades. Every trick in the book, plus some unheard of ones, were used to keep out foreign articles that might compete with local producers. Then, just for good measure, foreign manufacturers were prevented from investing in local production.[5]

MITI's role in the 1950s and 1960s was definitely significant, if not quite decisive. It thereby managed to salvage some of the power and prestige that had been enjoyed by the prewar Ministry of Commerce and Industry and the wartime Ministry of Munitions. But its position was gradually eroded as the economy developed. Once things were moving smoothly and other sources of finance were available, technology could be obtained readily, and companies built up their own funds, staff, R&D and marketing ability, there was not much that MITI could do for them.

The watershed would seem to be the years 1962–64, when MITI tried to have the Diet adopt a measure generally known as the "Designated Industries Promotion" law. This was presented as something between a controlled economy and *laissez faire,* prettily summed up as "cooperation between the public and private sectors."[6] But the legislation was fought relentlessly by the opposition, which probably mattered less than that it was also firmly rejected by business circles and only weakly supported by the cabinet.[7] Apparently no one other than its own bureaucrats wanted MITI to enlarge its competences further.

Consequently, MITI had to proceed on a case-by-case basis using persuasion and administrative guidance. But its advice could be spurned by private companies, and occasionally was unless they received something in return. MITI's pretensions to merge companies, encourage specialization, or reorganize whole industries were not generally approved by company executives. On the other hand, they continued to appreciate any access to funds, technology (through special research projects) and especially protection. The only companies that accepted greater control happened to be in the declining or "ailing" sectors and they hoped to obtain subsidies or protection in exchange for complying with industrial reorganization and rationalization plans.

So, any claim that MITI is still instrumental, or indeed had been the driving force over the past two or three decades, is woefully misplaced. While it provided a useful stimulus to those industries it chose to help, most industries, and the vast majority of companies, gained little from its efforts. Even those which benefited most never depended entirely on MITI and its aid was usually just a modest supplement to what they were doing on their own. The Japanese "miracle," if it existed, came first and foremost from the dynamic activities of the managers and workers.

But it would be incorrect to even stop at this point and speak of mutual aid or partnership. Even during the period of MITI's strongest influence, it was not really the bureaucrats who were calling the shots. How could they? MITI bureaucrats did not know more about the intricacies of industrial organization and production than EPA bureaucrats did about planning. It was even hard for them to learn on-the-job since they were rotated every few years. Rather, the predominant influence came from business circles, the ones they were supposed to help, and who knew best what kind of backing they wanted. This advice was passed on formally through the various deliberation councils and informally by private discussions with relevant officials.

This is shown most clearly by the targeting exercise. No matter how this has been embellished in the media, it was rarely if ever MITI which picked the "strategic" sectors. Automobile and electronics production got started without MITI support and, in some cases, against MITI advice. More recently, companies entered biotechnology massively even while the government maintained antiquated rules on genetic engineering experiments. "New materials" were being developed, and sold, before MITI ever seriously considered them.[8] Thus, industrialists usually took the first steps alone and only when they had proven their ability was MITI brought in. On the other hand, some items ambitiously targeted by MITI never quite worked, take aeronautics and undersea mining for example.

Similarly, when it came to promotion and protection, it was most often the companies concerned which informed MITI that they needed aid, a practice common everywhere else in the world but formally disclaimed by Japan. Yet, how could it have been otherwise? It is necessary to know an industry's needs and potential to know how to support it. No bureaucrat had the information first hand. And some of the non-tariff barriers were so ingenious that only specialists could have dreamed them up. That MITI failed to remove this structure readily and brought barriers down only under foreign pressure is amply known. This was only partly due to patriotism and the wish to defend its wards. More persuasive was that the removal of this support left MITI without much purpose or prestige.[9]

Recent years have seen MITI desperately seeking things to do, ways of creating a new clientele. Aside from its aid to ailing industries, few have materialized. Its "visions" are increasingly vague and illusory. It has ever less money to spend on research projects. And companies with their own R&D capabilities and intensely suspicious of rivals are less willing to work together. This has bedeviled its only major project, the development of a Fifth Generation Computer. The idea of establishing technopolises sounds good, and makes wonderful PR, but it will work only if the local authorities put up enough funds and manufacturers make enough investments. For MITI is providing little more than the catch phrase and the sponsorship.

Not only have the major, long-term operations become increasingly less effective, short-term management of the overall economy is notably worsening. It has always been hard to decide when business would turn up or down and if the government should intervene to cool an overheated situation or stimulate things in times of recession. The decisions were that much more difficult to reach in that each alternative had its own backers. MOF was congenitally cautious and hoped to avoid the expenses involved in stimulatory action and therefore urged that measures be held back. MITI, and the EPA in its wake, were ever ambitious and eagerly backed any possible measures to stir things up. This left the prime minister of two minds and the decision was perhaps swayed by his closer relations with bureaucrats of one ministry or another or a desire to avoid responsibility and do nothing, which was the most frequent course.

The result was an evident stop-go policy which was not the best for the economy and usually included a mixture of too little, too late and too much, too early.[10] But, at least there was some economic policy to speak of in the 1950s, 1960s and early 1970s. By the 1980s, the government found it hard to adopt any policy since the elementary tools were no longer available or effective. It was impossible to stimulate growth through public works or government spending in general, due to fiscal restraint. It was unwise to use monetary or interest policy because this could result in inflation or a flight of currency. And appeals to business to invest or consumers to buy more regularly went unheeded.

This inevitably caused a sharp decline in government economic activities. It would, in fact, be very hard to speak of it as leading the van and, in many ways, it is dragging its feet and slowing down the procession. Meanwhile, business leaders have clearly reversed the power relationship and either disdain government help or impose the form of aid they want. This is not the first time that has happened. A similar reversal occurred between the government's encouragement of industry in Meiji days and business domination of government during Taisho days. Only this time the turnabout was quicker.

Milking The Economy

While it is very interesting to see who runs the nation's economic policy, it is even more enlightening to see who gains most from this policy. Obviously, economic growth has brought benefits to all Japanese to a greater or lesser extent. There are more jobs, higher incomes, and a much improved standard of living. This progress also provided a boost for the people's self-esteem and the nation's reputation.

But there were also drawbacks. The defects in this case, however, were hardly coincidental or a result of fate. For, no matter what they are termed, industrial policy, targeting and planning involve a direct intervention in the normal course of economic events and a deviation from the so-called economic "laws." If not done carefully and wisely, there could be serious waste and distortion.

The underlying theory of much of the government's action was that a "dynamic" comparative advantage should be pursued rather than spontaneously following the market signals. Thus, and this was clearly shown by striving first for heavy-and-chemical sectors, it was sovereignly decided to neglect labor-intensive industries and promote capital-intensive ones. That was definitely not the most appropriate step just after the war, when it was taken, for Japan was saddled with excessive labor and had pitifully little capital. Such a policy therefore involved greater risks and greater sacrifices than any other.

On the surface, the outcome appeared eminently successful. That is, Japan managed to create most of the industries it targeted. It set up steel and metal-working branches, chemicals and petrochemicals, shipbuilding, automobiles, electronics and many others. But it is exceedingly difficult to tell if this was a genuine success since measures were adopted to artificially reduce the cost of capital and also facilitate exports through a cheap yen. Once sufficient incentives are given, just about any industry can prosper. It is not until the promotion and protection cease that one really knows how well they are doing.

Considering the existence of ailing sectors among the industries which were only launched in the 1950s and 1960s, it would appear that some were poorly chosen. This applies foremost to those that were not only capital-intensive but required imported raw materials and energy to run. It was probably foolish to target processing industries such as aluminum and other metals, pulp and paper or petrochemicals. Even steel is on the borderline and can get by only due to incredible economies of scale.

Furthermore, even if the industries targeted were well chosen, by throwing the government's weight behind them and offering multiple incentives, they probably became too attractive. Too many companies entered them and there was soon excess capacity. This sort of thing is all the more likely in a country like Japan, where group-think prevails and everyone wants to get into the act. Thus, there has been massive overcapacity in shipbuilding, light metals and steel, and certain electronics. The Ministry of International Trade and Industry, which originally helped build these sectors up, now has the less glorious task of helping them scale down.[11]

These distortions are reasonably visible. What is seen much less distinctly, but can be no less decisive, is what happens to those industries which are not targeted. By directing funds, personnel and efforts toward a number of "sunrise" sectors, they almost automatically rose. This took away necessary funds, personnel and efforts from other industries which fulfilled the prophecy of becoming "sunset" sectors. So, many seemingly old-fashioned and labor-intensive branches, the crafts, garments and others, suffered unduly and declined before their time.

So much for the question of efficacy. There is no less cause for doubt as regards equity. The government's decisions were hardly neutral in the economic sense. They artificially stimulated certain sectors and artificially stifled others. If there is a correlation between who is engaged in these two categories, then there were doubtlessly also social and political implications.[12]

As is well enough known, the companies involved in the heavy-and-chemical industries, MITI's first basic target, are huge. Indeed, how could it be otherwise? It takes a lot of capital to enter them, economies of scale are important, and advanced technologies are often needed. In addition, MITI insisted on further concentration. Thus, on the whole, the companies aided were those which already possessed more capital, larger staffs and better organization than most. The government was thereby helping those who could most readily help themselves.

Those who really needed help were, by and large, located in sectors which were not targeted. In fact, some of them were tacitly written off by the government. Almost all such were relatively small and undercapitalized, run by less influential entrepreneurs. Government policy was therefore a further blow against them. Admittedly, there were sops like a special agency and special banks and loans. But there was not enough to go around and not even enough to compensate for the artificial handicaps these companies faced. Gradually they sank to the lower rung in the "dual structure."[13]

If government support were just moderate, this would not have made much difference. But targeting was not a matter of mere recognition. Companies received valuable incentives, cheap loans, land, infrastructure and so on. Frequently, they sold their products to the public sector at special, read inflated, prices. Even more precious was to benefit from protection from imports during extensive periods which allowed them to charge more domestically than otherwise. And exporters were further supported by the cheap yen. This was all worth a fortune.

That explains why major companies were willing to follow MITI's lead. Even when they did not think that the programs were particularly wise or that a product was truly suited to Japanese conditions, they were offered enough incentives to overcome any initial qualms and probably also to guarantee a reasonable success. Then, as things progressed, they gradually imposed their own preferences on the bureaucracy and were even happier to get substantial backing.

What did the bureaucrats get out of the system? First of all, they enjoyed heightened prestige domestically and internationally for creating an economic "miracle" and delivering high growth by overfulfilling already ambitious plans. Few noticed that the early plans were actually quite prudent, with the target set at a lower rate than had been attained in the previous period. Alas, it was not long before this bubble burst as plans failed to reach their goals year after year and Prime Minister Nakasone finally decided to scrap planning as such.

Despite the slowdown, the bureaucracy could at least maintain an aura of patriotism by promoting new industries, boosting exports and preventing imports. Such acts were widely approved by the general public and bureaucrats who defended local industry from demands for liberalization were assured of gratefulness. Aside from this aspect, however, these various tasks, as well as the masses of rules and regulations they generated, were sources of work for thousands and thousands of bureaucrats. Any retrenchment meant a loss of jobs for them and they therefore had to justify the system.

Finally, much less nobly alas, by providing incentives and assorted advantages to the private sector, many bureaucrats were able to establish mutually beneficial relations. They could strengthen an industry or, even better, help a specific company, and look forward to suitable compensation, fancy entertainment or sometimes a cash bribe. But it was more often a comfortable *amakudari* job on retirement. Such delayed rewards were particularly abundant for just those ministries which aided the private sector most.

So, intervention was indubitably good for big business and the bureaucrats. For the politicians, it was a mixed blessing. They also promoted local industries, and called for protection, using their influence with the administration to gain this. Here, the recompense took the form of jobs for their followers and status with the electorate as well as political donations and support for themselves. But, when the time for liberalization finally came, they were caught between intense foreign pressure and fierce resistance at home. They were even more embarrassed when they had to force companies to accept export restraints. In both cases, the best policy seemed to be procrastination which avoided a formal commitment on their part and meanwhile enabled exporters to ship a bit more and imports to be held off longer. This approach did not go down well abroad, but it won them acclaim in Japan.

What about the people in all this? After all, they were also affected. While not denying the benefits of postwar development, it has to be remembered that there were also disadvantages to the specific strategies used which might not have accompanied other approaches. Massively channeling resources to business deprived citizens of funds they could have used for more or better housing, consumer goods or leisure. It also meant that they could put away less for security in old age. Promoting and protecting local industries resulted in domestic products that were more costly, both because more tax revenue was needed to finance the incentives and because higher prices could be charged due to lack of foreign competition. Keeping the yen cheap had the side-effect of making imports that much more costly.

The high priority on production as opposed to consumption, leisure, or welfare kept the living standards and lifestyles from improving as rapidly as otherwise. It further disrupted families and communities, accelerated the depopulation of backward areas and concentration in big cities and coastal zones. Production first, especially heavy-and-chemical production, contributed mightily to pollution. But the worst effect was probably to twist the Japanese psyche in such a way that time-honored traditions were dissipated and there was little time or thought to communion with nature or the inner life.

Politically, this approach further reinforced the position of the elite over the masses. There were major gains for big business (and lesser ones for small), the bureaucrats and politicians. Ordinary people had to foot the bill as taxpayers, consumers, citizens and individuals. Considering that big business already had enough clout, it might be asked whether it would not have been better for the government to take an intermediate stance between the goals of economic and social development, between the needs of businessmen and the rest of the population, between the strong and weak. Better or not, it is probably unreasonable to expect anything else than that business should ultimately coopt and dominate the establishment.

Mobilizing Funds

No amount of entrepreneurial fervor, no government plans or targets no matter how wise, would have made the slightest difference if Japan could not raise the necessary funds to invest in economic production. Over the years, it developed a mighty system of mobilizing resources, one which is probably unique in the world due to its odd mixture of voluntary saving and guided allocation. While this did get the money where it was desired, perhaps even more abundantly than was advisable, it had many troubling implications that were blithely ignored.

Everybody knows that the primary source of funds was the savings of millions of individual Japanese. This was particularly essential since, for political reasons, the government refused to rely on external loans or foreign investment. Thus, it was fortunate that due to traditions of frugality and the urge to guarantee their future, the people were truly prodigious savers. They managed to put aside as much as 20% of their income year after year. They also increasingly put money into life and other insurance policies and pension schemes for their old age. All this built up into absolutely extraordinary amounts of money.

What is much less widely known is how this money was channeled into economic investment. Naturally much of it flowed through the banks, especially the major city banks. They granted loans to what they regarded as deserving companies which could then expand. But this lending was not on the basis of normal interest rates as fixed by supply and demand. Rather, the interest rates on both sides were set by the Bank of Japan and Ministry of Finance, after consultation with the government and also the banks. The decision was consistently to keep interest rates for loans low so that companies could get relatively cheap money.

However, for lending rates to stay low, it was necessary for borrowing rates to be low as well. So, the banks regularly paid rather mediocre rates to the small savers whose money they used. These interest rates were defended as adequate since they usually exceeded inflation. This, of course, meant the official and artificially low CPI. Still, they were much lower than if market forces had prevailed and gave savers a rather mediocre return.

Some of the funds also flowed from the insurance firms and pension managers directly into the companies. They bought large amounts of stock in quoted companies, which made them—along with the banks—the major shareholders in the nation. But the investors were not really getting that much for their money because most of the companies paid quite modest dividends. There were many other uses that could have been made of the money to get a better return. Not doing so was again a disservice to the people who bought insurance or depended on pensions.

Through these mechanisms, the funds were indeed transferred efficiently and cheaply to the corporate sector. The losses of the savers and insured might have been justified if the money was then used as efficiently as possible and funds were distributed wisely and fairly. That would mean that companies with the most promising projects would get first crack.

Any hope of this was substantially reduced by the existence of *keiretsu*. The groups of companies revolving around major banks were certainly in a position to get more of the funds than outside companies. Banks therefore gave precedence when granting loans to related firms or others recommended by them. In so doing, they provided loans at nominal and sometimes even negative rates for those most closely related and still modest rates for the rest. But they rarely had enough money to go beyond a narrow circle of clients. Insurance firms also invested in banks and companies of the limited "family."

Companies beyond the pale of the *keiretsu* had tremendous difficulty in obtaining any credit, unless they had access to the government banks. Individuals who needed money for housing or consumer loans were even worse off. These borrowers could turn only to the unofficial market which was inhabited by unreliable institutions or loan sharks *(sarakin)*. The interest they had to pay showed just how imbalanced the money market was. It could easily run into 30% and more for reputable firms and 60%, 80% and even 110% in earlier days for individuals.

Thus, the beneficiaries of the system created by the government were, first of all, major companies which had easy access to cheap funds. This enabled them to move into new sectors, expand production and personnel, and capitalize on the tremendous possibilities of postwar growth. It gave them a further edge over all other companies, especially the smaller ones, which were often stymied by lack of funds. Indeed, the leading assemblers and trading companies sometimes borrowed huge amounts from the banks and fed smaller quantities to their suppliers and subsidiaries, further strengthening their control over these lesser firms.

The financial intermediaries also benefited from the system. The banks could lend quite safely to large and established companies which often invested in keeping with government policies, thereby absolving them of any criticism if the loan went sour. They were even more pleased to have a guaranteed spread between lending and borrowing rates, a spread which they furtively negotiated with the financial bureaucracy and proved very remunerative. For their part, the securities houses were able to collect big commissions and the insurance companies to charge high rates, again with the benediction of the Ministry of Finance. They, too, waxed fat.

But there was one further beneficiary, namely the financial bureaucracy in the MOF, BOJ, state banks and other agencies. There was nothing like regulation of financial intermediaries to enhance the position of the bureaucrats concerned, who soon appeared as an elite of sorts. They not only issued instructions, either through window or administrative guidance, they supervised many operations and sometimes inspected firms. This gave them considerable authority. They also assigned the various activities to each category, deciding what could be done by banks or securities houses, for example. A favorable revision of such boundary lines, often mooted and occasionally brought about, boosted their rating even higher.

In addition, by allowing the banks large spreads, the securities houses big commissions, and the insurance companies high rates, there was little if any chance that any of them would become insolvent or go bankrupt. This permitted the bureaucrats to look more like an "elite" since there were rarely troubles in their sector and they could not be accused of incompetence or creating confusion. The fact that many of their wards were inefficient and the excess costs had to be borne by the public was hardly noticed.

There was also the possibility of finding good *amakudari* jobs once they retired. Having heavily regulated the financial institutions, they were able to place one or another in their debt. Knowing how the complicated regulations worked or having younger colleagues who engaged in administrative guidance of some sort, they were still able to render valuable services after retirement. This was enough to earn them a post of advisor or auditor in a company or a cozy seat on a board of directors.

But this was not all. Although rarely mentioned, there was an additional source of funds which came almost directly under the control of the politicians and bureaucrats. This is the Fiscal Investment and Loan Program (FILP). Often referred to as the "second budget," its dimensions were most impressive, amounting to as much as two-fifths of the regular budget or some ¥20 trillion by the 1980s. It drew resources partly from the postal savings system, which explains why the MPT could get away with having higher interest rates than granted by MOF. The rest came from the civil servants' pension schemes. FILP money was funneled into the state banks and a multitude of public corporations. They included agencies for the construction of roads, railways, bridges, airports and so on as well as some regional development bodies.

Since they helped determine how this kitty should be spent, LDP bosses could use it as a form of patronage by offering additional public works to favored districts. The Ministry of Finance had the privilege of administering the FILP. But many other bureaucracies benefited from the existence of lavish funds that were poured into literally dozens of government-affiliated corporations and agencies which eventually offered post-retirement jobs, some quite lucrative. Yet, despite the huge sums involved, the fact that many of the corporations were inefficient or improvident, and also that the funds were invested in long-term, low yielding activities that were improper for savings or pensions schemes, there was little criticism in the Diet. Even the opposition remained suspiciously silent.

Thus, the peculiar system which evolved for allocating funds was clearly biased in favor of big business, the bureaucrats and the politicians. It also worked very much against the deeper interests of ordinary people. They received artificially low interest rates for savings, poor yields on stocks and bonds and mediocre appreciation of money paid into insurance and pension schemes. Meanwhile, they had to pay bloated rates for insurance, stocks and loans, assuming they could get them. In short, they not only provided the essential wherewithal, they got short-changed while doing so.

Despite this, the population at large did almost nothing to alter the situation. People only rarely sent money abroad, where the returns were better, perhaps due to restrictions or a lack of knowledge. They only showed a bit more imagination in seeking alternative investments. At most, they might cheat a bit by opening several tax exempt bank accounts under different names. But they did not organize and they did not protest. Even the consumers' movements failed to recognize the abuses or launch campaigns for improvement.

The only real hope was foreign pressure. While foreign banks, securities houses and insurance companies objected to some of the restrictions, they usually found the situation too cozy to complain. Then, in the mid-1980s, when massive amounts of Japanese funds—from banks and big companies primarily—flooded into the United States to benefit from higher interest rates, the value of the yen plummeted. This motivated Washington to demand a liberalization of the financial system which might ultimately, some years hence, result in interest rates for ordinary accounts being fixed by the market.

Yet, even this is unlikely to change the fact that small savers will probably still get somewhat less than they might or that most of the funds will still be directed to the large, well-connected companies. Admittedly, the banks, securities houses and insurance companies will have to reduce costs and work harder for their profits. But there is ample room for private collusion to replace some of the formal deregulation. The position of the individual will therefore improve only moderately.

Meanwhile, there are other emerging influences on the system which should have even greater effects. After having saved at length for their old age, more and more Japanese will be withdrawing their savings. This has already begun and the saving rate is falling. They will also start drawing on their life insurance and pension benefits. As money is paid out and used for consumption, less will be available for investment in plant and equipment.

While this could be expected, another threat is more untoward. With the government running massive budget deficits, and swamping the market with bonds, it will be necessary for the banks and other intermediaries to absorb these offerings whether they want to or not. Obliged to purchase these relatively low-yielding instruments, they will find it ever harder to raise enough money for corporations. Completely reversing trends that go back decades, the government will be harming rather than helping business. However, since bonds are particularly sterile investments, that does not mean that it will be helping the public in return.

Running Out Of Funds

Given their differing positions and interests, it was not surprising to encounter a continual tug-of-war between bureaucrats who had to manage Japan's financial resources, namely those in the Ministry of Finance and Bank of Japan, and others whose hopes of glory lay in new and more impressive projects. This was actually most of the rest, with MITI, Agriculture and Construction leading the pack. The tensions were greatly eased by a long period of economic growth during the 1950s, 1960s and into the

1970s. This made it possible for MOF to get more revenue and the others to gain more expenditures without the state being squeezed.

But this situation changed drastically with the oil shocks and resulting worldwide recession which reduced Japan's growth rate and made it harder to get ahead by exporting. For the first time, there were definite constraints on how much could be spent since revenue increases no longer came about almost automatically and funds had to be allocated more carefully. The time had come, or so it seemed, to control expenditures. This form of common sense reasoning, however, was countered by contrasting philosophies of how to overcome the crisis and bring about a recovery, with many pressing for stimulatory measures and pump-priming of one sort or another.

Influential bureaucrats and economists, and not only the most optimistic, argued that a good push was all that was needed for Japan to quickly resume a rapid cruising speed as it had done so often in the past. They do not appear to have grasped the seriousness of the downturn or how long the debilitating consequences would last. Thus, if it were only a question of increasing public works and granting loans or subsidies for a while, this was deemed feasible. It was even seen as a gesture of international solidarity when other advanced nations called on Japan to become a "locomotive" for world growth, along with the United States. This was accepted, with only slight regrets, by Prime Minister Fukuda in 1979.[14]

Instead, as it turned out, rather than pulling out of one crisis the nation was spending itself into another. Expenditures regularly exceeded revenue, and by very considerable amounts. The level of deficit financing rose to truly astounding levels, climbing from 11% in 1974 to nearly 35% in 1979, when it peaked and slipped a bit but remained high. This meant that costs could not be covered

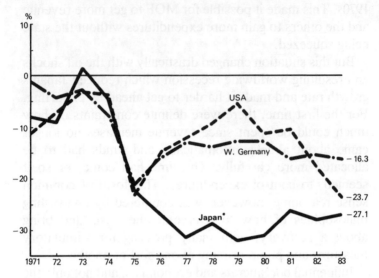

Plumbing greater depths in fiscal irresponsibility. Share of government expenditure *not* covered by tax revenue.

Source: Comparative International Statistics, Bank of Japan, 1984.
Credit: *Facts and Figures of Japan 1985*, p. 35.

without floating public bonds, a measure MOF had steadfastly pledged not to tolerate. Yet, it was gradually increasing the so-called construction bonds which had been used to mount desirable public works for some time. And, in 1975, it took the even more fateful step of issuing deficit-covering bonds.

With budget deficits remaining high, these two forms of bonds kept growing at an alarming pace. The Ministry of Finance tried to stem the flood, first promising to eliminate all new bond issues by 1984, then putting this off for 1990. Meanwhile, the amount spiraled ever higher. In 1984, it passed the symbolic point of ¥120 trillion which worked out to ¥1 million in debt for every man, woman and child in the country. But it could easily top the ¥200 trillion or even ¥400 trillion mark some day. This day was only advanced when, in 1984, MOF broke another pledge and began issuing refinancing bonds to redeem the old ones. With this, the visions of a stolid and frugal Japan evaporated as it ran deficits that were proportionately larger than in Europe and accumulated a national debt that might eventually rival that of the United States.[15]

Bad as this was, it was only part of the debt problem. For it was not only the central government which resorted to bond issues. This practice was increasingly adopted by local autonomies. Many towns and cities were living beyond their means and could cover expenses only by floating municipal bonds to cover some 10% to 15% of their budgets. These bonds already amounted to about ¥50 trillion and could be expected to rise further. Moreover, the government guaranteed bonds issued by certain public or special corporations. It was also responsible for the sums loaned to state bodies within the FILP. Among them were a number which could not possibly pay back the loans promptly or perhaps at all, such as the Japanese National Railways, Japan Railway Construction Corporation and assorted bridge, tunnel and other construction agencies. These various items probably doubled the total national debt.

With this, the Finance Ministry's policy and its very authority were in disarray. Its bureaucrats repeatedly urged political leaders to halt this progression before it was too late and they always met with a sympathetic hearing. But only on rare occasions was this turned into strong action. Prime Minister Ohira, himself a former Finance Minister, accepted the arguments presented and made a plea for greater revenue to cover the outlays. He went so far as to propose a "general excise tax" which was recommended by the Taxation System Council and made this a plank in the 1979 elections. This was a fatal mistake, for the opposition parties gleefully attacked a leader who campaigned for higher taxes and the LDP lost votes. No other prime minister since then has been willing to tackle the problem head on and, when they tried to boost taxes, it was always cautiously, piecemeal . . . and after elections. Also, like politicians everywhere, they were under pressure to grant tax cuts no matter how difficult the situation. The opposition parties did not hesitate to call for this and thereby become the champions of the common man. When the pressure built up adequately, the LDP would usually make a noble gesture to steal the opposition's thunder and announce its own grandiose reduction. It never amounted to much, and was often balanced by petty increases in other taxes, but it slowed down the return to fiscal responsibility.

If the situation had been painful in Ohira's day, it was certainly not getting any more comfortable. Seduced by events taking place across the Pacific, with a taxpayers' revolt in California and the advent of Reaganomics, the Japanese felt that it was appropriate to manifest their discontent. Admittedly, tax rates were still very low in Japan compared to the West. But people were being squeezed between slowly rising income and mounting taxes resulting from bracket creep. Dissatisfaction was strongest among the salaried employees whose taxes were deducted at the source. But it was clearly widespread. According to a survey of the Ministry of Home Affairs, 70% of the respondents felt that taxes were already too heavy and 60% were against any tax hike.[16] This was a clear message to the government.

Other grievances had less to do with the level of taxation than the manifest lack of equity. Salaried employees paid taxes on their whole earnings and got few deductions while the self-employed (including doctors, professionals and service operators) and farmers rarely declared their entire income and claimed huge, often unjustifiable expenses. This was commonly referred to as the 9:6:4 rule indicating which shares of their taxes were actually paid by the three categories. Meanwhile, the National Tax Administration Agency periodically reported on tax evasion which was reaching epidemic proportions. Prime offenders included not only small, somewhat disreputable operators but big names like Mitsui, Marubeni and Mitsubishi. Until something could be done to correct these abuses, raising income taxes would be resented. But it was hard to crack down seriously since most of the offenders came from groups which solidly supported the ruling party.

Still, it was not a tax revolt or annoyance among the people, let alone the meek salaryman class, that worried the government nearly as much as rumblings in the business community. Company executives complained bitterly of paying taxes at exceptionally high rates, or so they said. They also insisted that, after having made every effort to cut their own costs and pull in their belts, it was time for the government to do its part by reducing expenditures and personnel. A campaign for "administrative reform" was led by top business leaders, especially Toshiwo Doko, Yoshihiro Inayama and Bunpei Otsuki and enjoyed the backing of the *zaikai*. It was spectacularly successful since it was soon endorsed as official policy by Prime Ministers Suzuki and Nakasone.

Naturally, cutting costs aroused some opposition. But most of those hurt belonged to weak or disorganized groups and complaints from the opposition parties were anticipated no matter what. More irksome were criticisms voiced from within the LDP. Toshio Komoto, then EPA Director-General, repeatedly urged increased spending to stimulate the economy. Kiichi Miyazawa, playing to popular sentiment, proposed an "assets doubling plan" that was bound to cost a substantial amount. There were also divisions in the business community with small companies, and especially building contractors who lived off public works, calling for a prompt resumption of major programs and measures to shore up ailing companies. This ultimately found some echo in the broader Chamber of Commerce.

But none of this was enough to reverse the policy. After all, there was not much choice: either revenue had to be increased or expenditures decreased. The objections to the first were greater than to the second and it was adopted as the easier way out. It probably was . . . for the short term. So, without giving much thought to the long term, it was decided that rather than pursue MOF's tack of boosting revenue, it was better to follow the businessmen's approach of decreasing expenses.

As of fiscal 1982, efforts were made to block the rise in budgetary allocations, eventually bringing it down to about "zero" growth. Year after year, with amazing resolve, the government held the line and the increases were indeed minimal. But this was not a very pleasant task either since, within the overall limitations, some few items were allowed to increase marginally while others sank. The first to go were several social expenditures, such as the promised increase in teachers and free health care for the aged. Even public works sank somewhat. Among the items which rose, the most prominent was defense. Yet, while most of the clamor was concentrated on this breach, it only grew moderately. Where the biggest expansion occurred, although it was hardly noticed, was for debt servicing. This figure grew by as much as 30% or 40% a year, rising from a mere ¥443 billion in 1973 to ¥12,000 billion in 1985. This made it the largest single item in the national budget, accounting for 20% of the total.[17]

MOF officials rationing out the budget to other ministries.
No happy faces.
Credit: Foreign Press Center/Kyodo

Thus, while the policy of fiscal constraint was a success in its own terms, it was a failure in all others. It proved possible to hold down budgetary allocations more than had ever been expected. But this scuttled every alternative policy including economic measures aimed at recovery and social measures aimed at enhanced welfare. Yet, even then, additional bonds had to be issued, debts kept accumulating and debt servicing absorbed more of the budget. And, if it were to avoid sheer bankruptcy, the government would still have to impose substantial new taxes.

Japan's Political Farmers

Only one other sector enjoyed considerable support from the government, namely agriculture. This has been going on since the 1950s, at which time special attention was probably justified since the farmers were backward and numerous. To see they got a fair deal, and cover the risks of bad weather and crop failures, it was decided to purchase rice at a relatively high price. To avoid an excessive burden on the consumers, it was sold at a lower price (although still much above world rates). When there was overproduction, the surplus was stored at government expense. This triple subsidy left the state with substantial costs which could run as high as ¥1 trillion a year.

To avoid this, it was decided to encourage the farmers to switch to other crops and help them make the transition. Thus, they received a subsidy for taking land out of rice and further assistance for planting wheat, soya or other grains. Pushing ahead, efforts were also made to turn some of them into fruit growers or cattle breeders. This required additional subsidies. And, since domestic costs were so much higher, measures were taken to protect these crops from imports. Prices therefore rose to artificial levels which could be two, three and even four times the international rates.

The "solution" therefore created even greater problems than had existed to begin with. The farm sector was running, but it was doing so only because of massive subsidies which revolved around ¥2 trillion a year. And agriculture was dreadfully inefficient as compared to foreign competitors or domestic industry. To proceed yet further along this path was inane since every additional step involved crops for which the land was even less suited and would therefore require even greater investments. Yet, at the same time that most other assistance was being cut back, it was decided to strive for agricultural self-sufficiency. This was proposed by the Ministry of Agriculture, Forestry and Fisheries and ratified by the

Diet in 1980, at the behest of Prime Minister Suzuki whose interest in the sector was manifest.

There was a tenuous argument for such a concept. In the event of wars, port strikes or crop failures, Japan could be deprived of access to food. Something like this had happened with the soybean embargo in 1973 and a considerably less applicable parallel was the American grain embargo of the Soviet Union for invading Afghanistan. This was actually the pretext for adopting new plans to maintain "food national security" which could apparently only rest on self-sufficiency.[18] Few critics, and even fewer Diet members, bothered questioning such a move. Despite the lack of land, inappropriate climate and incredible costs, it was adopted as the nation's goal.

This does not mean that there were no alternatives. A far more sensible one was not to expand agriculture but rather effect an orderly retreat. It would be facilitated by the constantly shrinking farm population of about five million households, only 30% of which were largely farmers while the rest earned more from outside jobs. More could be imported to make up for any shortfalls. Or, yet better, productivity could be improved. This could be done easily enough by increasing the size of land holdings. But that was blocked by existing legislation, although shrewd farmers were already leasing land to one another. Still, what was the point to selling one's land or giving up farming when prices were so high?

The results of these policies were two-fold. On the one hand, the government was strapped with a heavy financial burden and the consumers had to bear exorbitant food costs. On the other, farm income was rising steadily. The once impoverished farmers were eventually faring better than the city dwellers. Their earnings were higher, their living costs were lower, and they possessed more household appliances, cars and other comforts than average and traveled more widely abroad. This was increasingly visible and created no small resentment in the rest of the population. But there was no policy reversal nor the slightest chance that the present supports would be seriously eroded.

Why have the farmers done so well? The answer is quite simple. While a minority of the population, they were better organized than most sectors thanks to the local cooperatives and the broader federations, like Zenchu. They also realized that more could be gained by backing the LDP which became increasingly dependent on the rural vote. But they could command support from other parties as well, including the Socialists and Communists who traditionally defended a peasantry that was hardly downtrodden any more. It was therefore possible to rally two hundred or more Dietmen to back them while few indeed had the temerity to question even the more extravagant demands.

Moreover, the farmers were not the only ones interested in supporting—or expanding—the present system. There were also the distributors of foodstuffs, and especially those who could import the limited quantities of citrus fruits, bananas, beef and other produce. For, with the domestic prices kept artificially high, it was possible to obtain inflated margins when buying cheap foreign products. These distributors were not just anyone but handpicked agents, most of them with excellent political connections, who did not hesitate to kick back to those who helped them and made handsome political contributions to the ruling party.

Then came the staff of the Ministry of Agriculture, Forestry and Fisheries, nearly 80,000 strong and one of the biggest contingents in the administration. They had staked their career on a flourishing agriculture and were always eager to launch new projects and programs. Diversification provided a fertile field for such, albeit often unsuccessful, experiments. And the goal of self-sufficiency meant that these activities could go on almost indefinitely. On the other hand, any weakening of the support structure or liberalization of imports would show how poorly they had done their job.

The only noteworthy opposition to the farm policy came from industrial circles, again led by Keidanren. It came out against raising the self-sufficiency rate and in favor of opening the market to let in cheaper food. But there was more talk than action and even Keidanren could not accomplish much against Zenchu. At best, it might slow down the expansion of subsidies or strengthen the government's will to increase quotas. For this it was portrayed as egoistically sacrificing the Japanese farmers to take the heat off Japanese manufacturers for exporting too much.

Surprisingly little was heard from the general public in these debates. It was the average consumer who was paying two, three or four times as much for most food-stuffs and had to go without beef or other delicacies more often than not. Yet, when the cards were down, few Japanese would do more than bring in the allotted quantity of frozen beef on returning from a trip abroad or mutter that, after all, fish is healthier than meat. Even the consumers' movements gradually swung into line behind the farmers and stressed that it was far more important to have reliable supplies of domestic food than to have cheaper imported food.

The only threat was therefore foreign pressure. This took the form of demands for liberalization of agricultural imports by Japan's trading partners. Such calls only became louder as producer nations ran growing trade deficits and desperately sought something to sell, something

Subsidizing rice production and then subsidizing storage of surplus rice.
Credit: Foreign Press Center/Kyodo

which they supplied better and cheaper. This certainly applied to just about all farm products, including even rice. But they were discreet enough not to tamper with the national staple and just request improvements for beef, citrus fruits and some minor items. These demands were resisted stubbornly by the farmers, seeing any concessions as merely the start of a move that could ultimately "destroy Japanese agriculture."

When such ominous threats arose, as they increasingly did, the farmers mobilized their political machinery. The cooperatives asked their members to send letters to the Dietmen, Zenchu and other groups organized thousands of farmers to visit Tokyo and protest in front of the Ministry, Diet and American embassy. It did not take long for the Agriculture Committee of the House of Representatives, for example, to adopt a resolution opposing liberalization of farm imports. And such resolutions were sponsored not only by the LDP but also Komeito, DSP, JSP, and JCP.[19] This pressure was then used by government negotiators to explain to their foreign counterparts why they could not conceivably make greater concessions.

Agriculture thereby became almost a caricature of what could happen when industrial policy and targeting got out of hand. It also laid bare the mechanisms for obtaining—and preserving—assistance even when such support lacked any rationale. Finally, it showed just how hard it was for the population as a whole to counter the efforts of a resolute and self-seeking pressure group.

NOTES

1. See *Consider Japan*, London, The Economist, 1963.
2. Jon Woronoff, *The Japan Syndrome*, pp. 120–4.
3. See Shinohara and Yanagihara, *The Japanese and Korean Experiences in Managing Development*.

4. See Johnson, *MITI and the Japanese Miracle.*
5. See Woronoff, *World Trade War.*
6. Shinohara and Yanagihara, *op. cit.,* p. 29.
7. Johnson, *op. cit.,* pp. 255–60.
8. Woronoff, *The Japan Syndrome,* pp. 137–46.
9. According to Chalmers Johnson, the top authority on the subject, "there is no question that MITI, as a bureaucracy, feared that liberalization might eliminate its raison d'etre, and for this reason, if no other, it sought to obtain new control powers." *(op. cit.,* p. 249.)
10. This is admitted even by a friendly observer and sometime participant Tatsuro Uchino, *Japan's Postwar Economy.*
11. Just how much money was wasted by targeting is hard to say. Still, given such gross errors as shipbuilding, shipping, aluminum smelting and petrochemical industries with massive overcapacity, it must have added up to trillions of yen in excessive investment and many more in subsidies or higher costs to domestic customers.
12. One of the first, and best, studies of this often negative relationship was Kozo Yamamura, *Economic Policy in Postwar Japan: Growth versus Democracy.*
13. On the dual structure, see Tadashi Fukutake, *Japanese Society Today,* pp. 83–7, and Takafusa Nakamura, *The Postwar Japanese Economy,* pp. 151–206.
14. See I.M. Destler and Hisao Mitsuya, "Locomotives on Different Tracks," in Destler and Sato (eds.), *Coping with U.S.-Japan Economic Conflicts,* pp. 243–70.
15. Woronoff, *op. cit.,* pp. 104–12.
16. *Japan Times,* July 23, 1980.
17. Woronoff, *op. cit.,* pp. 112–6.
18. *Japan Economic Journal,* June 10 and October 28, 1980.
19. *Japan Times,* April 23, 1982.

7

Social Issues

Re-Reforming Education

Educational reform was one of the foremost legacies of
the American Occupation when efforts were made to mold
a more democratic, equalitarian and individualistic population. To this end, the old prewar system was completely
reshaped, pretty much along American lines, with a structure based on 6 years of elementary, 3 years of lower
secondary, 3 years of higher secondary and 4 years of
university education. Schools were encouraged to become
coeducational, to teach more social and humanistic subjects and to cease their elitist tendencies. Greater grass-
roots participation was to be achieved by reducing central
control and instituting local school boards and parent-
teacher associations.[1]

These are some of the main features of the Fundamental
Law on Education which was adopted in 1947. While this
legislation and, even more so, the new spirit, were clearly
fashioned by American experts and advisors, implementation was left largely to the Japanese. After the Occupation,
the system could be remodeled by the authorities, with an
increasingly keen interest taken by the Liberal Democratic
Party. Under conservative pressure, the Ministry of Education gradually adopted more restrictive policies and
tried to reassert its former control. Many of its early

bureaucrats, by the way, were former hardliners who had been briefly purged or managed to dissimulate their views. Thus, with the passing years there was a partial rollback of the American reforms. Nothing was done to change the basic 6-3-3-4 structure, although it was sporadically criticized if for no other reason than being a remnant of foreign influence. The curricula, by and large, retained a stress on social and liberal subjects, although science and mathematics won pride of place. More notable concern was shown for enhancing "moral" education, which some felt was not only ignored but debased.[2] To this end, the Ministry of Education favored celebration of National Founding Day which was sometimes criticized as being reminiscent of the discredited Empire Day. It also checked, censored, and partly dictated the contents of textbooks although schools were still free to choose which ones they would use. And a system of "head teachers" *(shunin)* was introduced.

While reimposition of the central government's authority was relatively easy in most other areas, in education it was stubbornly resisted. Here, as nowhere else in society, it encountered stiff and organized opposition which was directed by the Japan Teachers' Union (Nikkyoso) representing just over half of all teachers. It fiercely defended the postwar advances and was often headed by outspoken leaders who enjoyed unusually vigorous support from the rank-and-file. While the confrontation between Nikkyoso and the Ministry of Education was most visible, skirmishes were carried on even more aggressively within the schools themselves where local chapters countered local boards and unionized teachers fought school principals and administrators.[3]

This struggle was even broader. Nikkyoso was not just any trade union but, in many ways, the backbone of Sohyo. Its long-time president Motofumi Makieda was a combative president of this leftist federation, itself allied with the Japan Socialist Party. The union therefore seized upon national policies related not only to education and youth but also foreign affairs and defense and especially any threat to the integrity of the constitution. It did not hesitate to blast "reactionary" steps or statements coming from the Liberal Democratic Party and more particularly its right wing. It thereby became the primary target of rightist organizations which regularly harassed its demonstrations and meetings.

To neutralize Nikkyoso, and impose its own views, the LDP did its best to split the union. New or splinter groups were encouraged, although none grew very large. The bigger threat was a spreading disinterest in politics, whether on the national level or within the schools, by two categories of teachers who made up almost half of the total and remained non-unionized. The more admirable were those who felt that teachers should keep out of politics so as to create a better school atmosphere and, if they had to intervene, should do so more for social and academic reasons. The others, the fastest growing contingent, regarded teaching purely as a job, one which offered considerable leisure which they did not want to waste on union meetings and campaigns.

Thus, an endless round of debates raged between conflicting philosophies and ideologies of education, the conservatives pressing for "reforms" which were frequently directed more toward the past than the future, the radicals seeking yet more democracy and freedom and clinging at least to the present system. Most ended in a deadlock, with occasional gains by one or the other, but no significant advance. This should not necessarily be seen as unfortunate, since there was little reason to believe that either side represented the general opinion of the nation. But it was terribly futile by generating anger and suspicion without any positive outcome. Worse, it was disrupting the smooth functioning of the school system and even the simple provision of proper education.

Meanwhile, completely different events were turning the system as it existed, as well as the improved versions proposed by the right and left, into a travesty of itself. This was brought about by the insidious return of elitism with children striving to get into the best possible high schools so as to enter the new elite of colleges and universities. To help them advance, private schools sprang up in profusion to offer cram courses and many pupils spent untold hours in these *juku* which, in their eyes, were not only as important but more helpful than regular schools. With the excessive stress on passing entrance examinations, it became impossible to even carry on normal class work or follow the prescribed curriculum because the sole interest of many pupils was to prepare for the exams and anything that did not contribute to that was given only cursory attention.

This, more than anything else, sapped both the form and spirit of modern education. It steadily undermined the apparent success of the system such as an increasing number of students moving on to higher education or doing brilliantly on international comparative tests. For those going to high school spent much of their time cramming to get into college, where they then proceeded to unwind and relax until they got a job. Their skills therefore consisted largely of an ability to memorize vast amounts of information and, more particularly, to pass multiple choice exams. While extremely good at answering specific questions, they were exceptionally poor at practical tasks or thinking for themselves. And what knowledge they did accumulate was often spurious and forgotten a few years later.[4]

Socially, the liabilities were even more serious. The

grind of examination hell not only deprived children of the joys of childhood, it made them fragile, oversensitive and unfriendly. They were unable to develop their physical skills or strength. Some got ulcers and psychological ailments which could result in severe depression or suicide. Those who did not make the grade, and at least realized this at an early date, quickly lost interest in learning and acquired a hatred for schools and teachers. Those who tried hard and failed were often alienated and resentful. By the 1980s, absenteeism, school violence and juvenile delinquency reached such proportions that they created national scandals.

Even the Japanese, who had obstinately disregarded the situation for decades, finally realized that something had to be done. But they were exceedingly slow in doing anything. While there was some talk of a need for reform in the early 1970s, that only concerned a change in the 6–3–3–4 format and not the basics. In the early 1980s, two minor steps were taken. One was to insert "free time" in the daily schedule to give pupils a chance to do something other than ingurgitate instruction. Alas, this often ended up as a further opportunity for cramming. The decision to have a uniform examination for entrance to the public universities just added one more test to the many individual ones that still had to be taken to get into specific colleges or universities. It was soon hated by students and teachers alike and intensified, rather than relieved, the pressures of examination hell.

Finally, in 1983, Prime Minister Yasuhiro Nakasone called for a fundamental reform. Ignoring the Central Council on Education, which had come up with few useful recommendations in over a decade, he set up his own advisory Council on Culture and Education, chaired by Masaru Ibuka of Sony. Then, going a big step further, he decided to establish an Ad-Hoc Council on Education designed to make a thorough investigation of the school system leading to a major overhaul. This was to be as sweeping, according to the press, as the introduction of the Western system in Meiji days and the postwar revamping. While it was rumored that this move was just a political ploy to stay in power longer, it was clear that Nakasone took a personal interest in education and had thought about the situation at length. This concerned not only things like morality and patriotism, which were highlighted, but also an end to cramming and elitism and more internationalism.

This was not the first time an attempt was made to reform the system. There had been others in the past, either partial or complete failures.[5] But the new Ad-Hoc Council was the most ambitious by far, examining all aspects of education and even the surrounding environment. It met as of September 1984 and began issuing reports and recommendations, with its final conclusions scheduled for the summer of 1987. Among the items that were stressed some applied to the mechanics. This included a reform of university entrance examinations, establishment of six-year middle schools and creation of unit-system high schools. Others dealt with broader issues like improving the quality of teachers, introducing more individualized teaching, changing the contents of curricula and upgrading research. The most significant aspects, however, affected the basic philosophy by fostering principles such as dignity, freedom and self-discipline, individualism and a sense of responsibility.

No matter how encouraging, there were reasons to doubt the ultimate success of this latest effort. One was that the Council's membership had been hand-picked by Prime Minister Nakasone. It included many academics and bureaucrats and supposed representatives of parents and citizens. It even had labor members, namely two

Domei trade union leaders. But it lacked anyone coming from the high schools, where the biggest troubles existed, nor anyone from the teachers' union Nikkyoso.

While the appointment of such a body showed that the crisis had been officially recognized and attempts were being made at finding solutions, it was hard to be overly optimistic about the results. One primary cause for concern is that it came at a time of great fiscal stringency when many useful recommendations could not be implemented due to lack of funds. Worse, even while the advisory bodies were deliberating, those in charge of administrative reform were trimming the education budget. One of the first things to go was funds for reducing classes in public schools to 40 pupils, a measure already promised. This meant that teachers could not possibly deal properly with their pupils, either academically or socially, and it made Japan look particularly bad when compared to classes of 25 or 30 in the West.

A further drawback to any efforts was that attention was concentrated on the system as it existed on paper. It was, of course, possible to change the 6-3-3-4 format, to introduce more language courses, to have children engage in extracurricular activities and even to change the contents of university entrance exams. But these were only adjustments in the official system. The worst damage arose from the parallel system of elite schools, cram courses and a brute urge to succeed in the entrance exams. This was not included in the formal system. In fact, it was precluded. Thus, any changes would be effective only if they reached much further than the Ministry of Education, the schools and the teachers into the community and even the worldview of the population.

In addition, there were definite political problems. The Japan Teachers' Union not only failed to provide a member to the Council, it repeatedly denounced Nakasone's proposals of educational reform and refused to cooperate in any way. The JSP and JCP were also opposed although the NLC, DSP and Domei conditionally supported the moves. This meant there could be considerable opposition in the Diet when it came time to approve any new legislation. Moreover, whatever reforms were eventually introduced into the school system, if Nikkyoso did not alter its position, they could easily be subverted or distorted by the teachers.

While less visible and tangible, it was rather disturbing that there was no great enthusiasm in business circles. Admittedly, there was no objection and Isao Nakauchi, head of Daiei, and several others were on the Council. But the degree of support was rather feeble compared to the way the *zaikai* massively backed the administrative reform. There was also reason to doubt that large corporations or government bureaucracies would drastically revise their employment practices which placed notable emphasis on educational background and often operated through old-boy networks. With their own in-house training or apprenticeship schemes, they seemed to care little about the candidate's knowledge. And many actually preferred a "blank sheet of paper" that could more readily be shaped after hiring and thereby deprived the school system of any real purpose.

The nation's parents were hardly more enthusiastic, which is even stranger. Many deeply regretted the punishment they were putting their children through in order to get into elite schools. But they nonetheless continued to do so and spared no effort to get around the existing system by resorting to private tutoring and *juku*. As for violence, delinquency, lack of family feeling or patriotism, they tended to blame that on the schools and tried to shift their parental responsibilities to the teachers. With more and more mothers working, and fathers returning home late, there was little hope they would provide the essential backing without which no educational reform could succeed.

Environmental Destruction

Japan, one of the world's smaller and more densely populated countries, is by far the most intensively industrialized. Factories and plants of every description, many of them engaged in processing of metals and chemicals, were strewn the length and breadth of the archipelago. They were not always located in clearly specified industrial zones but rather mixed in with residential and commercial districts. Under such conditions, it was almost inevitable that serious environmental problems should erupt.

While scarcely noticeable during the 1950s, already by the 1960s there were signs of what was increasingly called "environmental destruction" *(kankyo hakai)* here and there. In Minamata, people were suffering from mercury poisoning traced to Chisso's vinyl chloride plant. In Niigata, there was a second outbreak of "Minamata disease." Folks living along the Jinzu River contracted *itai-itai* on eating cadmium-infected fish. Yokkaichi, with its many oil refineries, became known as "asthma city" and was symbolic of many other spots. Even more broadly, the coastal waters and especially Inland Sea were visibly polluted and a pall of photochemical smog hung over major cities, like Tokyo and Osaka.[6]

Pollution had come to Japan, as it had come to the United States, Great Britain, Germany and all other heavily industrialized countries and was gradually spreading even in developing ones. Yet, although the evidence was manifestly there, the Japanese government was extremely slow in reacting. There was hardly any legislation, and that quite poorly policed, until the 1970s. Indeed, it took a long and painful struggle just to prove what should have been obvious, that pollution was a danger to the people and nation.

This demonstration was made by those at the grass roots, a rare occurrence in Japanese history. And it was not the work of prominent civic or political groups. Rather, the most active were those who suffered from one form of pollution or another and found no redress. When the Minamata disease, *itai-itai* and other afflictions arose, they were consciously ignored or denied by the management of the plants that caused them. In this, they were usually followed by the in-house unions, local authorities and even general population. The central government and MITI were unconcerned. It therefore took some time for the trouble to be recognized and anything done for the individuals.

With little help coming from the political side, they turned to the courts as their only hope. In one case after another, companies like Chisso, Toho Zinc, Sumitomo Mining, Nippon Chemical and others were accused of negligence for dumping dangerous waste in public waters or spewing it over private land and thereby contaminating them. Or they were sued for having their employees work under conditions they knew to be harmful. After carefully hearing the evidence, judges frequently ruled for the plaintiffs and sometimes awarded damages or solatia.[7]

Some of these were landmark decisions. In 1973, it was decided that Chisso Corporation was responsible for pollution and had to pay compensation to many Minamata sufferers. In 1980, a company that continued dumping toxic waste was tried criminally and punished. In 1982, a court recognized the polluter's voluntary negligence. Gradually, the Polluter Pays Principle (PPP) gained ground. But the courts were painstakingly slow in their proceedings, often taking a decade or more. And they were rarely very generous to the victims. Moreover, while ruling in favor of those who personally incurred some loss, they shied away from class action suits or plaintiffs who brought complaints on broader grounds such as that a given project violated their constitutional right "to maintain the minimum standards of wholesome and cultured living."[8]

While this progress was to the good, it was dreadfully limited. For, as long as it was only victims or potential victims of pollution who acted, there would be no generalized effort to improve the situation. This was shown by the fact that often, in preference to a long and costly trial, they entered into private negotiations with the polluter and accepted whatever compensation they could get. Farmers or fishermen whose land was sought for factories, villagers where a nuclear power plant would be built, or people living on land needed for railway lines, airports or other

Pollution kills. So do endless court trials and administrative formalities.
Credit: Foreign Press Center/Kyodo

major public works, and the like, were equally willing to accept what might come in return for a sufficiently generous counterpart.

Little could be expected without more personally disinterested and morally committed citizens who would fight for a better and healthier Japan. Eventually, activist groups sprang up. Among them were circles of friends or relatives of pollution victims, who spread the word of their griefs and supported their efforts. A growing number consisted of professionals and intellectuals trying to obtain more general solutions. And the leftist parties and trade unions pitched in. But this never grew into a mass movement like the Sierra Club or Greens and ecology remained a marginal issue.[9]

Still, the calamity was so noticeable and serious by the 1970s that the government felt obliged to act. There were thousands of complaints from citizens and even foreign visitors drew attention to the distressing signs of decay. Meanwhile, with other advanced countries adopting legislation and establishing supervisory bodies, Japan would appear out of step if it did not do so as well. Thus, it hesitantly introduced suitable regulations, often modeled after foreign laws if somewhat less stringent. Then, in 1970, a so-called "Pollution Diet" approved broader legislation and, in 1971, an Environment Agency was inaugurated.[10]

While the legislation and agency made it look as if Japan had turned a new page, that was not really the case. It was still necessary to fight for the slightest advance. Most of these struggles pitted the Environment Agency, a relatively small and low-status body, against the most powerful ministry in the field, MITI. The fight was not only unequal because of the difference in size and prestige. More decisive was that most of the EA's top officials were seconded by MITI, would later return to it, and therefore had to maintain proper relations. It took a full decade before EA could appoint a department head from among its own personnel.

MITI was basically fronting for its traditional clientele. Much of the legislation was opposed because it could create difficulties for private companies, either through an increase in running costs, restrictions on expanding facilities, or even withdrawal or refusal of the right to engage in certain operations. With notable frequency, the complaints of individual companies were taken up more broadly by Keidanren as the representative of business. Given its clout, it was backed by the relevant LDP committees which could torpedo objectionable bills or preferrably keep them from being tabled.

This occurred repeatedly. One example involved the regulations on nitrogen dioxide, one of the worst air pollutants, which had been set at a certain level per individual pollution source. Naturally, in areas where numerous sources were concentrated, the overall amounts could reach an intolerable level. The EA's plan to limit total NOx emissions in major cities was obstructed by MITI and the LDP, obviously on behalf of business interests. Even in the case of automobile exhaust regulations, which were very strict, the step was taken only after stringent American laws were announced that would also apply to Japanese exports. Truck emissions, a bothersome local problem, were only controlled much later.

Stiff opposition was also faced when the Environment Agency tried to tighten up a very loose Water Pollution Prevention Law. It covered only industrial waste, from larger factories, and limited the concentration of pollutants rather than the total amount. By diluting waste with water, virtually any amount could be dumped. In lakes and marshes, most of the pollution came from smaller factories, farms and households anyway. Although approved by other relevant ministries, MITI objected to stricter rules as this would hamper business and blocked the EA's original bill on the subject. Ultimately, a much weakened version was passed. It applied only to the bodies of water and not the surrounding land and lacked convincing penalties for violation. Fortunately, a civic movement to "Make Lake Biwa Clean" led to local bans on the use of detergents, a practice which spread but was occasionally obstructed in local assemblies.

It was the most crucial piece of legislation that was most adamantly fought. This was an Environmental Impact Bill which provided that special environmental assessments be conducted before undertaking large-scale construction works. Every year since 1976, the EA tried to present such a bill. In the first years, it was killed by some of a dozen other ministries and agencies before it could even reach the Diet. Then it was held up by LDP politicians concerned with commerce, industry, construction and so on. But the real obstacle was Keidanren. Thus, the bill was repeatedly altered to overcome some of the objections. The various types of pollution covered were decreased, then the list of projects was revised to drop power stations, later the concept of permitting views from third parties or hearing local opinions was discarded. Yet, this was not enough and the EA finally agreed to withdraw the bill in 1984 and work on the basis of what would probably be rather meek administrative guidance.

Without this key legislation, environmental activities could only consist of cleaning up the mess after it had been made rather than preventing unfortunate occurrences. This limited the EA's positive potential. But it was even on the defensive as regarded its permissible action. Most laws were only applied gradually, giving those concerned time to prepare, and it would seem that implementation was not terribly rigorous to judge by the smoke still pouring out of factories and waste dumped in rivers. In addition, the government appointed EA Directors General who were relatively tame and sometimes restrained its efforts. Meanwhile, the agency accepted the need for a direct "dialogue" with the business community.

Whatever impetus had been gained in the early 1970s was lost by the early 1980s. The Environment Agency, which had never been much of a watchdog, was being muzzled. And every effort was made to convince the public that pollution was no longer a serious problem. Much was made of the fall in levels of the most painful and visible pollutants, like sulfur dioxide, nitrogen dioxide and photochemical smog. Less was said about the tremendous quantities of industrial waste that were accumulating and contained traces of toxic chemicals, including dioxin. Or the continued contamination of rivers, lakes and even drinking water. And the government turned a blind eye to potential pollution from mercury in batteries or acid rain. The only remaining form which was conceded to be grave was noise pollution, something for which it could hardly be taken to task since it issued from the people at large.

This line would seem to have been swallowed to some extent by a population which was hardly sensitized to the dangers. While about 30% of those surveyed by the Prime Minister's Office stated that they were affected by pollution, as many as 70% did not. In the big cities, this was only 60%. Among the 30% or 40% which had complaints, the biggest group was disturbed by noise and lesser numbers complained of odors, water and vibration pollution. But even those who were annoyed by pollution admitted, for the most part (70%), that they chose to do nothing about it. Only in one way were these responses not very satisfying for the government—almost half of the respondents thought that pollution would get worse in the future.[11]

Consumers Beware!

When it comes to the interests of the consumers, Japan would seem to be in a much better position than for environmental issues. It has a rather impressive legal structure defining consumers' rights and producers' obligations such as the Misleading Representations Act of 1962 and the Consumer Protection Basic Act of 1968. Aside from the normal administrative machinery, the Fair Trade Commission also helps supervise this. In addition, the Prime Minister's Office has an advisory National Life Council, with a Consumer Policy Subcommittee, and there are other councils attached to MITI and the Ministry of Health and Welfare. There is even a government-run National Consumer Information Center with over 250 local "better living centers."

The whole paraphernalia is there. In theory, the laws and regulations should prevent any untoward occurrences and be kept abreast of developments by action of the government, based on advice from the deliberative councils. If any abuses were to arise, they would supposedly be spotted quickly by the bureaucracy and corrected. Instead, for all too explicable reasons, this system does not work that way. Worse, many of the government's responsibilities seem to have been delegated to those least likely to perform them properly, private businessmen.

For example, while it is essential to maintain quality, granting of JIS (Japan Industrial Standards) and SG (Safety Goods) marks is determined largely by the associations concerned under rather hazy direction from MITI. The former, applying to factories and not products, is particularly meaningless. Even decisions on the amount of potentially harmful ingredients to use in foods and beverages is often left to voluntary agreements among the producers, rather than a strict ruling of the MHW. It has long failed to fill in some gaps, such as regulations for baby foods and health foods. And, despite massive use of asbestos, nothing was done to curb its side-effects.

So, time and again, regrettable lapses have arisen. With regard to product safety, it was found that children's tricycles bearing the SG mark were defective and could cause bodily injury. Crayons and erasers, specially made for children with synthetic flavors, contained harmful substances.[12] Most striking by its absence, there were astonishingly few recalls of Japanese motorcycles or automobiles. This despite the fact that the very same models, in their usually superior export versions, were recalled in the United States and elsewhere as defective or dangerous. As for tobacco, nothing was done officially to warn consumers of any potential health hazards.

The health aspect was even more worrisome as regards items like dried baby foods, which a research group found to contain enough bacteria to cause food poisoning. Much more widespread were the supposed health drinks *(dorinku)* whose contents were more than dubious, but not subject to official supervision. The same applied to a flood of supposed "health foods." Due to harmful household goods in general, including synthetic detergents, clothes and accessories, to say nothing of cosmetics, an MHW report showed that about half-a-million patients visited hospitals annually with health problems. If those not going to the hospital were included, the figure would have been several times greater. Yet, that only prompted the ministry to urge manufacturers to make safer goods and the consumers to be more careful when using them.[13]

False labelling was rampant. For example, beverages were sold as "juices" when they actually contained no juice. Japanese *mikan* juice was, and still is, sold as orange juice although it is, at best, a mixture. Supposed "health drinks" were sold as remedies for "physical fatigue," "loss of appetite" and "a weak constitution," although there was nothing in them to warrant such claims. So-called ultrasound facial treatment vessels were sold to "get beautiful skin" even though they had no demonstrable effect. The top prize for misleading advertising, however, would have to go to the state tobacco monopoly for describing tobacco as "essential to life."[14]

Just as vital for good health is proper medical treatment. Yet, there was increasing reason to doubt that this was being provided given the decline of medical education and the growing number of doctors in it for money or to succeed their parents. Just how bad the malpractices could be was shown by reports of hospitals which used untrained and unauthorized personnel or undertook unnecessary operations to collect bigger fees. Considering that many doctors ran a pharmacy on the side, there was even more cause to suspect excessive prescribing of drugs, preferably expensive ones.

This meant that the official system was of little use in many instances. Those who learned this to their personal disadvantage were among the few who challenged it. Again, the most effective recourse was the courts. While not that many cases were handled, some were sufficiently important to affect the general situation. In 1971, victims of a nerve paralyzing disease known as SMON sued several pharmaceutical firms which sold quinoform to which it was traced. In a compromise settlement, they obtained modest compensation. The Ministry of Health and Welfare was also reprimanded for not having checked the efficacy of the drug carefully enough. In the rice bran cooking oil case, a 1984 ruling held not only the manufacturers but also the state responsible, since effective action by the MAFF and MHW could have prevented many of the poisonings.[15] Recently, more malpractice suits have been brought against physicians and hospitals.

This provided more telling warnings to potential misdoers than the manifestly lenient supervision and administrative guidance of the government. But it was necessary to push further if Japan were to avoid many other nasty occurrences. This could only be achieved by active participation of the population. Fortunately, or so it would seem, there were many, perhaps too many, small consumers' movements and some central organizations, such as the Japan Housewives' Association (Shufuren), Consumers' Union of Japan (Nihon Shohisha Renmei), National Liaison Committee of Consumers' Organizations (Shodanren) and Japan Consumers' Association (Nihon Shohisha Kyokai).

But these groups were rarely very large, claiming perhaps tens of thousands of nominal members but only small numbers of activists. They were also not engaged in that many projects, ignoring the vast number of ordinary articles or broader principles and focusing on some more spectacular cases, such as the ultrasound cleaners, certain cosmetics, and so on. Oddly enough, they were sometimes more acutely concerned about threats from abroad, warning against imported drugs or foods rather than militating actively against the vastly larger flow of dangerous products and noxious substances coming from local manufacturers.

What was more disheartening was that the consumers' movements did not get more than rather half-hearted backing from the population at large. There should have been far bigger numbers of supporters, either as contributors or merely following their activities. It would have been thought that special consumer magazines would detail the dangers and be read widely before making purchases. Instead, there was again apathy and passiveness. Repeated surveys by the Prime Minister's Office showed that some 70% of the consumers who were dissatisfied with products, services and door-to-door salesmen resigned themselves to unpleasant experiences and losses. Some regarded this as "bad luck" while others, who would have liked to complain, did not know how or where. Only 7% contacted the distributors or manufacturers and a mere 1% used the official organizations set up to receive their grievances.[16]

There was only one place where the authorities seemed to be defending the people's interests with any zeal. That was the Fair Trade Commission, established as a "watchdog" for the Antimonopoly Law of 1947. This law had already undergone some vicissitudes. It was imposed during the Occupation and then, in 1953, revised to relax some of the wording and permit the industrial reorganization promoted by MITI. In 1977, it was again revised, this time to strengthen it in certain respects. The FTC's actions and influence have varied with its chairmen, the times, and the mood of public opinion. Waning during the early postwar recovery, it waxed with the oil crisis and accompanying inflation, only to stabilize downward with the recession and business stagnation of the 1980s.

The FTC has several major functions. One is to prevent excessive concentration of economic power which could take the form of monopolies or oligopolies in specific branches or control of one company over others. If abused, this could result in manipulation of production, sales or prices which would harm the consumers' interests. In particular, there was a fear of "illegal cartels" among producers to jack up prices or less formal arrangements to bring about parallel price hikes. More positively, it tries to encourage competition which should bring a fair deal for both producers and consumers.

The introduction of antitrust machinery was not a fluke. It was imposed by Occupation advisors because Japan's mighty *zaibatsu* and tight government control of business were seen as causes of the war. Cartelization had an even longer tradition, going back to Meiji and Tokugawa days. And it quickly assumed a new guise as *keiretsu* and other groupings emerged. So, when the new legislation was adopted it encountered fierce resistance from executives, bureaucrats and politicians who praised the virtues of cooperation among businessmen and between business and government. Thus, the FTC faced daunting challenges and tremendous veiled or indirect opposition.

But it went about its work as diligently as it could, tackling one violation after the other. Indeed, it had to handle as many as 200 or 300 cases a year, the propensity for cartels, parallel price hikes and other collusive arrangements being so strong. Among those it dealt with were steel, sheet glass, cement, alcohol, pharmaceuticals, gypsum board, paper, color film, automobile tires, and many other industrial products. It then moved on to marketing, disapproving of practices such as resale price maintenance, sales territory and sole agency arrangements, and any abuse of dominant positions by suppliers or distributors. It also took a crack at collusion for public works. More recently, it finally expressed an intention to push deregulation of essential services, including banking, securities and insurance, transportation, warehousing, electric power and data communications.[17]

Most FTC action took the form of so-called "administrative corrective measures" such as consent decrees and recommendations asking the suspected culprits to cease any improper activities. But it could raid offices, impound documents, and impose fines. It could also bring cases to court, albeit a relatively rare tactic. Still, one such case enhanced its status immeasurably. This concerned a dozen major oil firms accused of forming a cartel at the time of the 1973 oil crisis and sharply raising prices, an action which sparked extraordinary price spirals throughout the economy. While admitting that the companies, and the Japan Petroleum Industry Association, were adjusting production in keeping with MITI's administrative guidance, the Tokyo High Court in 1980 and the Supreme Court in 1984 held that they were wrong to boost prices on their own. These rulings also called for criminal punishment of the participants, for the first time in Japan's history.[18]

This case, like some of its other operations, brought the FTC into direct conflict with MITI. This time, both sides gained a point. MITI was tacitly allowed to introduce administrative guidance, although it had no legal basis, as long as it was socially necessary and did not run counter to the public interest. But its intervention also had to be consistent with the purposes of the Antimonopoly Law. Whether this was true of MITI's massive restructuring of ailing industries, which included recession cartels, was an open question. The FTC thought not and criticized these plans in that they might put the consumers at a disadvantage and pose antitrust problems. It even went further and noted that such policies, which were often inefficient and defective, resolved the difficulties much less effectively than healthy competition.[19]

This activism, striking as it was amidst the otherwise placid bureaucratic routine, did not make the Fair Trade Commission a real threat to business. There was still a tremendous amount of concentration, more than in other liberal economies, and there was also a lot of amicable collusion which went unnoticed. When one means of evading the law was blocked, powerful companies quickly found another. Meanwhile, the various ministries and agencies learned to live with the FTC which, more than a true "watchdog," was just a gadfly in most cases. MITI had no trouble carrying out its restructuring policies and, without too much ado, the Antimonopoly Law was waived for a transitional period which could be rather extensive. Nor did the calls for deregulation stampede the Ministries of Transport, Posts and Telecommunications, Construction or Finance in that direction.

While the other bureaucracies found ways of getting along with the FTC, and still maintaining their prerogatives, certain business leaders were more piqued. Chief among them was Yoshihiro Inayama, often referred to as "Mr. Cartel," who argued that in the harsh economic climate of the times it was necessary for companies to cooperate. Keidanren angrily launched a campaign in 1983 to prune the Antimonopoly Law or, at least, lop off the 1977 additions. It also urged that the FTC cease being an independent body and be brought under the control of a cabinet minister so that industrial and antitrust policy could be coordinated for the good of the economy.[20]

For some time, it looked as if the LDP would go along with this approach. The relevant committee blithely claimed that Japan's antitrust regulations were even stricter than those in the West.[21] But the government did not wish to rock the boat and feared domestic and foreign criticism of any rash action. Like MITI, it felt that most problems could be overcome in practice and should be dealt with on a case-by-case basis. It also realized that, while big business was irked by the FTC, smaller firms regarded it as a vital form of protection. They, too, were a persuasive component of its political constituency.

This contest showed the importance of popular backing for the second prong of consumerism. Yet, here the consumers' movements were even feebler than when it came to product safety. They only occasionally campaigned for lower prices or criticized sudden price hikes of some few articles. This was strange on the background of overall high price levels and a failure to demand that imports of agricultural or manufactured goods be permitted to bring prices down more generally. Presumably, they were not so unpatriotic as to plead foreign causes. Nor, indeed, was the FTC, claiming that Japan's marketing system was open and fair despite all the proof it had accumulated to the contrary.[22] But they all had to admit that the only reason antitrust ever came to Japan, and one reason why it could not readily be suppressed, was that this would arouse considerable ire abroad.

Labor Aristocrats And Coolies

Before the war, Japan's labor conditions were horrible, with operatives working endless hours under ghastly conditions, having scant job security or personal freedom, and paid miserably low wages. This was not only a result of the prevailing poverty in a then developing country but rather the pressure and exploitation of a managerial elite very closely tied up with the governing elite. The wartime experience was even worse. Thus, the postwar democratization was like a miracle, providing gains that could never have been attained by the efforts of the most valiant trade unionists or socialists on their own.

However, when impatient militants tried to push too far, there was a concerted rollback in the face of strikes that SCAP feared might paralyze the country and often had a more political than labor thrust. At that time, the old-guard company executives tried to reassert their control and conservatives replaced reformists in the Ministry of Labor.[23] Unexpectedly, it was not the hardliners but a moderately liberal group that won the day. Keizai Doyukai, representing younger and more enlightened managers, pressed for a fairer deal that would bind workers more closely to management in their mutual interest. This evolved into the present renowned "Japanese employment system."[24]

Still, while the new order brought a vast improvement for some, it was not equally beneficial to others. For this wondrous system prevails essentially among the large companies which account for only 1% of the total and 30% of the labor force. Moreover, even in large companies, not all employees are members of the "company family." Not included are part-timers, temporary workers and, on the whole, women. Thus, taking both large and medium-sized companies with some form of modified "Japanese" system, those enjoying its advantages would add up to only about a quarter of the labor force. Smaller firms, and the bulk of the workers, therefore endure much less generous treatment.[25]

One way of improving the conditions of the less favored is by enhancing the status of the smaller firms which employ them, an indirect but quite purposeful approach. This has been attempted partially through the Small and Medium Enterprise Agency, a subsidiary body of MITI. It provides a certain amount of guidance and, more precious, low-cost loans and other support through related financial, insurance and investment corporations. But this funding is rather modest compared to the vast amounts mobilized by MITI for projects of interest to major companies and direct access to commercial banks.

While this aid is welcome, and creates a certain clientele for the bureaucracy concerned, it does nothing to prevent or correct the abuses which are bound to arise within the Japanese system. The most prevalent occur where larger companies have some control over smaller ones, whether their subsidiaries, suppliers or subcontractors. Given the state of dependence, and lack of bargaining power, smaller enterprises have frequently seen their situation worsen with the years. They have regularly been forced to accept lower prices, stricter quality demands, tighter delivery schedules and the like. During the recession, or when they could be replaced by new machinery, they simply lost their orders. Since most functioned without written contracts, it was exceedingly easy to alter conditions or cease relations at any time.

This sort of treatment was regularly noted by the SMEA, and duly included in its reports, but nothing special was done.[26] It counseled the smaller firms on how to get by, not how to defend their rights. If it had tried to do so, it would have encountered stiff opposition from its own patron, MITI. With little political backing, there was not much the small fry could do anyway. They were at best petty members of the Chamber of Commerce, a body with too many other interests and less clout than Keidanren, whose primary concern was big business. In only one instance, the limitation on opening local branches of chain stores, was the small business community very successful due to the sizable numbers of irate voters involved.

The situation of the individual workers could be improved by organizing. They enjoyed the support of the trade union movement which had swollen after the war and then declined somewhat, but still represented about 30% of the labor force. Collective bargaining allowed labor to make demands regarding wages, bonuses, job security, working conditions and hours, even if they were not always attained. But this applied only to the minority of unionized workers, which often coincided with the minority of regular workers in larger companies. Thus, in certain ways, trade unionism actually contributed to enhancing the position of the elite of workers or "labor aristocracy" over against the others.

This was particularly notable in Japan, where unions were organized by enterprises and therefore had very narrow interests. They were concerned primarily with the workers in their own factory, or perhaps company, but not even in the whole trade or industry and certainly not workers in general. They even ignored those on their own premises who, for one reason or another, could not join the union or stayed only briefly. This included part-time workers, frequently women, and the numerous employees of subcontractors. Only Sohyo showed a broader, more ideological concern for the working class, but it was less helpful because most of its members were in the public sector. Domei, which would have been a more appropriate leader, was more moderate and cautious politically and rarely advanced other than "bread-and-butter" issues.

Labor's ineffectual and fragmented efforts were resolutely opposed by two powerful organizations that worked in tandem: Keidanren for political issues, Nikkeiren for labor-management relations. Under the direction of Bunpei Otsuki, Nikkeiren proved a particularly stubborn and determined opponent which almost systematically obstructed labor's calls for better pay and conditions. It habitually approached each contest as a last-ditch struggle to maintain management's prerogatives intact and grant as few concessions as possible. Fortunately for all, this inflexible position was rarely adopted by the individual companies when they had to negotiate with their house unions and thus tolerable compromises could ordinarily be reached.

The arbiters between labor and management should have been the government and Ministry of Labor. In both cases, they tended to come much more under the sway of business circles than the unions. Yet, even LDP politicians realized that it was necessary, for various reasons, to improve the lot of the mass of workers and some of them collected part of the labor vote. When their majorities wore thin, they might also make suitable modifications in pending legislation to gain socialist or at least centrist support. As for the Labor Ministry bureaucrats, they were rarely personally sympathetic to the cause of their wards, let alone the more radical views of the unions, but they did want things to run calmly and outwardly well in their sector.

This precarious balance explains why the impact of foreign public opinion has occasionally been effective. With a bad prewar experience, and a need to avoid any charges of social dumping at present, it was necessary for Japan's employment system to appear at least on a par with those in other advanced countries. The pressure was only greater due to membership in the International Labour Organisation, which met regularly to scrutinize the situation of its member states, and where there were direct representatives of labor. They did not hesitate, if they thought it would do some good, to embarrass the government and seek international support. In other cases, it was Japan's trading partners that stumbled across questionable practices. While less directly related, decisions by the United Nations to hold a "year of the handicapped" or "women's decade" also had labor implications.

Thus, progress was slow, partial and not very steady, but still noticeable, during the period of rapid growth, when Japan could readily afford such improvements. During the more recent phase of slow growth, however, even that has been undercut somewhat and on certain fronts there is barely any advance at all. Whether the situation will get any better in the future—for the majority and not the minority—remains to be seen.

Basically, the government does not intervene in the setting of wages, this being achieved through bargaining between labor and management. That wage hikes have fallen to unprecedentedly low levels was noticed, but not severely criticized, by any party. The government does, however, set the minimum wages and could use them to raise levels, especially for the more disadvantaged segments. Instead, it has tended to keep them so low that the concept is meaningless. It should also take some interest in the fact that, after narrowing, the gap between wages for large and small companies was now widening. But this was noted only by specialists in the field.

In a way, the government is responsible for unemployment, since there is a form of insurance and benefits are socially desirable to avoid unnecessary hardship. Still, the amounts provided have remained modest and restricted to short periods. More surprisingly, the aid has often gone to large companies which are retraining their workers rather than to small firms, or individual workers, who are in much harsher straits. The scope of this assistance has been limited not only due to fiscal restraints but also because the Ministry of Labor deliberately applies a definition of unemployment that is strict and underestimates the numbers.[27] And it is abundantly clear that Nikkeiren objects to any action that could conceivably undermine the vital work will.

Regulation of working hours would seem to be a suitable task for the Labor Ministry. That the Japanese work long hours, put in considerable overtime and have little vacation are things the bureaucrats must cope with. But they have, on the whole, preferred to act through administrative guidance rather than laws in an effort to avoid undue strains on their corporate clientele. Thus, it has been urged for over a decade that companies should introduce a five-day week, with the result that by now some half offer one or more Saturdays off. They also have to grant paid vacations, the average amount being 15 days, of which most workers take only half. And this has been partially compensated for by more overtime.

So, despite the pressure, the Japanese still work well

over 2,000 hours a year which is about the same level as a decade ago.[28] That is 100, 200, 300 and even 400 hours more than are common in most of its Western counterparts and even some developing countries. At last, in 1984, it was decided to adopt new statutory working hours which, it was assumed, would curtail them. Instead, the advisory panel proposed officially decreasing the work week to five days *but* increasing the working day to nine hours. Anything less was regarded as "premature," a view warmly applauded by the management team led by Bunpei Otsuki. This was regarded as "anachronistic" by Sohyo and the other unions which refused to accept the recommendation. Indeed, such a move would run counter to the ILO Convention and make Japan stand out even more. For many Japanese workers, it was actually a step backward.[29]

Working conditions are an even more essential part of the Ministry's activities. Considering that, in the dual economy, a "labor aristocracy" employed by the big companies is reasonably well organized and enjoys relatively decent treatment, it would be assumed that ample time could be devoted to those less well off. Yet, they appear to be largely forgotten.

Part-timers, some 10% of the labor force, often worked as long, and sometimes longer, than regulars. Yet, they had no written contract, no paid annual leave, no accident insurance and no job security. To remedy the situation, finally, in 1984, the bureaucrats began preparing suitable regulations. The plight of homeworkers, of which there were over a million, was worse yet. They had no contract, no paid holidays, no accident insurance and they could be dropped at any time. The piece wages were abysmally low and many did not even have the prescribed log to record their work. For them, however, the ministry was only willing to offer administrative guidance and an annual "be kind to homeworkers" week.

Women on the whole were usually subjected to inferior treatment and, since they were a good 35% of the labor force, should also have elicited a special effort. They were systematically hired for specific jobs, many of them quite menial, that were regarded as fit for females. They found it very difficult to gain promotions no matter how hard they worked. They were often forced to retire early and thus deprived of the benefits of seniority when, as increasingly happened, they rejoined the labor force later on. And the wage differential was large and growing.[30] In addition, they provided the largest contingent of part-time employees and homeworkers. Yet, the bureaucrats did nothing to improve their status. They did not even bother dispensing administrative guidance. This despite the fact that there were literally hundreds of regulations forbidding such discrimination and guaranteeing equal treatment for women.

Even the health and safety regulations were either very inadequate or poorly observed. This was shown by repeated industrial and mining disasters which could probably have been avoided.[31] More concretely, a survey by the Administrative Management Agency revealed that the existing labor codes were regularly violated. It indicated that in factories with considerable dust or using vibration-causing equipment, namely those subject to special supervision, many companies did not provide the appropriate devices, take the necessary precautions, or give their workers the prescribed medical check-ups. This was partly because the local labor standards inspectors did not carry out all the on-site inspections scheduled and evidently failed to notice violations that did occur.[32]

But these are not the only instances of regulations being

freely and persistently flaunted. Such behavior is customary with regard to part-timers, homeworkers, and women in general. Efforts to impose rules for recruiting elderly and handicapped workers were equally a sham since the quotas were rarely met, with large companies often the worst culprits. It is widely known that employees put in more overtime than allowed and are forced to give up their paid leave, at the strong request of management. That all sorts of health and safety codes are repeatedly ignored can be proven by the serious accidents, occupational diseases, and broader disasters that arise. This widespread violation of the existing regulations makes the unwillingness to add new ones even more disconcerting. And it leads one to wonder whether the supposed progress has been real or illusory.

Once again, further progress—or prevention of backsliding—could come only from determined action by the population. Yet, despite dissatisfaction with many aspects of the employment system, as shown in countless surveys, not many workers were willing to take the initiative. They could engage more energetically in trade union activities or simply stand up for their rights. It was possible to appeal to the courts, a step rarely taken but reasonably effective.[33] Political action could also be resorted to, quite simply by voting for the appropriate parties or politicians. But few even bothered finding out what the issues were, who took which position, and what could be done. Thus, a poll of working women found that, while 85% knew of the equal employment bill, less than 30% bothered finding out what it was about. And the majority was more afraid of radical change even in their favor than the *status quo*.[34] This seems to sum up the general attitude and at least partially explains why most workers remain relatively indifferent onlookers rather than actively shaping their own fate.

To Welfare And Back

Aside from poor laws, dating back to Meiji days, and desultory pension plans, introduced in the midst of the Pacific War, Japan had not done much in the way of welfare. This, too, was rectified during the Occupation, based on recommendations drafted along the lines of the American system. Slowly but surely, Japanese governments began creating a "safety net" of appropriate institutions, with livelihood assistance, employment insurance, and social security, followed by health insurance and pensions. This was done during the late 1940s, 1950s and 1960s. In the early 1970s, there was a further expansion of many of these schemes, increasing the coverage and benefits. This was to usher in a "welfare age."[35]

While this was a big step in the right direction, there was some difficulty resulting from the piecemeal approach, with laws adopted at different times, covering different categories of persons, and offering different advantages. There were, for example, almost twenty separate pension and health schemes. On the whole, those run by the state for farmers, fishermen and self-employed were not as good as was offered to public servants while those arranged by private companies, partly under government supervision, were considerably more generous. The former were not only less advantageous, they were often less well financed and managed, while the latter did reasonably well.

Had the initial plans worked out, Japan would now boast one of the finest welfare systems in the world. Alas, just when things were looking up, the domestic and world economies slowed down and less funds were available to finance these operations, whether public or private. This was particularly unfortunate since some of them, notably the state-run health insurance scheme and the JNR pension fund, were amassing huge deficits. In fact, the former, the *kanko hoken,* was one of the "three Ks" which were draining the national budget, along with rice subsidies *(kome)* and JNR *(kokutetsu).*

These troubles were just a forewarning of the serious crunch that was coming. Over the years, the costs of the health insurance, pensions and public assistance had grown with incredible speed. Simply during the 1970s, the costs for health increased 5-fold and those for pensions 11-fold. Such increments could readily be charted into the future to show that the coming decades would only compound the difficulties. According to a study by Professor Naohiro Ogawa for the International Labour Organisation, health care spending would increase more than 7 times and pension benefits 13 times by 2010. Smaller, but still impressive, figures came from the MHW's Pension Bureau which expected national pensions to rise another 4 times and welfare pensions 10 times by 2020.[36] Similar explosive growth could be anticipated further into the 21st century.

The reasons for this were perfectly clear. Most could be traced back to the dramatic aging of the population. While only 5% of the people were 65 and over in 1950, this rose to 9% by 1980, and was projected to reach 22% by 2020. This meant that, whereas previously twelve persons had to provide for each elderly person, this rose to seven by 1980 and would reach three in 2020. From a system in which most (younger) members were paying premiums into the various funds, there would be a traumatic shift to one in which most (older) members would be drawing benefits. From a mere 10% of national income devoted to funding health and pensions in 1980, the figure should—in theory—rise to 20% in the year 2000 and 32% by 2025.[37]

Despite somewhat different figures in the various studies, there was not the slightest doubt that costs would

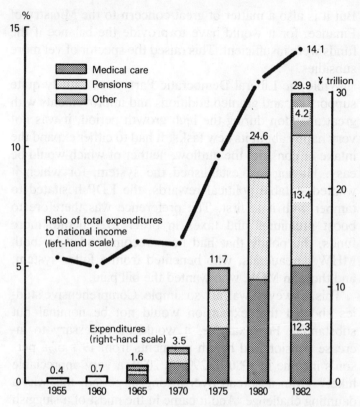

% (left-hand scale)
15

14.1

29.9   ¥ trillion
30

4.2

10

24.6

13.4   20

Ratio of total expenditures
to national income
(left-hand scale)

11.7

5

Expenditures
(right-hand scale)   3.5

10

12.3

1.6

0.4   0.7

0

0

1955   1960   1965   1970   1975   1980   1982

What if funding cannot keep up with spending? Social security
expenditures on the rise.

Source: White Paper on Health and Welfare,
Ministry of Health and Welfare, 1984.
Credit: *Facts and Figures of Japan 1985*, p. 94.

swell immensely and within a relatively short period. It
was thus of the utmost importance that the government
make every effort to collect the necessary funds as soon
as possible so the money will be there on time. The
responsibility lies primarily with the Ministry of Health
and Welfare, which administers many of the schemes and
provides the overall supervision of the welfare system.

But it is also a matter of great concern to the Ministry of Finance, for it would have to provide the balance if the funds were insufficient. This raised the spector of yet more subsidies.

While the Liberal Democratic Party was initially quite supportive, and granted additions and improvements with great abandon during the high growth period, it was not very happy about its new tasks. It had to either expand the intake or constrict the outflow, neither of which would be easy. Having just established the system, for which it wanted suitable political rewards, the LDP hesitated to tamper with it at first. The preference was therefore to boost premiums and taxes in order to generate more funds, the policy that had been recommended by both MHW bureaucrats, who benefited from a fatter system, and those in MOF, who wanted the bill paid.

This, however, was not so simple. Comprehensive studies showed that expansion would not be nominal but substantial. For example, it would be necessary to increase pension and health payments from 19% of a person's income in 1980 to 29% in 2020, a very appreciable hike.[38] Even if spread over a longish period, this was a daunting challenge. And it came in the midst of a sluggish economy. Thus, the first proposals were rejected all around. Business circles alluded to their already considerable welfare and fringe benefits and complained that little more could be done without ruining the companies. The trade unions, for once agreeing with management, insisted that the individual worker could not make the effort either. The population as a whole, while wishing to have more welfare, did not want to pay the price. Of those polled by the Prime Minister's Office, 40% were opposed to raising taxes for that purpose while only 24% were willing to pay more.[39]

Sensing the political dangers, the government changed

its tack. This time going more with the MOF than the MHW bureaucrats, it decided to do away with what were regarded as unessential or superfluous aspects of the system and save a bit of money. There were decreases in payments to fatherless families, disqualification of wealthier people from some services, and a more radical decision to cease free medical care for the aged. Remuneration of doctors was "rationalized" and pharmaceutical prices were reduced. It was also planned to postpone the age for receiving the employee's pension from 60 to 65, which proved to be a particularly unpopular measure. With an election approaching, Prime Minister Ohira was unwilling to accept the risks and withdrew the proposal . . . which surfaced again after the election.

This approach was no more acceptable in certain circles. The trade unions, most conspicuously Sohyo, objected to every reduction in medical benefits or pensions since that would impose a heavier burden on the people. The public, seeing that the whole system was now under attack, became somewhat more anxious about their future welfare. Replies to another poll showed that 66% of the respondents were uneasy about the coming of an aged society, particularly as concerned pensions, health services, and employment opportunities.[40] But they did not put up any serious resistance to the moves. Nor did they bother organizing. There were some clubs and associations, often sponsored by local governments, but few that arose at the grass roots or fought for the interests of pensioners or the aged in general. Despite millions of old people, there was nothing even vaguely resembling a "grey power" and most seemed resigned to their fate.

There was a much sharper reaction from the doctors and hospital administrators, whose financial interests were at stake. Most outspoken was the Japan Medical Association, especially under the forceful leadership of Taro Takemi, its long-time president. It criticized the government for proposing cutbacks in the health scheme. It lambasted the administrators of health insurance societies for inefficient management. And it gleefully scolded the MHW bureaucrats for lack of imagination in seeking other solutions to the problems than retrenchment. The JMA did not propose many practical solutions of its own, but two were of note, namely elimination of waste and more preventive medicine to keep costs from rising so rapidly.[41]

It was not surprising that there was some influence here from the outside world. Japan was continually comparing itself to the West, as concerned economic growth and productivity, and on social achievements as well. It was not pleased to be shown lacking at various international bodies, such as the UN, OECD and ILO. This reinforced the urge to upgrade its health and pension systems until the former was on a par and the latter at least approaching the same level. But it was also appalled by what had happened to Western countries which went too far. Thus, while its existing tax and social security burdens were much smaller than in the West, it was not so eager to reach those levels.

What was surprising, given the crucial nature of this issue, was that the opposition parties did not play a more constructive role. They all claimed to defend the interests of the people, including those less well off, and the Socialists and Communists were exceedingly fond of talking of welfare. But none of them came up with a concrete and comprehensive counter-proposal to the government's demands for reduction. They merely denounced each LDP action, and got what political gains they could from such a visible stance, and then tacitly accepted the legislation after obtaining minor concessions. In so doing, they missed a golden opportunity to offer a valid alternative and enhance their following in threatened segments of the population.

This meant there was really nothing to withstand the concerted efforts of business circles, this time led by Keidanren and Nikkeiren together, in their push for a leaner administration. They resolutely insisted that the government carry out a fiscal reform without tax hikes, which meant that some budget items would have to go. Nothing was slashed as ruthlessly as welfare. This was done by some of the measures already mentioned but went into high gear with a decision to make patients bear part of the cost of their health scheme. The Ministry of Finance initially aimed at 10% for 1984 and 20% for 1986. But the government was forced to leave the latter pending in order to obtain opposition approval for the former. So, with broad Diet support and not merely LDP backing, the first major breach was made in the welfare system.

The second was even more decisive, although cleverly disguised as a mere measure to unify the various pension schemes. Already in 1983, the heavily deficit JNR fund was merged with the richer NTT and tobacco monopoly funds. As of 1986, a basic pension was to replace the separate *kosei nenkin* for salaried workers and *kokumin nenkin* for self-employed and non-employed persons. Here, too, the more prosperous fund would help carry the less affluent, a fairly decent gesture except that the subscribers were never consulted on the matter. But the primary purpose was not social justice or even financial solvency so much as to reduce the costs—and benefits— sharply. Under the new system, beneficiaries would receive 15–30% less than otherwise. Meanwhile, premiums would be raised making the whole system considerably less useful than before.

Meanwhile, the government launched a more aggressive campaign to convince the general public that the age of state welfare had come and gone and that in the future the individual would have to do more for himself. This was billed positively as the age of "self-reliance" and "self-help" and much stress was placed on family solidarity and the wish of children to look after their parents, in keeping with good old traditions. In addition, elderly people were urged to work longer—because it was good for them. Such ideas were regularly expressed in speeches by the prime minister and other ministers. They were underlined even more extensively in the MHW's White Papers for 1983 and 1984. The first claimed that the Japanese were already rich enough to bear heavier welfare burdens and the second added that, if they wanted more than the state could provide, they should make their own arrangements.

While it sounded reasonable, and did appeal to some Japanese, there was little chance that a workable solution could be found on that basis. First of all, even if the government did eliminate some health and pension benefits, the projected increases in needs were so great that more funds would still be required. If, on the other hand, it were decided to restrict the services to available revenue, the whole system would simply collapse or people would suffer grievously. That was not desired by the population, nor was it politically feasible action for the ruling party. Thus, it would probably have to call on the people to make a major financial effort. This left it in the same dilemma as before.

Even if the individuals, alone or with their families, could shoulder more of the burden, there were definite limits to this. Aging was taking place so swiftly that there would soon be vast numbers of aged who were seriously ill, mentally unbalanced or senile and would require professional care that no family could provide. Moreover, the trend toward nuclear families had not ceased, and there were ever more older people living alone. Indeed, with small and crowded dwellings, and little excess money, it was not easy for even devoted children to look after their parents. Also, with a life expectancy of 80, it was no longer just a question of caring for parents but grandparents as well. As for elderly people working, it would be hard for most to find satisfactory jobs, and the difficulties were bound to grow with the prevailing unemployment.

Nowhere was the failure of the political mechanism more evident. It was known with certainty, not just shortly in advance but decades ahead of time, that there would be a crisis for the welfare system in Japan. This had already been encountered in more advanced countries and, to some extent at least, overcome. Yet, the government could not gather the courage either to increase taxes or fairly readjust the burden. In fact, it was running away from the problem. At the same time, there was not even a consensus within the population as to what to do although at long last, there seemed to be agreement that something should be done. Alas, what was being done was to weaken and actually tear apart the "safety net" at the very time it would be needed most.

Administrative Retrogression

All of the social movements which evolved during the 1960s and 1970s were directed toward increasing government action for the good of the ordinary people. The progress was often slow and erratic, but it was real. In the 1980s, however, it was countered by another movement initiated to bring about "administrative reform" *(gyosei kaikaku)*. The sponsors of this effort presented laudable reasons for the new direction. The government was getting involved in too many activities, it was looking after things that had hitherto been the concern of private citizens and it was becoming increasingly invasive. This "big government," in addition, was very inefficient and costly. It was pointed out that other advanced countries had already reacted, such as the United States under Ronald Reagan and Great Britain under Margaret Thatcher. It was now time for Japan to get in step.

While appealing, this reasoning was very misleading. Japan had only about half as many civil servants per 1,000 inhabitants as the Western countries. Its environmental and consumer protection machinery was still very rudimentary. The welfare system was incomplete and, although only partial, already clearly underfinanced. The Japanese were paying much less for social security and old age care than their Western counterparts. So, the reference to Reaganism and Thatcherism was sorely misplaced. Those were countries which had perhaps gone too far while Japan had not yet gone far enough.

But such arguments were rarely heard and easily muffled in the active and noisy campaign launched by big business. That administrative reform was the pet project of the *zaikai* could not be more evident. The original ideas, and many of the specific measures, were suggested to the LDP by business organizations. Toshiwo Doko, the honorary president of Keidanren, was appointed chairman of the Ad Hoc Commission on Administrative Reform that was established in March 1981. He presided over the work of the expert committees which included many businessmen and pro-business academics. He presented the reports to the government and strongly urged that they be acted on. Subsequently, he became head of the Special Reform Council set up to supervise implementation. His assistant there was Bunpei Otsuki, president of Nikkeiren.

The purpose of this operation was to reduce the size and cost of government in various ways. It intended to shrink the administration partly by merging or abolishing many of the 200-odd government-affiliated enterprises, public corporations and other agencies. It sought to trim or cease many of the subsidies granted by the state, not only for agriculture but also school lunches and free textbooks. It aimed to hold down the mounting costs of social services and welfare and trim the health insurance system. While focused largely on the central administration, it was also desired to cut costs and personnel at the local level and have the local autonomies assume more of the responsibilities . . . and costs. Finally, it was proposed to mobilize the private sector to make up for any shortcomings in government action.

While, in public at least, it was possible to get broad backing on the general goals, as soon as it came to specific measures there were bound to be objections and resistance. This had been the case in the past and it was never certain how far this new attempt would get. After all, administrative reform had been tried before. In 1962, a Special Administrative Research Council was set up under Prime Minister Ikeda. Directed by the Chairman of Mitsui Bank, it took nearly three years to present proposals for sweeping reforms. But Prime Minister Sato, who succeeded Ikeda, was not willing to push them through. Many subsequent efforts were made to dispose of one body or another. Prime Minister Ohira grandly announced a plan to scrap or rationalize many government-affiliated enterprises in 1970. But nothing came of it.

This time around, however, the situation looked more auspicious. Prime Minister Suzuki stated that he would "stake his political life" on carrying out the administrative reform. When he resigned in 1982, this was a tacit admission that he could not do the job. Yasuhiro Nakasone, first as head of the Administrative Management Agency, and thus directly in charge of the exercise, and then as prime minister, made more vigorous efforts. He brought the government into line on the issue, at least formally.

This pitted the government and big business against a number of opponents, some open and others less visible. The strongest were obviously the bureaucrats themselves who had a vested interest in a perpetuation of the system. Professionally, they could hardly approve of cuts in wages or numbers of personnel or even controls on wage hikes and recruitment of new personnel. More personally, having worked their way into a given branch, they did not look forward to mergers or reforms that might prejudice their career chances. And they certainly did not want the many state corporations and other bodies which provided post-retirement jobs to disappear. Finally, they did not like the bureaucracy as a whole coming under attack or being singled out as a prime cause of the economy's difficulties.

The bureaucrats were backed by many LDP Dietmen who had risen from the bureaucracy and still maintained close ties. They also established cooperative relations with most others, especially prominent politicians who had been ministers at one time or another. As for slashing subsidies and scrapping state corporations, the biggest foes of these reforms were in the Liberal Democratic Party. They were the ones who created the whole system on which they depended as plentiful sources of funds and patronage.

The most resolute bloc of adversaries was found in the Japan Socialist Party because it was supported by the public sector labor organizations, and especially the Sohyo-related Kankoro (National Council of Government and Public Workers' Unions). Many JSP Dietmen came from this group and all had to back the unions. The DSP, related to the private sector unions, actually spoke out in favor of the reform and it was tolerated by the NLC and

Komeito. But the three of them, and the JCP, did not hesitate to berate the government vociferously for its disregard of the social needs of the population.

There was not much sign of concern among the people at large, although opinion polls showed they did not like some of the measures proposed. But the pressure groups which felt their specific interests might be hurt were quickly mobilized. The doctors' and dentists' associations roundly condemned the limitations on health services. The PTAs criticized the idea of ceasing free textbooks or school lunches. Most energetically, the farm lobby worked to block any reduction, let alone elimination, of subsidies its members benefited from. On this, it was even backed by the Agriculture Ministry, the only breach in the cabinet's ranks. Aside from public protests, they naturally also engaged in far more effective private approaches.

Thus, the reform was watered down even in its forma-

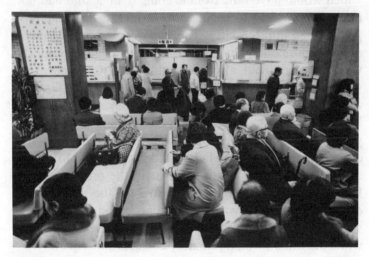

No matter how long they wait, there won't be enough hospitals and old age homes.

Credit: Foreign Press Center/Kyodo

tive stage as the bold proposals somewhat lightly announced to the press were quietly forgotten during the deliberations and never appeared in the formal reports. Of the 33 subsidies that were originally mooted for abolition, only one was actually recommended. Not many specific mergers or abolitions of state bodies were actually proposed. One of the few was to combine part of the Prime Minister's Office and the Administrative Management Agency in a new Management and Coordination Agency, a largely symbolic gesture. The only effective action was to contain civil service wage hikes and slow down (but not stop) the growth in personnel. Transfers to the local autonomies were also cut, leaving them to grapple with their own problems.

Only three public corporations were slated for privatization. The one that was easiest to engineer was Nippon Telegraph and Telephone, a still highly profitable company which would have little trouble going it alone and had not really been a drag to begin with. In fact, it had regularly paid money into the kitty. The Tobacco and Salt Monopoly was more anomalous, profitable only because imports were restricted but also not a drain. It was, however, somewhat of an embarrassment in a time of trade liberalization. The sticking point was the Japanese National Railways which had been losing money hand over fist for years. Every attempt at rationalization (i.e., reducing costs and personnel) had failed, and it was hoped to get rid of this headache by turning it over to the private sector. However, nobody would want to buy the JNR in its existing form and it was therefore proposed to cut it into several smaller units, some of which might be appealing while the others would probably collapse subsequently.[42]

While little palpable emerged, there was much talk of giving a new vitality to the private sector and encouraging it to play a bigger role, thus relieving the government of some of its burden. This was promoted partly through privatization of the public corporations and deregulation of the telecommunications field. It was thought that some erstwhile government services might be provided by private companies, obviously for a fee. But it was unlikely that private entrepreneurs would undertake major public works, whose costs would be hard to recuperate and would take decades to reimburse, without state backing and perhaps subsidies. It was further hoped to enhance the vitality of the private sector by revising or scrapping some annoying rules and regulations.

So, the "second" administrative reform was certainly more dynamic and successful than its predecessors. But it never really got as far as had been intended and the results were relatively modest. Actually, there was less to show for it as concerns what had been done away with than that the disturbing trend toward an even bigger government had been interrupted, if not halted. This gave the business leaders some cause for cheer. It even heartened the average citizen to see that the bureaucracy could be kept from running things much as it pleased and expanding its role and perquisites.

Yet, even if the administrative reform was a modest success in its own terms, it was a lamentable failure in most other terms. The exercise was oriented toward freezing the staffing, funding and programs on the existing basis rather than shrinking old aspects and enlarging new and necessary ones. This means that the bureaucracy preserved its old structure geared to helping industry and agriculture rather than promoting things like health, welfare and amenities which would be needed in the future.[43] In this sense, the administrative reform was more retrogressive than progressive and marked a high point in the second postwar rollback.

It must therefore have appeared slightly bizarre for the

man who forced it through to proclaim an era of "resilient culture and welfare." And Nakasone's attempts at presenting this as a positive course were probably just as ludicrous and misleading.

"Having gained material affluence, the people now crave spiritual affluence and richness of culture. At the same time, there are fervent calls for a bountiful Japanese-style and family-centered welfare, which differs from the West European concept of the welfare state. . . . I firmly believe that it is respect for the home as the basis of this happiness and the enriching of this basic unit of Japanese society which are at root of our quest for culture and welfare. This ideal society must be constructed in close cooperation between the government and the people. Each citizen's acting in the spirit of self-reliance and self-help to fulfill his own responsibilities in cooperation with others is the driving force facilitating smooth political progress."[44]

NOTES

1. Thomas P. Rohlen, *Japan's High Schools,* pp. 63–76.
2. It was, alas, hard to convincingly press "moral education" when the loudest proponents came from a political party known for its questionable practices and corruption.
3. Rohlen, *op. cit.,* pp. 210–40.
4. See Rohlen, *op. cit.,* and Woronoff, *Japan: The Coming Social Crisis* and *Japan's Wasted Workers.*
5. Amano Ikuo, "Educational Reform in Historical Perspective," *Japan Echo,* Vol. XI, No. 3, pp. 9–16.
6. See Margaret A. McKean, *Environmental Protest and Citizen Politics in Japan.*
7. See Ellis S. Krauss and Bradford L. Simcock, "Citizens' Movements: The Growth and Impact of Environmental Protest in Japan," in Kurt Steiner et al., *Political Opposition and Local Politics in Japan,* pp. 187–227, and Hiroshi Nishimura, "Environmental Pollu-

tion Cases," in De Vos, *Institutions for Change in Japanese Society,* pp. 41–52.

8. Article 25.
9. For information about their activities, see *Kogai, Newsletter From Polluted Japan.*
10. Background on government policy is provided in T.J. Pempel, *Policy and Politics in Japan,* pp. 218–54.
11. *Japan Times,* October 28, 1984.
12. *Ibid.,* October 1, 1980 and January 15, 1983.
13. *Ibid.,* November 16, 1980, December 15, 1981, August 30, 1983, and *Japan Economic Journal,* June 7, 1983.
14. *Japan Times,* December 15, 1981, September 13, 1980 and February 22, 1981.
15. *Ibid.,* March 17, 1984.
16. *Ibid.,* March 16, 1981 and September 6, 1983.
17. *Ibid.,* March 19, 1980 and *Japan Economic Journal,* August 24, 1982.
18. *Japan Times,* September 27, 1980 and February 25, 1984.
19. *Ibid.,* December 4, 1982 and *Japan Economic Journal,* November 23, 1982.
20. *Japan Times,* March 9 and July 27, 1983 and *Japan Economic Journal,* October 11, 1983.
21. *Ibid.,* October 18, 1983.
22. *Ibid.,* April 26, 1983.
23. Sheldon M. Garon, "The Imperial Bureaucracy and Labor Policy in Postwar Japan," *Journal of Asian Studies,* May 1984, pp. 441–57.
24. See Joe Moore, *Japanese Workers and the Struggle for Power.*
25. See Tadashi Fukutake, *Japanese Society Today.*
26. MITI, *White Paper on Small and Medium Enterprises,* annual.
27. Jon Woronoff, *Japan's Wasted Workers,* pp. 229–61.
28. Ministry of Labor, *Survey of Working Hours,* annual.
29. *Japan Times,* August 29 and September 21, 1984.
30. Woronoff, *op. cit.,* pp. 111–47.
31. Consider the Hokutan Yubari, Ariake and other recent coal mine disasters which took hundreds of lives.
32. *Japan Times,* October 10, 1983.
33. Alice Cook and Hiroko Hayashi, *Working Women in Japan,* and Tadashi Hanami, *Labor Relations in Japan Today.*
34. *Japan Times,* June 24, 1984.
35. The path to welfare is traced in T.J. Pempel, *op. cit.,* pp. 132–70. The way back has yet to be described more fully.
36. *Japan Times,* July 14, 1983 and April 7, 1982 and *Focus Japan,* August 1984.
37. *Look Japan,* August 10, 1984 and *Japan Times,* June 3, 1982.
38. *Japan Times,* December 12, 1982.
39. *Japan Times,* April 21, 1980.

40. *Japan Times,* April 8, 1983.
41. *Japan Times,* March 1 and November 22, 1980, July 9 and October 21, 1981.
42. It was also decided to sell the government's stake in Japan Airlines, but for other reasons including a string of accidents and pressure from competing airlines.
43. Woronoff, *The Japan Syndrome,* pp. 188–98.
44. Speech to the 97th Session of the National Diet, December 3, 1982.

8
Political Issues

Public Works, Private Gain

Ordinarily, public works should come under the heading of economic activities. After all, the ostensible purpose was to equip the country with essential infrastructure such as roads and railways, bridges and tunnels, harbors and other useful infrastructure. There was also some lesser concern with providing public housing and amenities which improved living conditions. These projects, in addition to any intrinsic value, generated work for numerous employees and business for countless companies. But there were always political implications which repeatedly overshadowed any economic rationale and strongly affected the selection of projects, allocation of funds and organization of the actual work.

To be most effective, such programs should have been integrated in some sort of formal or at least conceptual master plan. On occasion, this seemed to be done. Various prime ministers presented grandiose concepts for making Japan the site of "garden cities" or "regional plazas" which would embellish urban and rural living.[1] Prime Minister Tanaka sponsored an even more ambitious "remodeling of the archipelago."[2] The National Land Administration and other bodies proposed the creation of green belts around the cities or a transfer of government activities out of Tokyo.

If these plans had materialized, Japan would have become the earthly paradise described by, among others, Prime Minister Ohira.

"As nation-building concept for the 21st century, I have proposed the garden-state. . . . In promoting the garden-state concept, I feel it is necessary to aim for the creation of vigorous and diverse local societies by advancing richly verdant redevelopment while heeding protection from natural disaster in the cities and by advancing the creation of culturally attractive villages in the rural areas. In developing the specifics, I hope first to harmonize man and nature by utilizing our natural foliage to create verdant expanses linking city and country and by seeking to restore greenery to our daily lives. Second is to promote the development of regional cultural activities by seeking to enrich and activate arts, community education, physical education, and other cultural facilities, by training community activity leaders, and by other means. Third is to promote the development of region-appropriate technologies, to seek to encourage diverse regional industry, and to secure attractive employment opportunities in all regions."[3]

Alas, nothing ever came of this. In fact, even the most pedestrian tasks of urban planning were regularly botched as a handful of cities grew to sprawling megalopolises that embraced over half the population while many towns and villages were depopulated.[4] Traffic, transport, crowding, sanitation, pollution, noise and other problems abounded in the cities and were expected to get worse. The distance to the havens of nature and culture were longer. Even local zoning laws were haphazard and regularly violated as residential, commercial and industrial districts spilled over into one another. With this, the quality of life continued degrading and Japan had little to boast of on that account.

If ever there was a country that needed overall physical planning, it was Japan. But there was a hopeless breakdown of coordination between the many different central and local governments, the various special agencies and corporations and what was being done by the private sector. This resulted in a remarkably patchy network with too much infrastructure in some places and too little in others, to say nothing of duplication and some rather grotesque "white elephants." It also entailed excessive costs on occasion. Part of this was due to a tendency to launch prestige projects more often than necessary while ignoring smaller, less impressive ones that could more directly benefit people at the grass roots.

Among the more deplorable instances were some of the largest ventures ever. Superfluous JNR lines, many making losses, some soon to be closed down, should probably have been avoided from the outset. It was possible to expand the old Haneda airport in Tokyo for a third the cost of ¥1,800 billion needed to build a completely new one in Narita. The projected Osaka airport at ¥1,000 billion looks like another unavoidable boondoggle. But this is nothing compared to the Seikan Tunnel linking Honshu and Hokkaido, which cost ¥700 billion to construct but cannot be properly used until the *shinkansen* line is extended, for another ¥1,600 billion. Even then, with much of the traffic now carried by aircraft, there is little real need and some question as to how it should be used.

High costs also derived from inefficiency or incompetence in overseeing the actual work. This was shown by the annual reports of the Board of Audit which revealed that among the billions of yen wasted each year, a disproportionately large share was related to construction works. They arose from a broad range of irregularities. Some were sheer dishonesty, such as padding bills. Others were officially traced to negligence, as when paying for more units than were needed. In other cases, the project just did not work out as when the JRCC designed a special heavy-duty tunnel borer that continually broke down. While usually comprehensible, they could be bewildering as when the JRCC unnecessarily built part of the suspended *shinkansen* line to Narita airport. Other problems arose from the fact that most of the actual execution was not even handled by the official contractors. More often than not, they won major awards and then proceeded to distribute the work among hordes of smaller building firms that depended on them. These subcontractors further down paid back some of the money and had correspondingly less to get the job done. Forced to skimp, they produced defective construction as shown by use of inferior materials, poor design and execution, improper welding and generally shoddy workmanship reflected by leaks or cracks in cement. Such failings severely plagued the JHC's public housing projects.

Part of this disorganization and waste can be traced back to the bureaucrats. Another portion is largely attributable to the politicians. Far from thinking in national terms, they were exceptionally oriented toward the specific wishes of their home constituency and perhaps some others of general interest to their party. They paid little attention to what happened elsewhere and were certainly not upset by glaring omissions or duplication . . . as long as they got something out of the pork barrel. Nowhere was this more flagrant than in the urge to establish new railway lines and stations, in keeping with the political adage that "a new station means a lifetime guarantee and a new line two generations."[5]

The fact that highly successful operators, like Kakuei Tanaka and his fellow prime ministers and ministers, managed to get not only railway lines but schools, local offices and other spoils for their electoral district only incited the others.[6] They would lobby in every possible

Celebrating completion of the Seikan Tunnel with sake and subsidies.
Credit: Foreign Press Center/Kyodo

ministry and agency, use pressure when possible or offer a return in the form of Diet support. Some special agencies, like the highway, railroad construction and regional development bodies, were actually created to provide just such goodies. It was not surprising that this distorted the selection and distribution of public works, a hazard in most democracies but more pronounced in Japan.

Unfortunate as it was, this is not where the abuses stopped. For, to the nation's half million builders, nothing was more important than getting some of the public works which usually paid better than jobs for the private sector and left room for wangling. It was worth a fortune to be included in the restricted lists of contractors approved for bidding that were kept by the ministries, corporations and local autonomies. It was even more precious to actually get some lucrative business.

Various special relations therefore developed between the parties concerned. One linked the ministries and the special corporations which hoped to get bigger budgets to carry on more projects. There was always an additional strand to the Ministry of Finance, which approved the overall budget, controlled the hefty "second budget," and periodically inspected for irregularities. This led the corporations to set aside huge funds for entertaining key MOF or other ministry officials.

Even closer ties existed between the bureaucrats in the ministries and agencies ordering works and the construction companies which handled them. There were many instances of outright bribes and kickbacks. But they were probably less damaging than the almost systematic hiring of bureaucrats when they retired. The most notable case was uncovered in the Defense Facilities Administration Agency where several generations of officials were adopted as executive directors and entrusted with getting more work.[7] But it was not only there, this sort of thing was rife in Agriculture, Posts and Telecommunications and especially Construction and public corporations like JHC, JRCC and highway agencies. In some cases, the bureaucrats simply enjoyed their fat *amakudari* salaries, in others they apparently pocketed a commission for jobs obtained.

Since politicians also had a major say on how projects were distributed, there was another series of links with them. There was a certain amount of pure graft. But, once again, it was more discreet to contribute to the candidate's war chest or encourage construction workers, of which there were many, to vote for him. This took place blatantly at the local level, with many mayors and councilmen implicated. It reached much further up as well, since major construction companies contributed lavishly to the campaign funds of leading LDP politicians and to the party as a whole.

Of course, the contractors could make such contributions out of money that had been fairly and lawfully earned from their business activities. But the tight profits normal jobs generated hardly left much room. Instead, they were able to dip into much richer sources of funds through a system that embraced politicians, bureaucrats and contractors. Known as *dangoh,* and almost regarded as an intangible national custom by those concerned, it consisted of what is locally called "adjusting orders" but elsewhere known as bid rigging.[8] And it is believed to have been involved in virtually all major and many lesser public works in the country.

Since the number of approved contractors was small to begin with, and only about ten or so usually bid for any given project (after a careful preselection), it was possible for the chosen few to take the preselection a bit further. Rather than competing aggressively, and bringing the price down, they came to agreements with one another as to who should do which projects. Through some leak, they often had advance knowledge of the frequently generous price officially regarded as acceptable. This is essentially the price they bid at and they had little trouble in winning those tenders which had been allocated to them. The excess earnings, which were considerable, could then go to paying off helpful bureaucrats and politicians.[9]

This practice, alas, was clearly illegal. First of all, the Public Accounts Law provides that bidding for public works has to be open to all contractors in principle, so governmental preselection was not even permissible. And collusion to apportion jobs and fix prices is strictly forbidden by other laws. Yet, nothing was done about this for decades until, in 1982, the Fair Trade Commission cracked down on a particularly notorious case. The matter was then brought to the Diet and a lengthy investigation undertaken. The report of the Central Construction Industry Council, however, recommended no major changes in the tendering system and simply urged more careful policing to avoid mishaps.

Thus, there seemed to be little chance that the many abuses referred to would ever be eliminated. The Board of Audit found new irregularities, the media kept turning up examples of *dangoh,* cabinet ministers were periodically interpellated in the Diet, it was generally admitted that there were problems. But there was minimal follow-up. Some minor bureaucrats or politicos were arrested, even fewer contractors were fined or barred from bidding for a short while, the contractors' association made a formal apology and things continued as ever. In this charade, the JCP provided most of the leads to especially grievous cases, the press then uncovered many more, and the JSP pitched in whenever bureaucrats in its following were not involved. The other parties, especially those which benefited most from the misbehavior, remained silent. The public read the reports with interest and did nothing of note.[10]

If this were a minor matter, such a reaction could perhaps be understood. But the construction industry is the country's largest sector, bar none. It generates about a fifth of total GNP. Public works represent almost half of that. The sums involved are in the tens of trillions and the amount that is wasted, inefficiently used and turned into bribes or more subtly passed on through *amakudari* is in the trillions of yen each year. This is therefore a primary source of dirty money and it is generally known that contractors surpass even top manufacturers in their political influence. Yet, none of this leads to a reform. Actually, it probably explains why so little has been done and not much more can be expected in the future.

Even more distressing in some ways is what is loosely called "land speculation" but is considerably more structured. Insiders such as bureaucrats and politicians who knew what land would be needed for public works regularly passed on tips to speculators who bought the land cheap and sold it to the local, prefectural or national government dear. These speculators were not just small-timers but some of the most reputable real estate companies including, on occasion, firms owned by or related to influential politicians. While this practice was extremely widespread and misbehavior periodically came to light, there was almost no prosecution. The authorities were too deeply implicated themselves and the bureaucrats counted on retirement jobs and politicians on campaign funds or kickbacks from those involved.

This naturally increased the costs of public works which had to be borne by the taxpayers. In addition, it artificially restricted the number of projects which could be launched and hindered the spread of infrastructure and amenities. For the land component of any project could absorb half or three-quarters of the total budget and reached heights that could no longer be afforded by many communities. An even more baneful effect was the swift rise in land prices for every purpose, including commercial, industrial and residential premises. This became most notable when Tanaka's plan was being mooted and speculators bought up every scrap of land in the target regions, doubling, tripling and quadrupling prices in short order. Oddly enough, although the plan was never enacted and the market was periodically sluggish, land prices continued rising and rarely sank. That is because the real estate firms were also well-organized and controlled so much land and property that they could determine prices. While this squeezed the average citizen, many of whom could no longer buy a home due to exorbitant price tags, there was relatively little reaction. And it was ignored by political parties which depended heavily on donations from the industry.

Institutionalizing Corruption

Unfortunately, while this is not one of their more agreeable tasks, the Diet and other bodies have repeatedly had to deal with a very delicate matter, corruption.[11]

Locally, there have been countless cases of bribery of town mayors and other officials, most of them tied up with granting contracts for public works or providing services. And there have been more and more charges raised in connection with efforts by power companies to have nuclear power plants built, in which case it may be not only a few officials but far larger numbers and, as it were, the whole town which received gifts. There have also been numerous charges, and arrests, for massive vote buying or gift giving in towns and cities, with some of the more notorious located in Chiba, Niigata and Kofu Prefectures.

But this often went higher. Half-a-dozen governors were involved in vote buying or bribery in the past decade.

Hundreds of national-level politicians, in both houses of the Diet, have been accused, and sometimes convicted (although not too often), of similar practices. In some cases, it was not merely that money was offered for a specific favor but that the Dietmen, including even ministers, were expected to influence legislation or regulations under discussion or already adopted. Usually, of course, the money was passed on in the form of political donations, but the intent was clear. Former Agriculture Minister Ichiro Nakagawa received donations from a trading house handling marine products. In the Fujita case, donations were made to Dietmen to avoid a tax examination of that company. And a former Health Minister received money from a local hospital accused of malpractices.

There have also been some amazingly extensive examples in which not one but dozens of politicians have been involved regarding major legislation or operations. In 1979, the Japan Political League of Authorized Tax Accountants distributed donations to 101 Dietmen, including members of all parties except the JCP, in sums ranging as high as ¥5 million. This coincided with deliberations on a bill to vastly expand their scope of business. The most extraordinary case, however, arose with Kokusai Denshin Denwa, the international telecommunications monopoly, from 1975-79. In order to keep its rates unduly high, and hide its huge profits, KDD's president distributed gifts to top MPT officials and 190 Diet members of most parties, and especially those on bodies dealing with communications, including ministers.[12]

As for the bureaucracy, it, too, was unfortunately tarnished on more than one occasion. In fact, scores of abuses were mentioned in any report of the Board of Audit. Most prevalent were accounting irregularities in which bills were padded. For example, overtime which had not been worked was listed, official trips with related travel, meals and accomodation were reported although they had never been taken, wages were entered as paid out to non-existent workers, or there were indications of fictitious purchases (along with the corresponding fake vouchers). Such practices were traced to the JHC, JNR, JRCC, NTT, Environment Agency, Education Ministry and even the Prime Minister's Office.

There were two basic purposes to this. One was to illegally increase the earnings of the agency's personnel. They were allowed to collect for this overtime or travel and thereby supplement their income. Just as often, the money was channeled into slush funds which were used to maintain proper relations with other bureaucracies or politicians. The money was spent on lavish entertainment with those whose favors were sought. This was particularly disturbing when it included staff of MOF's Budget and Financial Bureaus, which approved the budgets of and granted loans to said agencies, as was done in the notorious JRCC scandal. Perhaps the most embarrassing moment came when it turned out that members of the Board of Audit had also been treated to such wining and dining by several ministries, including Construction, Transport and the Defense Agency.

On a more mundane, and cruder level, there were cases of outright bribery and graft among the bureaucrats. One of the most serious instances involved an MHW inspector who routinely approved new drugs although they had not undergone suitable testing. Another was caught leaking information on new drugs from some companies to their competitor. In a more direct way, the National Personnel Authority reported annually on the several thousand cases of theft and embezzlement of national properties or funds by public servants. Similarly, the Ministry of Home Affairs made its annual report on incidents of corruption in local governments, most of them involved bribes from contractors, which ran into several hundred a year. One of the more intriguing samples was the chief accountant of a small town who managed to embezzle more than the town's whole budget.[13]

Such events, taken up repeatedly in Diet debates or the media, were sufficiently frequent to be almost commonplace. But they were overshadowed by a number of major scandals which had deeper political ramifications. An early one arose in 1948 from the attempt of Showa Denko to buy the influence of Japanese officials and resulted in the fall of the Ashida Cabinet. Far more extensive was the shipbuilding scandal which grew out of overly close government-business cooperation to strengthen the industry by providing tremendous state funds. To get a larger share, some shipyards bribed high officials, especially in the Transport Ministry. In addition, shipbuilders and shipping lines, which wanted cheaper ships, offered massive political donations and bribes to politicians to have a bill adopted by the Diet in 1953 which cut the interest on these funds in half and reduced taxes on the industry. These activities were noticed by the prosecutors who began an investigation into the doings of numerous government and party officials. They even asked Justice Minister Takeru Inukai to arrest the then LDP Secretary General Eisaku Sato. This was blocked by Prime Minister Shigeru Yoshida and further action was obstructed.

In 1965-66, another series of scandals of startling proportions was revealed. One involved two Dietmen who received political donations from the Taxi Drivers Association to prevent a tax hike on liquefied petroleum gas, widely used in taxis. Another was a huge swindle in the sugar industry. More significant was the bribery scandal involving Nippon Express, the biggest forwarding company, and 47 Diet members, most of them from the LDP, including then Prime Minister Sato. In the end, however, only two Dietmen were found guilty. A bit whimsical, but no less annoying, the transport minister was asked to resign for obliging JNR express trains to stop in his home town. This all resulted in talk of "black mist" *(kuroi kiri)* emanating from the Sato government.

For some while, there was relative calm until Kakuei Tanaka became prime minister on the basis of what was generally called "money politics" *(kinken seiji)*. As per usual, there were rumors, allusions, guesses, but nothing very clear as to what was afoot in the press. Finally, deciding to follow things up, *Bungei Shunju* issued one of Japan's rare investigative reports into Tanaka's conduct as a politician, businessman and property owner. It brought to light many cases of questionable land and property deals, influence peddling and the like, which have been added to since. One such was the purchase of an apparently worthless dry riverbed whose value suddenly increased 200-fold when it was bought for a government project. The resulting clamor was sufficient to make Tanaka resign in December 1974.[14]

However, it ultimately turned out that the calm was not due to a lack of devious activities but that the perpetrators had proceeded more cautiously and secretively than before. In fact, the only reason the Japanese ever found out about them was that allegations were made at U.S. Senate hearings in February 1976 that Japanese officials had received bribes from Lockheed. Then, in 1978-9, Securities and Exchange Commission material was made public in the hearings of the Church Committee, which incidently aroused suspicions about illegal doings in sales of aircraft to other companies such as McDonnell Douglas.

The McDonnell Douglas case dated back to the late 1960s, when it was trying to sell its F-4E Phantom jet

One resigned, the other stayed on. Two men with different fates:
Nixon and Tanaka.

fighters to the Defense Agency. In so doing, the trading
company it worked through, Nissho-Iwai, bought the
influence of a number of politicians, including conceivably
Kakuei Tanaka and Nobusuke Kishi. But most of them
could not be tried due to the statute of limitations and
prosecution was limited largely to Raizo Matsuno, a
former Director General of the Defense Agency who

received ￥500 million for his help in clinching the deal. Since both Matsuno and Hachiro Kaifu, a Nissho-Iwai vice-president, admitted the bribery, the case was settled quickly enough. In 1980, they were given short suspended sentences due to their cooperation and Kaifu's "dedication" to company business, as it were.

The most notorious postwar scandal arose from Lockheed's efforts to sell aircraft during the early 1970s. The primary goal was to have All Nippon Airways, the leading domestic airline, purchase TriStars, which resulted in a complex operation. It was first necessary to convince ANA to buy Lockheed planes rather than McDonnell Douglas DC-10s or Boeing 747s, which were also in the running. To do this, two business tycoons and fixers with good political connections, Yoshio Kodama and Kenji Osano were recruited as largely secret agents to introduce the right people and pull strings. Lockheed worked more officially through Marubeni Corporation, another top trading company, which sought further support in the form of none other than Prime Minister Tanaka. Finally, since ANA was afraid that its archrival JAL might introduce larger aircraft, a further route passed through the Ministry of Transport, where former Minister Tomisaburo Hashimoto and Parliamentary Vice-Minister Takayuki Sato manipulated government aviation policies to delay the introduction of wide-bodied aircraft on domestic routes.

All of this, alas, was done for money. Hashimoto and Sato were accused of accepting ￥500 million and ￥2 million respectively. Kodama allegedly received something like ￥2.4 billion in consultant fees and commissions and Osano an uncertain, but doubtlessly handsome sum. Kakuei Tanaka was charged with asking ￥500 million for his services. The money came from Lockheed but was partly channeled through Marubeni, which was drawn deeper into the reckless plot. However, it would be foolish to regard this as nothing more than a bribery case. At stake were much more significant principles. For, in order to attain their ends, the prime minister and other officials were using—or rather abusing—the powers of their office and particularly the ability to issue administrative guidance which is a pillar of the whole Japanese system.

Some of the criminal acts were dealt with by the courts, admittedly at a snail's pace. Eventually, several Marubeni executives were given suspended sentences for violation of the foreign exchange control law, perjury and bribery. Osano was convicted of perjury and Kodama of tax evasion, both getting rather light sentences. Hashimoto and Sato were found guilty of bribery. Susumo Nikaido and a dozen "grey" Dietmen were not even tried because the money they received was deemed a "gift" or "donation." Tanaka's case was tougher, for he pleaded innocent, and fought the prosecutors year after year. Using shrewd lawyers, he presented one defense after another. Each was ultimately demolished. Finally, in 1984, he was found guilty of bribery and sentenced to prison. Rejecting this, he appealed and prepared to fight the case for many more years.[15]

Corruption at home was often coupled with corruption abroad. Japanese companies seeking foreign business paid kickbacks to local politicians and sometimes donated money to Japanese politicians who helped them win contracts. Much of this was done in projects undertaken with Japanese foreign aid. Such practices were almost routine in parts of Asia, where links between prominent LDP politicians and Asian leaders like Korea's Park and Indonesia's Suharto were notorious. Yet, only in the case of the Philippines did much of this come to light. After Marcos' fall in early 1986, information was revealed showing massive bribes to Philippine politicians, most coming from Japanese trading companies. There were also rumors that, to maintain good relations, Marcos made donations to Japanese leaders, including Tanaka. Despite lively press coverage and Nakasone's pledge of a complete probe, the whole affair was quickly covered over.

The major scandals, implicating the highest authorities in the land, and the many lesser ones, involving national and local politicians and bureaucrats, showed that corruption was uncommonly widespread. But certain aspects of these cases indicated that there was much more. For example, some involved dozens or even hundreds of persons and yet went unnoticed—or, at any rate, unreported—for extended periods of time. Moreover, the Board of Audit, National Tax Administration Agency and other supposed "watchdogs" only examined a small fraction of the incidents each year and were reputedly inefficient. This led one to believe that most of the misconduct never came to light and therefore what had been perceived was, as the press never tired of saying, the "tip of the iceberg." Yet, even if those which were uncovered were the true extent of the phenomenon, this could be regarded as a very serious problem. If there were really many more, then the situation would be shocking for a supposedly advanced nation.

That the latter is more likely can be concluded not only from the acts but the ineffectual efforts at stopping them. The most notable attempt was to avoid bribery not by prohibiting or punishing it but by reforming the campaign fund law so that money could be passed along legitimately to politicians. This was done by a Public Office Election Law of 1948 which laid down procedures to ensure fair and honest elections. But it was so obviously ineffective that pressure built up for a revision, which was resisted by the LDP until 1975, when a new Political Funds Control Law was finally adopted. This provided for public disclosure of funding and set limits on amounts that could be granted to parties, factions and individual politicians by specific sources. It also limited the total amount of political contributions that could be made by any company depending on the amount of capital.

This new law was basically flawed in three essential ways. First of all, it was full of loopholes. While only a limited amount could be donated to the support organization of a politician or faction, there was no limit to how many such "organizations" they might create. Businesses could also buy costly tickets to special parties and fund-raising events. While large contributions had to be reported, smaller ones—or many repeated small ones—were not. More intriguing, only the person who received money was liable for any improprieties. Politicians could thus keep their hands clean by routing funds through their secretaries and assistants. Considerably more serious, the limits were set at absurdly low levels. Most candidates were therefore forced to stretch the laws and, in so doing, were less concerned about how much they violated it since a little or a lot were equally illegal. Their reasoning was apparently followed by the public and the authorities entrusted with monitoring campaign expenses.

But the biggest drawback was that just about anything could be claimed as a political contribution, including things that might be regarded as illegal, or at least unethical, in many foreign countries. Worse, funds which were not duly recorded as donations when made could be, and regularly were, claimed as such later on. It was widely felt that if Tanaka had not denied the existence of the Lockheed kickback and instead said that it was really just campaign funds (as Matsuno did), he could have gotten away with it. Moreover, and this is almost always forgotten, the most important race, given the LDP's perennial rule, was for party president and there absolutely no rules applied to the amount of money that could be spent . . . or how.

Given the gravity of the Lockheed case, and the feeling that something had to be done to restore faith in the political system, the various parties began discussing a code of ethics. While the LDP held back, the opposition made exaggerated demands. The result was a deadlock. Unlike the United States, which adopted strict rules immediately after Watergate, the Japanese hardly moved at all. The government's proposals were turned down because they did not include public disclosure of the personal assets of Diet members or means of punishing those convicted of crimes, the two principal demands of the opposition. This was not compensated for by Prime Minister Nakasone's decision to have his cabinet members submit statements of their wealth. Among other things, they did not have to disclose the wealth of their wife and children or declare their worth after stepping down, which made it impossible to determine if their assets had grown. Nor were a new code of ethics and Diet councils to police it, adopted in 1985 after a decade of wrangling, expected to clean up the situation.

In addition, there was little point to knowing whether a person has misbehaved if nothing much could be done to punish him. The initial laws were extremely lenient and certainly no real deterrent. In 1980, the LDP was persuaded to stiffen the criminal code, raising the maximum penalty for taking graft to five years and, for offering bribes, seven. But, in practice, it turned out that most politicians were not prosecuted, any money simply being written off as another form of political donation in the case of the tax accountants league, KDD and so on. Even where there was clear criminal intent, as in the McDonnell Douglas and Lockheed cases, businessmen were often given suspended sentences and those who showed "repentence" and cooperated with the prosecutors got off very lightly indeed.

If few businessmen, and almost no politicians, suffered grievously for their misdeeds, the bureaucrats usually escaped with even less injury. Admittedly, there was a code of conduct that was tightened up in 1979 and made yet stricter in 1983. But the formal rules were rarely implemented and penalties were hardly ever applied. Most often the bureaucrats were merely given a warning or reprimand. Some actually faced a minor or temporary pay cut. Only outright criminal action resulted in more. When noisome scandals arose, as they periodically did, some high official might have to resign in a show of regret. Somewhat later, however, he was more than likely to be rewarded with an even better posting or at least get very substantial retirement benefits.

The only real hope for improvement lay in the political process. But events were not very encouraging. True, Tanaka was forced to step down as prime minister and the NLC broke away due partly to the Lockheed scandal. But Tanaka remained in the Diet, as did other incriminated politicians, and he gradually increased the power he wielded in the LDP, of which he was no longer a member. Periodically, the opposition parties demanded some punishment or even expulsion from the Diet, but this was always refused by the government. On occasion, the opposition even brought all Diet proceedings to a halt. In addition, the JSP and JCP continued attacking lesser cases of corruption in politics or the bureaucracy, often thanks to information leaked by the trade unions. This could lead to very nasty and embarrassing interpellations for the ministers concerned. But there was no deeper recognition of the need for political ethics.

There was, of course, the possible wrath of the people

turning on politicians who had misbehaved and had to run for reelection. Yet, amazingly few were hurt. Most bounced back, including Tanaka, Hashimoto, Sato and others, although Matsuno was defeated, and those incriminated had to run as independents rather than LDP members. This recovery was often regarded as a "restoration" or people's verdict, it being felt that reelection, especially with large majorities, meant that the misbehavior had been forgiven or even, in the case of Tanaka, had never existed. Actually, this only showed approval on the part of those in the local constituency, many of whom probably gained from the politician's actions.[16]

On the whole, the Japanese people did not approve of corruption and "money politics." But they were very poor at expressing this in any concrete way. Three elections were actually fought on the issue of political ethics, the 1967 "black mist" election, the 1976 Lockheed election, and the 1983 election after Tanaka's sentencing. In each case, the LDP did lose some popular support, although this could also be traced to other, completely extraneous causes. And none showed a notable gain for the opposition. The 1983 election was particularly instructive, because it was formally regarded as a setback for the LDP. However, as soon as Nakasone made an apology and promised to remove Tanaka's inflence (which he did not), it was apparently forgotten and the popularity rating climbed higher than ever.[17]

Thus, Japan seems condemned to live with massive corruption at many levels. In some ways, this is "structural" (kozo oshoku), as propounded by political analyst Tetsuro Murofushi.[18] It results from the LDP's long stay in office which allows it to get away with many things that would be far riskier if it had to fear the reaction of the opposition when it came to power. It is also "structural" because it has become an inseparable part of the system. Ruling party politicians and bureaucrats expect something in return for their favors, although in theory they are nothing more than services that must be rendered. And those who can afford it are not displeased to pay the price since it gives them a distinct advantage.

Would this cease if the LDP were voted out? Certainly, it would be altered and perhaps mitigated. But it is not very likely that the practice would cease. After all, opposition politicians also receive gifts, donations and bribes, only much less because they have less to offer. Many of the bureaucrats who were caught in the various scandals were Sohyo members, in which case the JSP promptly attenuated its criticism. While an alternation in office would lead the political parties to keep a sharper watch on one another, they might also settle into a pattern of mutual indifference, if not collusion.

The only real hope lies with a more energetic response from the public. Alas, the Japanese simply do not seem to care that much about political ethics and remain unwilling to make convincing efforts to correct the abuses. Indeed, all too many are so concerned about what the politicians can do for them that they pay little attention to how this affects others. They also engage in an exchange of gifts and favors to get what they want in their private lives. This makes the people perpetrators as opposed to mere victims and places a fair share of the blame on them. As Ichiro Kawasaki pointed out:

"Much of the political corruption stems from the traditional reliance in Japanese communities on personal connections in all social activities. It is an attitude that expects special, private favors in return for forming personal ties with others as distinguished from public or contractual relationship. . . . The fact remains, however, that if a Diet member merely had lofty national interests uppermost in his mind, he would most likely not survive in the complicated scenes of political struggle."[19]

Sidestepping The Constitution

While, over the course of years, most Japanese have gotten used to living with the 1946 Constitution, there have always been those who opposed it. Scornfully labelled the MacArthur Constitution (*Makku Kenpo*), it was belittled for being foisted upon Japan by the victorious Americans and criticized for disregarding its traditional ways and virtues. The complaints were strongest in the early period because, by and large, they were voiced by people who had been brought up—and often been in authoritative positions—under the old regime. But constitutional revision has remained a minor chord in national politics to the present day.

Naturally, the most outspoken support came from the Liberal Democratic Party. In its two official documents, the party's "Mission" and "Platform," adopted in 1955 when it was founded, reference is made to amending or rewriting the constitution. The idea was to replace this "imposed" charter with a "self-determined" one. Such views were expressed even more emphatically by an LDP Dietmen's League for an Independently-Written Constitution, which was founded in the following year. There has also been an LDP Constitutional Problems Research Council, gathering those most committed, to discuss and draft possible amendments.

While such views came from certain LDP members, it would be wrong to claim that they represented a majority, let alone a consensus, in the party. Most were content to let sleeping dogs lie, as it were, and saw little gain in pressing such an issue. Thus, much of the support came from right-wing groups or others of a nationalist hue. One of the most significant was the bereaved families of the war dead, who formed associations which actively backed the LDP. There were also broader circles, more often in the villages than cities, which approved of some of the sentiments if not always the actual proposals.

Opposition to revision has come from various sources. Roughly, it could be attributed to more "liberal" quarters, which consists essentially of the "reformist" camp covering a broad spectrum from Socialist and Communist to considerably more middle-of-the-road. There were also many who were basically apolitical and simply did not want to open old wounds or upset a comfortable *status quo*. The most steadfast opponents, in some ways, were minority groups defending human rights and religious freedom, especially the Christians. But those who fielded the demonstrators to attend rallies and march were usually the trade unions, led by Sohyo.

While the conservatives managed to have their way on most matters, they patently failed in this case. The reason may have been that much of the LDP was not sufficiently committed and it never brought its full strength to bear. This could be seen within the party from the fact that, despite the formal declaration in its founding documents, the plank of constitutional revision was not always included in the annual action policy statement, disappearing from 1976-80 and rarely a major thrust even when it was there.

In 1981, it made a spectacular reappearance in the action program and the party's research panel, led by former Prime Minister Kishi, drew up several amendments. The most important sought to make the Self-Defense Forces constitutional by revising Article 9. It was also proposed that the emperor should become the head of state rather than merely a "symbol of the state," as expressed by Article 1.[20] Meanwhile, the rightists began organizing a nationwide drive to revise the "foreign" constitution, holding local and regional conventions and trying to get more sympathetic Dietmen elected. But nothing came of this. No amendments were ever presented to the Diet. And, under pressure from the JSP, Prime Minister Suzuki conceded that his government had no intention of revising the constitution.

That Zenko Suzuki caved in to the opposition was not surprising, given his customary approach of shunning confrontation. What if a more resolute leader were elected? Such a man is Yasuhiro Nakasone, who advocated changes ever since he entered politics in 1946 and was widely viewed as a "hawk" on most points, including rearmament. During much of his career, he remained close to those pressing for revision. Yet, as prime minister, he failed to take action and merely suggested that the issue be further discussed among the people. "Unless we have a consensus and until the time becomes ripe, we should refrain from indiscreet statements (about amending the constitution)."[21]

This comment showed just how slender the chances of revision actually were. For, as on so many other topics, there was no consensus among the Japanese people and, moreover, there was not even much of a national debate. There were occasional blustering proposals by reactionary politicians or military rightists, immediately rebutted by liberals and "progressives," but no movement in either direction conceptually. There was, however, a shift in the population during the passing years. Those with any nostalgia for the former system, those urging more patriotism or nationalism, were on the whole remnants of older generations that were rapidly dying out. As they disappeared, so would the force behind any revisionist lobby.

In addition, amendments had to be adopted by two-thirds of both houses of the Diet and then ratified by a majority of the voters in a special referendum. There were few issues that could unite that many Diet members or even that many members of the LDP. And it was hard to imagine that the people would then ratify anything the least bit controversial. But there were other ways of bringing about change which required much less effort and could be done more quietly and craftily. In some cases, such moves seriously warped the word or spirit of the constitution.

The most striking obviously concerns Article 9, which provides that "land, sea, and air forces, as well as other war potential, will never be maintained." The prohibition is so categoric and the wording so strict that it was impossible to interpret the constitution loosely. Thus, turning to the UN Charter and traditional customs, it was decided that forces could be established for the purpose of "self-defense." This step was rejected by many constitutional lawyers and scholars as well as by opponents of the government. But such quibbling could not prevent the creation of the Self-Defense Force or its subsequent expansion and reinforcement. Nor did it keep the bulk of the population from growing accustomed to the institution and forgetting its doubtful origin.

Other subtle, and as yet incomplete, maneuvers were undertaken that could vitiate the separation between state and religion, provided by Article 20. One arose in connection with the celebration of National Founding Day, on February 11, which was instituted in 1967. It was sponsored by the government and, although not initially attended by prime ministers, it was observed by other ministers and LDP executives. In 1985, after the ceremonies were somewhat modified, Prime Minister Nakasone came. This celebration was rejected by the reformists as a revival of the prewar Kigensetsu rites marking the supposed accession of Emperor Jimmu and deeply rooted in Shinto. It was seen more generally as a return to discredited nationalism and therefore boycotted by the JSP and Sohyo which organized their own counter-rallies and meetings. Memorial services for the war dead, on August 15, were even more sensitive. The official one, held ever since 1963, was sponsored by the government and attended by the prime minister as well as the emperor. It was also boycotted by the JSP and leftists who organized a separate memorial ceremony. But the sharpest criticism was leveled at Yasukuni Shrine, dedicated to the war dead including some war criminals. Visits there were made increasingly by prime ministers and other ministers and Dietmen. At first coming in their private capacity, they gradually appeared in a more official capacity which incited waves of protest from reformist as well as Christian, Buddhist, and other non-Shinto religious groups. But it was the bitter reaction from China which made Nakasone reverse his position on official visits.

Oddly enough, less fervor was aroused by the failure to guarantee equal voting rights for many, which went against fundamental principles of democracy. This derived from the maldistribution of votes due to demographic changes which left certain electoral districts relatively depopulated and others, in the cities, with a greatly expanded population. Since the former chose as many Diet members as the latter, the inequality in the value of votes could amount to as much as 1:5 before rezoning in 1975, when it fell to 1:3, only to rise to 1:5 again by the mid-1980s. Such disparities existed not only on the national but also prefectural and municipal levels.

While this was severely criticized in liberal circles, and by the press, the politicians proved unable to rectify the situation. To defend their rights, individual citizens and

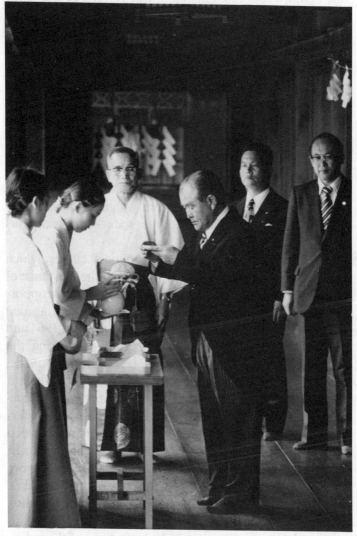

Zenko Suzuki worshipping at Yasakuni shrine—in a private capacity, of course.

Credit: Foreign Press Center/Kyodo

small groups lodged complaints with various courts to the effect that their guarantee of equality under the law, as per Article 14, was violated and therefore the corresponding Diet or local elections were unconstitutional. When rulings came they were by and large mixed. It was admitted by all courts that representation was disporportionate and the uneven distribution of seats impermissible. The Supreme Court ruled, in November 1983, that the existing difference was "so great as to contravene the constitutional requirement of equality of franchise." But most courts limited themselves to stating that a disparity of 1:3 (for some, 1:2) was tolerable and urging the Diet to make suitable arrangements. None were willing to declare specific elections invalid due to the social confusion this would create.[22]

This returned the problem to political circles which usually took much time to settle it despite the existence of a Public Offices Election Law which provided for reapportionment of Diet seats every five years. Instead, a good decade might pass while disparities grew until, in 1964 and 1975, the number of seats was increased to bring the difference to a more acceptable level. By the 1980s, however, the number of Diet seats stood at 511, which it was felt should not be exceeded. It was therefore necessary to undertake the more delicate exercise of transferring seats from less populated districts to more crowded ones. This aroused desperate resistance from Dietmen who risked losing their seat. There was also a more general tendency in the government to drag its feet since most of the "rotten boroughs," in rural and farming districts, voted LDP. That it was contravening the constitution and disregarding repeated admonitions of the judiciary was hardly considered.

Another manipulation which passed almost unnoticed also had a far-reaching effect on the working of the political system. While no distinction was made in the constitution between the membership and functions of the two houses, it was widely felt that the House of Councillors should in some way be different from the more decisive House of Representatives. It should perhaps have more mature members with a broader outlook and conceivably representing people directly rather than as party hacks. This, at least, was roughly how it operated for decades until 1983. For that election, it was decided that rather than national constituencies for some members, a proportional representation system should be introduced. In addition, the candidacy of independents was prohibited which forced Councillors to create their own parties or join existing ones. These measures were eagerly voted by professional politicians of all parties, who thereby cast out many unwanted interlopers. But it left Japan with two houses that were quite alike and with an upper house, in particular, that no longer served much purpose.

It was even more surprising that so little agitation arose in connection with the human rights that were guaranteed by Articles 10-40 of the constitution. This was a cornerstone of the whole political edifice and if these rights were not preserved there was little hope that the system would operate as intended. Yet, the most superficial examination of events turned up numerous cases in which the equality of race, creed, sex, social status and family were flaunted and specific guarantees grossly violated. This, however, seemed to be passively accepted by most Japanese who either regarded such rights as little more than lofty principles or felt they could hardly impose them in practice.

The group which suffered the worst treatment was the *burakumin,* the progeny of the former "outcastes." Although emancipated over a century ago, they continued facing serious discrimination in education, marriage, housing and employment. While some tried to pass into society and others accepted their fate, several organizations formed to defend their cause. In the mid-1960s, the government acceded to some of their demands. Funds were provided to upgrade the social and economic facilities in their neighborhoods and improve the material environment in general. This was to the good. But the other thrust failed. Most efforts for integration *(dowa)* were half-hearted and resisted by the majority. This left the huge community of between one and three million largely marginal.[23]

Two other minorities were formed by approximately 200,000 Chinese and 800,000 Koreans. Despite two or three generations in the country, many were not integrated socially or economically. Proud of their own heritage, and annoyed at the second-rate treatment, many refused to take out Japanese citizenship. This latter category was handled as rank foreigners and, among the more unpleasant aspects, had to be registered and fingerprinted every five years. In the mid-1980s, some refused this and launched a campaign that was joined by other foreigners and backed by the Korean government. Even this was not enough to bring about better treatment and the bureaucracy held fast as long as it could. After all, according to Justice Minister Hitoshi Shimasaki, "regulations and humanitarian concerns are separate issues."[24]

Although representing over half the population and guaranteed equality, it was obvious that women were also openly and systematically discriminated against as regards employment, politics and social activities. Yet, they did not even react as much as the minorities. The principal women's organizations were mainly engaged in traditional causes, such as reducing food costs or avoiding local pollution. Run by older women with scant sympathy for modern feminism, they steered clear of political issues. As for the parties, the LDP was almost closed while the JSP and JCP had modest numbers of female members and at least discussed the crucial points. Hopes of real advances remained dim as few young activists arose to replace the prewar suffragists and most women became increasingly indifferent or apathetic.

Thus, during the 1950s, 1960s and 1970s, women's rights was not really a concern and women's lib hardly a cause. In fact, it was only due to the proclamation of a United Nations "women's decade" in 1980 that the matter had to be faced squarely. To show its good will, the government created a special committee and a division in the Prime Minister's Office. Japanese delegations attended international conferences and the public relations machine launched a campaign to make the status of women look better. Women were given subsidiary managerial posts, one was named an ambassador and another actually ap-

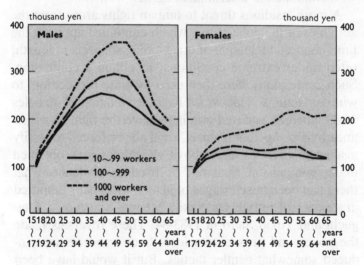

Profile of discrimination by sex, age and company size. Monthly wages in 1982.

Source: Ministry of Labor.
Credit: Statistical *Handbook of Japan 1984*, p. 109.

pointed minister (for the first time in 22 years). But the exceedingly small share of women in positions of authority barely increased and female workers were even worse off than before.[25]

In the field of labor, it was therefore necessary to achieve visible gains to quiet the criticism in the International Labour Organization and also to fulfill a commitment made when signing the UN Convention on the Elimination of All Forms of Discrimination Against Women. To do away with abuses like gaping wage differentials, assignment to specific job categories, limited promotions and pressure to retire after marriage, an Equal Employment Law was finally adopted in 1985 after being blocked by Nikkeiren.[26] However, to gain business acceptance, any improvements were left to the discretion of employers and no penalties could be imposed on those who continued to discriminate against women.

A more insidious threat to human rights arose from the activities of the police force which continued applying the time-honored technique of questioning suspects at length, often under extreme conditions, to obtain a confession. Such confessions were then used by state prosecutors to win convictions. This was a flagrant violation of Articles 36-39 whereby accused criminals have the right to assistance by a competent counsel, shall not be forced to testify against themselves and, above all, confessions obtained under compulsion shall not be used as evidence. That there had been miscarriages of justice was finally admitted in a series of retrials for Sakae Menda, Shigeyoshi Taniguchi and Yukio Saito in 1983-84. These reversals made the police and prosecutors lose "face" and perhaps induced somewhat gentler tactics. But it would have been better if the constitutional guarantees were more rigorously enforced.

These few examples, and there are many more, lead one

to reflect on the constitution and legality in general. It is perfectly evident that innumerable rights and guarantees are being regularly violated, relativized or ignored by politicians, bureaucrats and businessmen and not even pursued too diligently by the judiciary. If this could happen to the highest law in the land, what was occurring with more ordinary legislation and regulations?

NOTES

1. Woronoff, *Inside Japan, Inc.*, pp. 258-64.
2. For full details of the master plan, see Kakuei Tanaka, *Building A New Japan*.
3. Speech to the 96th Session of the National Diet, January 25, 1982.
4. These trends have still not ceased. Metropolitan Tokyo alone is projected to house a quarter of the population by the year 2000.
5. Despite the massive debts and losses, the LDP is still pumping more money into new railway lines.
6. Thanks to Tanaka, Niigata was regularly among the top prefectures in terms of per capita central government spending on public works.
7. As per usual, all the newspapers pounced on the same story. For all the news that was fit to print, see the vernacular and English-language press of January 1982.
8. Woronoff, *op. cit.*, pp. 78-85.
9. Numerous stories of the scandals, with photos, evidence, and lurid details appeared in the press during late 1981 and early 1982, only to fade away thereafter although no one assumed the practices had ceased.
10. What is most intriguing is that the press obviously had more than enough material to seriously embarrass the political and business establishment, but kept it in the files except when other sources brought up the issue.
11. This section is essential despite the views of some leading Japanapologists. Ezra Vogel claimed that "the distortions of public policy to favor certain vested interest groups on the basis of political contributions is probably not great." (*Japan as No. 1*, p. 126.) And even more categorically, according to Edwin O. Reischauer, "political corruption is not widespread in Japan." (*The Japanese*, p. 309.)
12. For a more detailed description of the KDD caper, see Woronoff, *op. cit.*, pp. 65-77.
13. *Japan Times*, December 16, 1983 and November 19, 1984.

14. *Bungei Shunju*, "Tanaka Kakuei Kenkyu," November 1974.

15. If not for a cerebral stroke, it is probable that Tanaka would have continued fighting the case to the highest court and, if still sentenced, sought to induce an amnesty or Imperial pardon.

16. As much as 91% of the respondents to a *Mainichi* poll in October 1983, when Tanaka was found guilty of corruption, felt that he should resign. Nearly half of the LDP Diet members polled agreed. But this had no effect and was soon forgotten.

17. One of the most farcical episodes was Nakasone's grudging decision to ask Tanaka to resign from the Diet in October 1983. Overcome with emotion, he never exactly used the word "resign" and Tanaka failed to take the hint. This formality duly accomplished, the whole matter was dropped.

18. *Japan Times,* April 5, 1979.

19. Ichiro Kawasaki, *Japan Unmasked,* p. 201.

20. *Japan Times,* April 29 and October 23, 1981.

21. *Ibid,* January 14, 1983.

22. *Ibid,* November 8, 1983 and March 15, 1984.

23. See George De Vos and Hiroshi Wagatsuma, *Japan's Invisible Race.*

24. *Far Eastern Economic Review,* May 30, 1985, p. 22.

25. Oddly enough, there were actually more female Diet members in the 1940s and 1950s than the 1970s and 1980s and both previous female ministers were appointed in the early 1960s.

26. It might be mentioned that the wage gap (women only earn 53% as much as men) was the largest in the OECD and Japan was the only place where it increased rather than declining in the past decade.

9
Foreign Policy (And Defense)

Foreign Affairs In A Skewed World

The postwar world has witnessed an unparalleled increase in the scale and intensity of international relations. This arose initially from the establishment of alliances deemed useful to prevent a future war or, if necessary, to win it. It was then overlaid by a network of organizations embracing all sovereign states and giving them at last theoretical equality. This opportunity was rapidly seized by the former Axis powers once they were accepted back into the international community and, even more vigorously, by innumerable new states which threw off colonialism.

One of the few relative exceptions to the rule was Japan. True, it did belong to most of the international organizations and positioned itself with regard to the East-West conflict and the North-South split. But, while Tokyo possessed a foreign policy, it was not very enterprising. The government rarely took noteworthy initiatives or got involved in burning issues. Often, the Japanese seemed more like onlookers, patiently watching and waiting until a consensus had been reached by the others—or they came under pressure from their partners—to join in a general chorus.

The contents of much of the policy was vague and superficial. It could almost be summed up by the title of a book by former Foreign Minister Sunao Sunoda—"The

World, Japan, Love." A more extensive, if not much more explicit, definition was provided by Prime Minister Fukuda.

"The problems confronting the nations of the world today, such as the problem of resources and energy, the North-South problem, increasing trade friction, unemployment and so forth, are issues which cannot be managed by a single country. They can only be resolved through international cooperation and solidarity. Each individual country has to seek the realization of its own national interests through the resolution of these problems by helping each other, accomodating each other and complementing each other and thus through the attainment of peace and prosperity of the entire world."[1]

Finally, the outreach was somewhat constricted geographically. For an amazingly long time, indeed much longer than was necessary for other former enemy states or quite primitive developing ones, Japan remained tied to and followed in the wake of American policy. In fact, as much as possible, it tried not even to take a stand on relations with other countries and seemed obsessed with how it got along with the United States.[2] Its contacts expanded more often as a function of additional countries seeking intercourse with it rather than the other way around.

This did make some sense, given the historical situation. The American army occupied Japan and SCAP, under the influence of General MacArthur, helped shape the political system. This new Japan was less self-assured than the old one whose failure was still remembered. It was also worried by the eastward movement of Communism, like its American mentor. The Liberal Democratic Party therefore agreed to cast its lot with the "free world." This naturally included support of the capitalist system and its current interest in free trade, one of whose greatest promoters and beneficiaries was Japan.

While much of this proceeded with relatively few hitches the situation regarding military links was more troublesome. As a matter of fact, the insertion of Japan in the Western alliance sparked the most serious domestic conflicts the nation had seen. The Japan-U.S. Security Treaty was angrily rejected by the Socialists, Communists and more widely and resulted in fighting in the Diet and violent demonstrations in the streets. Renewal of the treaty again provoked bitter resistance. Not until the 1970s was it more or less accepted by the general population. Creation of the Self-Defense Force, then its expansion, and the ongoing need to finance it generated another series of clashes.[3]

Yet, in all these dealings, it was almost systematically the United States which gave the most. The Americans provided aid, funds and technology for Japanese economic growth. They absorbed vast amounts of imports even when it hurt their own economy and as late as the 1980s Japanese growth was heavily dependent on American business. Its traders could sell their wares within an economic structure forged and fortified by American efforts. The military setup was even more lopsided. While the two countries were supposedly "allies," only the United States was bound to come to the aid of Japan which had no reciprocal commitment. American troops were stationed in Japan to back it up and an American "nuclear umbrella" was a key element in Japan's defense.

This odd relationship has often been traced to the Japanese characteristic of *amae* or roughly "dependence," in which the weaker partner makes insistent demands on the stronger. The protector, in this view, is responsible toward the protégé. While such an attitude was appealing in earlier years, since no one really wanted an assertive and aggressive Japan, it became ever less comprehensible as Japan developed economically and became the world's most dynamic economy. It was assumed that it should gradually participate more effectively in world affairs, hopefully carrying some of the crushing burden the Americans had trouble bearing.

This shift never really came about. As long as it possibly could, Japan tried to benefit from American backing without making undue efforts of its own. Worse, its economic policy was actually creating serious difficulties for the United States which traced its trade imbalances directly to Japan and placed the blame for the collapse of certain industries and spread of unemployment there as well. Indeed, by the 1980s, there was a constant stream of grievances which often resulted in open conflicts. The

Keeping the fearsome ally at bay: the Ron-Yasu relationship.
Credit: Foreign Press Center/Kyodo

once generally positive views of ordinary citizens were turning against Japan. In specific sectors, like big business, the trade unions and Congress, resentment was welling up.[4]

But little happened because Japan had—or cultivated—friends in the United States. Many of the ambassadors sent to Tokyo were selected for their knowledge of and sometimes sympathy with the Japanese. This occasionally degenerated into a tendency to defend Japanese interests in Washington more forcefully than American interests in Tokyo. Ambassador Edwin A. Reischauer led the way in the 1960s, followed even more fawningly by Ambassador Mike Mansfield in the 1980s. The Japanese won over other opinion-makers by inviting them for visits, hiring them as consultants or using them as lobbyists. It did not take long for Japan to spend more money on keeping America sweet than any other supposed ally.

Partly because this relationship had its ups and downs (the most noticeable being the Nixon shock in 1973), Washington was pushing Tokyo to assume more responsibilities and it was patently absurd to have such a limited and skewed foreign policy, Japan gradually did broaden its circle of contacts. The first steps were taken toward Europe. The earliest were economic as trade grew and Japan was eventually admitted into what were until then essentially Western organizations, such as GATT and the OECD. There was some talk of its eventually joining NATO, but that was only talk and was probably made to please its Western partners.

This tilt westward seemed almost natural to most Japanese who had more difficulty in conceiving of closer ties with other Asian countries. Some of them were initially opponents, including North Korea, Vietnam and the People's Republic of China. Others were merely former colonies like South Korea and Taiwan. Those further south were looked down upon as relatively backward while Australia and New Zealand were merely second-rate Western nations. That relations were not resumed more quickly was mutual since most of these countries were still aggrieved by Japan's wartime aggression and its apparent lack of contrition. Indeed, it hardly compensated for the material damage it had inflicted and tried to shirk any moral responsibility. It took until 1985 for the emperor to express an incredibly weak apology as concerns the domination of Korea:

". . . it is indeed regrettable that there was an unfortunate past between us for a period in this century and I believe that it should not be repeated again."

Finally, in the late 1970s, Japan added a second prong to its diplomacy. This was an opening toward the rest of Asia. In the meanwhile, these countries had recovered and some of them boasted solid economic achievements. Others, even if not quite as successful, were attractive as sources of raw materials and markets for exports. Diplomatic relations were resumed with South Korea in 1965. After Nixon's switch, relations were also restored with Peking in 1977. The most fashionable goal became the creation of a Pacific Basin Community of some sort. This would be more economic than political, it would initially include the more amenable states and perhaps later more difficult partners, and it would be buttressed on Japan and the United States. Thus, in certain ways, it was really just an extension of older patterns.

Aside from the United States, some European and Asian partners, most other countries were disregarded. Even lesser European countries had to send periodic missions to remind Tokyo of their existence. There were yet fewer political contacts with Eastern Europe. When it came to Latin America or the Caribbean, connections were even more tenuous aside from Brazil where some

Japanese had migrated. Africa was still a very dark continent of little note aside from periodic refugee or famine crises. Southern Asia was not even on the map for most. Only the Middle East, long neglected, was absorbed into Japan's world system with any alacrity. This showed most clearly that the motives were hardly morality or "love" but very practical and material concerns. Its intelligence was so poor that Japan did not realize the bitterness toward Israel or even the region's strategic importance. When faced with a loss of oil in 1973, Tokyo immediately sent off high-level delegations to plead its cause. It endorsed the Arab views, advanced enormous loans and quickly downgraded relations with Israel. It continued toadying to any Arab leaders, even those opposed to American policy (such as Iran), as long as the oil flowed.

While it took a long time to figure out who its friends were, it was much easier to identify its enemies. For some time, this appeared to include Communist China. But it was obvious from the outset that the real threat came from its traditional rival, Russia.[5] The Soviet Union, which fought against Japan in its last days of agony, took over part of its Asian realm and absorbed a few islands that were regarded as Japanese territory, was soon at odds with it. Soviet opposition kept Japan out of the United Nations for years until 1956, when the two countries finally restored diplomatic relations. This antagonism grew ever stronger during the Vietnam War. When Japan resumed relations with China and accepted an "anti-hegemony" clause, there was a second cause for anger. Despite some trade and a desire to have Japan help develop Siberia, full normalization was stymied and a peace treaty could not be signed.[6]

By the 1980s, Japan had finally created links with much of the international community. Few of these were entirely unambiguous since it tended to trade with foes as well as friends and disliked the concept of having any adversary, even the Soviet Union. To smooth things over, as frequently happened in Japanese society, the government scrupulously avoided putting its views too clearly. Just what it thought of its allies' policies was hard to fathom and approval was sometimes only verbal. It also subscribed to all the good intentions and pure sentiments expressed in the international organizations and joined every high-sounding movement.

Yet, even when it said the right things, Japan rarely took very meaningful actions unless pushed to do so by others. Thus, it required pressure from the advanced countries to get it to help the developing countries with grants or other aid. It took equally strong pressure to make it open its home market or stop flooding external ones. And it took more pressure to make it prove its commitment to a military alliance by strengthening its forces. This everlasting need to convince the Japanese to follow their words with deeds was most disconcerting to its counterparts.

To show its good will, periodically "initiatives" were launched by more spirited foreign ministers or prime ministers. Japan, so it was claimed, would work for disarmament and international stability. It would double its assistance, and then double it again, to create prosperity. It hoped to bring about peace between Iran and Iraq, in the Middle East or Indochina. But these were often empty gestures. They consisted of a supportive speech but no consistent campaign to meet with the opposing parties, bring them to the negotiating table, exert pressure to make concessions or offer major benefits if they did. Indeed, once uttered, the supposed initiatives just dissipated into nothingness.

The only way in which Japan managed to act with any

consistency or impact arose from its attempts to win friends with favors. Of course, as in domestic politics, these favors were almost always material and usually took the form of massive loans that were graciously proferred by top leaders to countries they visited and wished to impress. Brazil, Iraq, Iran, ASEAN and China received $1 billion or more each. Admittedly, these sums could only be spent over a number of years and each specific segment still had to be approved by Tokyo. But this appeared as a generous gesture when it was made. And it looked even nicer when presented in the right spirit, such as that of the "Fukuda doctrine," which was supposed to change Japan's earlier calculated approach.

". . . I have been keeпny aware of the importance of restructuring our ties with this region, ties which have more often than not tended towards a relationship with a bias to economic aspects, into a relationship of equal partners based on true mutual understanding, into a relationship of true friends with 'heart-to-heart' understanding."[7]

This left Tokyo a relatively marginal player on the world political scene as much as four decades after the war. Such behavior did not arise out of a blind commitment to its own goals or even pure self-interest. It was more an awkwardness in dealing with other countries and becoming just another one of them. For centuries, foreign relations had been minimal aside from periodic intercourse with China, Korea and ultimately the West. Japan was not really accustomed to the need to relate to others and many of its past experiences were negative. This did not arouse a very keen desire to resume the process. And much of what it did do was geared to the earlier practice of boosting its ranking in an international hierarchy based on greater and lesser nations as opposed to the new, more open and equalitarian world society. "Odd man out" was therefore a better description of its position than "splendid isolation."

Economic Relations Uber Alles

When military adventurism crumbled at war's end, much of the vacuum was filled with economic endeavors. Indeed, the Japanese threw themselves into the task of economic development with such fervor that it often appeared to be their only concern. It could thus come to pass that a Japanese prime minister visiting French President de Gaulle would be dismissed as a mere "transistor radio salesman."[8]

This did not seem to disturb the Japanese. If anything, they regarded the new tack as almost impeccable. This time foreigners could not possibly accuse them of being warmongers. As their economy improved, it was possible to raise the living standards of the Japanese people. Meanwhile, manufacturers were turning out a profusion of good and cheap consumer products which were exported to other countries. This was followed by some aid and investment. In this way Japan could be portrayed as a model country whose contributions were overwhelmingly beneficial. In time, such a policy should reap nothing but praise.

The turn to an economics first approach was taken by Prime Minister Ikeda in 1961, when he launched the "income doubling plan." While this was primarily directed toward the domestic situation it naturally had a tremendous external impact since the economy was heavily export-oriented. In short order, huge amounts of consumer goods were being shipped all around the world. To market and service them, and to find new customers, Japanese companies set up offices in city after city and country after country. Most prominent were the trading companies (*sogo shosha*) and the banks, soon followed by manufacturers, securities houses and even retailers.

During the initial period, this policy seemed to bear the desired fruit. Japan won growing admiration for its rapid and enviable recovery. Its products were welcomed and the country itself was judged by their quality. It was not particularly difficult to induce greater sales and everything seemed to be for the best. If exporting had been a normal activity and Japan had imported roughly as much as it exported, probably the policy would have continued making friends. But it was pushed with a vengeance as Japan became hooked on exporting and its manufacturers and traders competed ruthlessly with one another to boost sales. This led them to engage in practices which were less popular.

By the 1960s already, the trade balance began shifting against most of Japan's trading partners with the exception of those supplying oil or other indispensable raw materials. The first to feel the pressure was the United States. But it was quickly followed by the European countries and some Asian ones. South Korea, Taiwan and Hong Kong, closely tied to Japan as purchasers of intermediate goods, ran a constant and swelling deficit. Even developing countries were soon in debt. Meanwhile, it was accused of contributing to growing unemployment and the collapse of certain industries in advanced nations and, in the Third World, stifling the attempts to industrialize.

The 1970s therefore witnessed an unending procession of trade conflicts. In the United States there were disputes over televisions, textiles, steel and automobiles, among others. Europe was worried about shipbuilding and electronics. In Southeast Asia there were complaints about impediments to tropical produce and in Australia, Canada and the United States about blocking beef imports. There was hardly a trading partner which did not have some gripe. And the discontent gradually spread from individual cases to more general patterns which indicated that Japan was not treating others as well as it had been treated.[9]

In response to these grievances, the Japanese took various corrective measures or tolerated whatever penalties were imposed on them. Textile manufacturers accepted quotas and steelmakers obeyed the trigger price mechanism. Shipbuilders agreed to share the market with their competitors and electronics manufacturers held back on shipments or adjusted their prices upward. The automobile industry made the biggest concession by undergoing five years of "voluntary restraint" on the American market. In fact, when problems did arise, the first reaction tended to be to hold back.

But this sort of adjustment limited overall trade. A much better solution, in the eyes of most foreigners, was for the Japanese economy itself to be liberalized so that more imports could flow into the market and a balance be attained at a higher level. This view was not often shared by the government, or rather the business circles which influenced the government. Despite the many complications it proved easier to control exports than to liberalize effectively. Still, steps were also taken in this direction. During the 1960s, numerous tariffs and quotas were dismantled and currency restrictions withdrawn. During the 1970s and 1980s, however, it proved necessary to go further by abolishing nontariff barriers and truly freeing the financial system.

To appease the developing countries, it was imperative to adopt a second series of measures. This consisted of providing aid of one sort or another. Under pressure from United Nations bodies, and also its Western partners in the OECD, Tokyo was convinced to boost its official development assistance. The effort made in early years was really quite mediocre and thus the pressure had to be

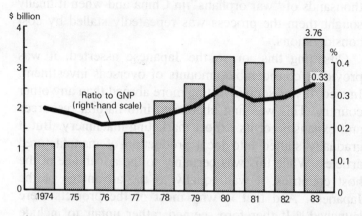

$ billion

Ratio to GNP
(right-hand scale)

3.76

0.33

1974 75 76 77 78 79 80 81 82 83

Japan's official development assistance. A very strange doubling and
redoubling of efforts.

Source: Diplomatic Bluebook, Ministry of Foreign Affairs, 1984.
Credit: *Facts and Figures of Japan 1985*, p. 43.

kept up. Not until the late 1970s was Japan ready to make
striking gestures in the form of three "aid doubling"
exercises. While the aid was not actually doubled three
times, it at least rose substantially. Yet, even then, Japan
was making one of the lowest per capita contributions and
its grant element was particularly meager.

A third type of giving was even harder to come by since
most Japanese failed to grasp its intrinsic value and had to
be convinced to participate. This involved humanitarian
aid to those suffering from natural and man-made disasters. Japan habitually made token offers unless called
upon to do more. The clearest example was for the
Vietnamese refugees and "boat people," modest numbers
of which were received but hardly welcomed. For this as
well as African refugees and the food crisis, the government regularly preferred making monetary rather than
human contributions. Even for its own kin, it was not
overly generous. For decades, it ignored the existence of

thousands of "war orphans" in China and when it finally sought them the process was repeatedly stalled by cost considerations.

Offsetting this, or so the Japanese asserted, it was providing considerable amounts of overseas investment. Indeed, it was soon investing more abroad than any other country. This was first channeled into natural resources and expansion of its export marketing machinery. But it gradually shifted into local production of manufactured articles. While this was certainly to the advantage of the host countries, it was equally to the advantage of the Japanese. And that is why most of the projects were launched.[10] It therefore seemed rather unfair to include investment and even trade in Japan's aid package, as was frequently done.

Looking back, it eventually became obvious that the Japanese had been very naive in assuming that economic activities would endear them to the rest of the world. Instead, overly aggressive trade practices aroused waves of anti-Japanese sentiment which could result in trade conflicts. On occasion, there were even riots and attacks on Japanese interests, especially in Southeast Asia. Its attempts to compensate through loans, grants or investments were of some use but hardly adequate.[11] And Japan's apparent "free ride" here was also castigated. Looking forward, much more pressing demands could be expected in the future.

The basic mistake had been to assume that trade and aid activities were enough to win hearts and minds. But this was exacerbated by the failure of the government to dominate the situation. The Foreign Ministry did not really know what the businessmen were doing or how and it only dawned on them rather late that the frenzy for sales had to be toned down or sweetened with other actions.

Meanwhile, even the aid operations were marred by a failure to grasp the true needs of the host countries. All too often, it was not really the local government which decided on the projects but Japanese companies that wished to launch them and then persuaded locals to apply for aid, subsequently pulling strings to see that it was approved.

Throughout the process, it was painfully evident that it was the flag which followed trade and not the other way around. It was the corporate community that first staked out a country and then dragged the government in. And it was always the businessmen who knew more about what was going on than the diplomats. Commercial interests actually had more far-reaching effects on overall foreign policy. For example, traders and manufacturers seeking sales behind the Iron Curtain or in the Third World convinced the government that closer ties were necessary and sometimes obtained trade credits, development assistance or other benefits to facilitate business.

This did not apply just marginally or incidentally. There were strong lobbies for economic relations with the Soviet Union, which attenuated government policy and argued against boycotts and the like. Businessmen reminded the politicians of the advisability of dealing with South Korea or Taiwan. Others, seeing the greater gains to be made in the People's Republic, were avid supporters of normalizing relations. When this could not be obtained, they at least managed to get informal trade agreements that opened the market. Business interests also promoted a rapprochement with the ASEAN countries, in particular the Philippines and Indonesia. And, of course, they were instrumental in keeping channels open with the Middle Eastern oil producers.[12]

Beyond the action of the various companies, *zaikai* organizations played a role and developed a parallel diplomacy that supplemented or supplanted normal government activities. Keidanren sent innumerable missions to countries which had to be cultivated in order to obtain trade or natural resources. It later sent off other missions to reconcile those which felt that Japanese markets were closed or wanted compensation in the form of more aid or investment. Foreign dignitaries were regularly received in Japan and treated extremely well, a gesture they rarely forgot.

As for the Japanese people, they were not terribly interested in this aspect of foreign policy either. It took a very long time to inculcate an understanding of the need to grant foreign aid. It was conveniently forgotten that Japan itself had benefited from substantial American aid in the early postwar years. Success made the hardworking and self-satisfied citizens forget the difficulties that plagued the development process. They were often dismayed by foreign leaders who appeared foolish or failed to get their priorities right and populations that looked lazy or venal. This inhibited the rise of a popular lobby for development aid or other humanitarian concerns.

When it came to complaints of a closed market or trouble in selling to Japan, people again tended to place most of the onus on the foreigners. They did not realize just how open other markets were or that this greatly facilitated penetration. Although they sensed that the Japanese situation was different, they still felt that foreign producers should be blamed for not making sufficient efforts. However, if faced by demonstrably irate reactions, they conceded the need for noble gestures and accepted token government measures. Oddly enough, they never seemed to grasp that opening the market was actually to their own advantage as consumers. So the generalized contempt for foreigners only grew.

Easy-Riding on Defense

Ever since the immediate postwar period, once the Conservatives took over and consolidated their position, it was evident that Japan was part of the "free world." Its leaders were emphatically pro-American and they espoused the virtues of democracy and pluralism as they saw them. They condemned the antithetical goals of Communism even more sharply. Despite that, it still took some doing to bring Japan into the Western alliance even loosely.

The man who engineered much of this was the strong-willed Prime Minister Shigeru Yoshida who rammed through a Japan-U.S. Security Treaty in 1951. This treaty bound the United States to come to Japan's aid in the event of a military threat and allowed it to maintain troops on Japanese territory to that end. The treaty was renewed, in a somewhat modified version, by Prime Minister Nobosuke Kishi, an equally prominent hardliner. And it has been maintained as a cornerstone of Japanese policy to the present day. However, as the older generation of politicians withdrew, the vigor of the commitment seemed to weaken. It reached a nadir under Zenko Suzuki who was denounced by the opposition for speaking of an "alliance" and then ridiculed by the press for backing down on this claim. It was only with Prime Minister Yasuhiro Nakasone, a reputed "hawk," that new warmth was breathed into the relationship.

Of course, it took more than a security treaty to create a viable defense. It was necessary to have some military establishment. And this was seemingly blocked by Article 9 of the constitution which prohibited the maintenance of armed forces. For some time, this was a definite obstacle, especially since there was a large pacifist contingent in the

Diet and nation. As the situation changed, however, and the "cold war" set in, ways were found. It was eventually agreed that Article 9 did not deny the right of legitimate self-defense, an inalienable right of every state and part of the United Nations Charter.

Thus, in 1950, a paramilitary National Police Reserve of 75,000 men was established. In 1954, it was reorganized into a Self-Defense Force which came under the direction of the civilian Defense Agency. By 1960, the SDF consisted of three arms with 200,000 men; by 1985, it had expanded to 250,000. Over the years, it was equipped with modern ships, aircraft and weaponry and became a notable fighting force, whatever its name.[13]

Yet, despite the acceptance of the alliance and the existence of a military establishment, the Japanese leaders did not go as far as had been feared.[14] If anything, they tended to hold back due to opposition from other parties and anxiety within the electorate as well as their own sense of priorities. None of the politicians wished to come under the domination of the military again, not even the most die-hard. Nor did they want to devote more men, effort and money than necessary to what appeared an intrinsically sterile occupation.[15] If Japan were to assume a place of significance, it could no longer be through military might but rather economic prowess. And it was necessary to reserve more resources for that.

Even Yoshida originally resisted rearmament and Ikeda tried to keep the cost of defense as low as possible. This track was followed by most ensuing LDP leaders. In early years, it seemed impossible to spare more than 1% of gross national product for such expenditures and, under Takeo Miki in 1976, this was made a ceiling although the country was then quite rich. In practice, the real figure was somewhat higher, closer to 1.3% of GNP if counted the same way as elsewhere. But even then it was quite modest compared to the 3%, 4%, 5%, 6% and more that was being spent in Europe, the United States and Soviet Union, Korea and Taiwan.

While the decision to restrain the defense budget was frequently presented in political terms as a measure to prevent a resurgence of militarism or avoid alarming neighboring countries, it definitely had economic advantages. The amount of money that could be saved by keeping expenditures to 1% (or 1.3%) was colossal. This was several percent of gross national product which amounted to trillions of yen every year. That could then be used to boost production or welfare and made it possible to keep taxes down. Without a doubt, it was this extra money which stimulated the type of development that made Japan a formidable economic power.

Going a step further, ostensibly to abide by the spirit of the constitution, severe restrictions were placed on the use of force. Not only were military capabilities designed for defensive purposes, curious gestures were made to preclude offensive operations. For example, the range of aircraft and ships was limited to short distances and planes flew without the missiles needed for combat. In addition, the nation repudiated the use of nuclear weapons through the "three non-nuclear principles" of Prime Minister Sato. Japan would neither make, possess, nor permit the introduction of nuclear weapons.

Thanks to such measures, and even more so to the passage of time, defense policy received an increasing degree of acceptance. A rough consensus was first attained within the LDP. While it was the more conservative party, included a coterie of former militarists and several avowed "hawks", they did not represent the majority. Many more were simply indifferent to military matters and some few were "doves." In fact, once the older leadership passed from the scene, there were only sporadic signs of a desire for a more beligerent policy. This was shown by the calls of the "Blue Storm Society" and then by Yasuhiro Nakasone, one of their number, when he came to office. Yet, even he did not much change the policy in practice although his comments were often provocative, as when he compared Japan to an "unsinkable aircraft carrier."

Even in Japan's political system, it is necessary to reach some sort of understanding with the opposition parties. In earlier days, this rule had been slighted and the result was fierce battles in the Diet and raucous demonstrations in the streets. This did not block government policy but it did induce a desire to find more acceptable solutions. That explains some of the measures mentioned above. But the opposition gradually took even more steps in the direction of the LDP. First middle-of-the-road parties like Komeito and the DSP accepted the existence of the alliance and the preservation of the SDF. Eventually the Japan Socialist Party came around to a similar view with the proviso that it should merely be a transition to a better state of things when the military establishment could be disbanded and the treaty dissolved in the midst of worldwide amity.

This position of the Socialists was more than lukewarm. Yet, even that was a remarkable switch from the former insistence on "unarmed neutrality." It had been claimed that the best way Japan could ensure its security was to have no military forces whatsoever and thereby be a threat to no other country. It was also urged to break off the treaty with the United States and remain self-reliant and independent. That it would also become isolated and undefended, an easy target for nuclear blackmail, was hardly considered. After all, this scenario was not rooted in rational arguments but faith and ideology.[16] It was not until Masashi Ishibashi headed the JSP that more realistic concepts were mooted.

It was only when the Liberal Democratic Party seemed to revert back to a more aggressive stance that the opposition reacted, as it repeatedly did with the coming of Nakasone. Before he took any initiative, he was roundly condemned in leftist circles as a warmonger who could drag the nation into deep waters. Some of his comments encouraged this view. But few of his actions did. While he boldly pledged to increase defense spending, cooperate more closely with the United States and defend the sea lanes up to 1,000 miles, little came of it. The defense buildup proceeded according to earlier plans and well behind schedule, amounts voted to the budget were only

Biting the hand that defends you. Protesting port calls by American ships.

Credit: Foreign Press Center/Kyodo

marginally higher, and the air force and navy were never in a position to defend the sea lanes. As per usual, much of the political sparring was verbal.

A consensus also gradually set in among public opinion. The security treaty had been around for a long time and the Self-Defense Force was a reality. Neither had done much to damage Japan and they seemed to be moderately positive on the balance without entailing unbearable costs. It was gradually felt that this status quo should be maintained. According to the periodic surveys, each year a few percent more agreed with this stand and they eventually became a considerable majority. The other side of the consensus, however, was that it was unwise to proceed any further. Hardly anybody wanted a more ambitious army, any dangerous commitment to Western aims or an increase in the risks of retaliation. Most of all, there was no desire to spend a yen more on defense than necessary.[17]

Admittedly, there was a large and vocal "pacifist" movement. One branch arose among the victims of the attacks on Hiroshima and Nagasaki, still over 300,000 people represented by the Japan Confederation of A- and H-Bomb Sufferers Organizations (Hidankyo). A broader movement against nuclear weapons arose in 1955 when a group of housewives launched a signature campaign that attracted many supporters at the grass roots and resulted in the Japan Council Against Atomic and Hydrogen Bombs (Gensuikyo). After it was infiltrated by the Communists, the Socialists set up a Japan Conference Against Atomic and Hydrogen Bombs (Gensuikin). The two bodies agreed only on some general principles and differed on most practical measures. Even the annual Ban-The-Bomb Conferences, attended by foreign counterparts, were wrent by these divisions. Meanwhile, new and small grassroots formations were created to get away from the rivalry and politicization. This welter of organizations staged meetings, rallies, marches, demonstrations and signature campaigns. Yet, despite a hypothetical membership of six million or more, the peace movement became increasingly ritualistic and ineffective.

It was not openly opposed by any other movement since there was no desire in the population for militarism and war. Some right-wing extremists held their own rallies, rode about the country in loudspeaker vans spouting propaganda or disrupted the activities of the leftists. For a long time, however, there was no other sign of interest even in conservative circles. Finally, in the 1980s, some businessmen began lobbying for enhanced military strength and preparedness. They spoke out on the need to recognize potential threats and share the burden of meeting them. Such views came not only from cranks but respected *zaikai* figures in bodies such as Keidanren, the Chamber of Commerce and especially the Junior Chamber. Admittedly, part of the interest derived from a desire for more defense contracts, especially in sluggish economic times and for depressed industries. But almost as much could be traced to a feeling that not enough attention was being paid to vital issues. Still, while the comments created a flurry of interest, they were not enough to reverse the trend toward complacency.

This consensus, like most others in the external sector, was therefore an inherently passive one that consisted of accepting what there was and what one had grown accustomed to while avoiding any noteworthy changes. It stuck more to generalities than practicalities. And even decisive details were casually overlooked. Thus, while there was an agreement that the total defense budget should not exceed 1%, there was hardly any concern as to how that 1% was spent.[18] Even more anomolous, while the nuclear principles included a rejection of the introduction of nu-

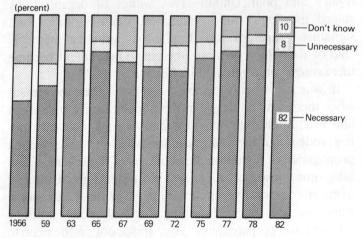

Do you think the Self-Defense Forces are necessary?
(percent)

10 — Don't know
8 — Unnecessary

82 — Necessary

1956 59 63 65 67 69 72 75 77 78 82

Forging a grudging consensus. The primary question.

Source: Public Opinion Survey on Defense Problems,
Prime Minister's Office, May 1982.
Credit: *Facts and Figures of Japan 1985*, p. 147.

clear weapons, nothing was done to control this. The government never bothered asking the Americans whether their ships carried such weapons and the Americans never volunteered the information.

Even essentials were blithely ignored. For example, the troops were chronically short of ammunition. Too much of the budget went into paying wages and too much of the personnel was elderly or non-combatant. The units were widely dispersed and few were located in Hokkaido, the most logical target. Contingency plans were inadequate and the military could not even commandeer land or facilities if attacked. But the most telling point was that the armed forces could not really accomplish their restricted mission. Even assuming that they were designed for purely defensive purposes, it was most unlikely that the SDF could actually defend the country for long. Most military experts assumed that at best it could hold off the

What do you think about Japan's defense budget?
(percent)

20	47	15	18
Want an increase	Want to maintain present level	Want a reduction	Don't know

How helpful you think the Japan-U.S. security treaty is to Japan's security?
(percent)

30	36	12	22
Very helpful	Somewhat helpful	Not helpful	No answer

What, if any, danger do you see of Japan's becoming involved in a war in the near future?
(percent)

28	32	21	19
Some danger	Slight danger	No danger	Don't know

Source: *Jieitai, boei mondai ni kansuru yoron chosa* (Public Opinion Survey on the Self-Defense Forces and Defense Problems), Prime Minister's Office, May 1982.
Note: Survey was conducted in December 1981.

The consensus stalls. Subsidiary questions.

Source: Public Opinion Survey on Defense Problems,
Prime Minister's Office, May 1982.
Credit: *Facts and Figures of Japan 1985*, p. 146.

enemy for a few days, perhaps not even that much. This left Japan basically undefended or dependent on American protection.

This is what distinguished the limp Japanese consensus from the much more virile one in places like Sweden and Switzerland. These countries were not only neutral but willing to defend that neutrality. The Japanese public, on the other hand, left much of the chore to officials, politicians and soldiers and otherwise washed their hands of the matter. Indeed, most ordinary citizens seemed incapable of conceiving of situations where they might have to fight for their rights or merely find refuge in the event of hostilities.[19] This made the intermittent defense debate, among the liveliest in Japan, quite empty and futile. Everybody knew the positions of the LDP and opposition and the outcome was a foregone conclusion . . . more of the same.

What permitted the Japanese consensus, such as it was, was not Japan's own efforts but the American alliance. It was possible to forgo nuclear weapons not because of some idealistic streak or a "nuclear allergy" arising out of Hiroshima and Nagasaki. This was enabled by the existence of the American nuclear arsenal and the nuclear umbrella. It was possible to keep the army to a minimum because the Americans had built up their own forces. It was possible to pay 1% of GNP or so for military expenses because the Americans were paying over 6%. If forced to carry its own burden and work out its own policy, it is unlikely that such a cozy and easygoing solution could have been found.

While the American ally accepted this posture at the outset, it was rapidly changing its attitude. Once upon a time Washington was simply relieved that Japan had shed its earlier aggressiveness and might no longer be a threat. In addition, the United States then possessed the world's premier military capabilities and a monopoly on nuclear weaponry. As this preeminence faded and it faced more arduous difficulties in defending itself and its allies, there was some annoyance that Japan did not share more of the burden. This was only aggravated when Japan first hesitated to cooperate by boosting its own forces, participating in joint military maneuvers or transferring military technology. Worst was the low budget. This inevitably led to charges of a "free ride."

This reticence was increasingly getting Japan into trouble with an ally it sorely depended on. For some while, it was compensated by keeping on better terms with other countries in the region which had suffered from Japanese militarism in the past. Still, as American strength waned, it became obvious that someone had to make up the difference and no other country was in a position to do so. With time, the calls to curtail the SDF were replaced by appeals to play a more vigorous role in regional security. This came not only from places like Taiwan and Korea, Singapore and the Philippines, but even China.

Meanwhile, the low posture was not winning points with the Soviet Union. The Kremlin's suspicion and distrust were so deep that its leaders continued picturing Japan as an unredeemed and unredeemable military power whose threat could only be checked by countermeasures. Each time the Japanese promised to beef up their armed forces, or talked of raising expenditures, the Soviets beat them to it. That the Japanese rarely followed through was hardly noticed. So, over the years, Soviet forces in the Far East expanded at a terrific pace and far exceeded any Japanese build-up. Tokyo ended up worse off than before and faced a truly redoubtable opponent. This made the policy even more absurd and counterproductive than otherwise.

Aspirations To Leadership

This rather anomolous situation of a major nation playing a minor part in international affairs repeatedly caused other countries to urge Japan to throw off its apparent reluctance and assume greater responsibilities. It was called on to become a pillar of the Western alliance along with the United States and Europe. Even more insistently, it was asked to stimulate economic growth in the industrial countries or help the developing countries progress. If nothing more, it was expected to boost its aid contributions. Otherwise, Japan was condemned to remain an "economic giant and a political midget."

These appeals were very tempting since the Japanese were inately proud of their achievements and secretly wished to enjoy a more elevated standing in the world community. Politicians waxed poetic about Japan's potential role and especially all the good it could do for others. Naturally, there were hopes that such a promotion would also help Japan and let it enter the small circle of leading powers. This was clearly shown by the efforts to join more exclusive groups such as the OECD or the summits of industrialized countries. The highest aspiration for the moment was to obtain a permanent seat in the United Nations Security Council.

Yet, while there has been some upgrading, Japan's position has not undergone a drastic change politically despite four decades of economic progress. This was so noticeable that the Foreign Ministry had to admit in its 1985 diplomatic blue book that the country had not yet become a full-fledged "international state." It was still necessary for Japan to become more "socially, economically and psychologically" open to the world.[20]

The reasons for this are as numerous as they are compelling. The foremost is probably the astounding lack of consensus. The Liberal Democratic Party, as a coalition of factions, found it hard to agree on its own exact position although it was clearly in favor of the American alliance, a defense force and more trade. But it included some with very strong American ties and others who flirted with a Chinese connection or improvement in relations with the Soviet Union. Some were "hawks" on military matters and others "doves." And many followed personal designs that had little in common with the official policy. It therefore appeared so hard to bring the assorted views into line that it was deemed wiser to leave foreign policy sufficiently vague and amorphous to satisfy a majority.

Even this nebulous LDP policy, however, was enough to arouse tremendous acrimony in leftist circles, especially among the Socialists and Communists. They could not agree with the most basic elements of Japan's position. For example, they resolutely opposed the Japan-U.S.

Security Treaty and the Self-Defense Force, which made them antagonistic to an American partnership in general. In fact, they were so adamant that they rarely traveled to the United States. On relations with the Soviet Union and People's Republic of China, they were not much more help. While wanting them as a counterbalance, the JSP and JCP were either too closely aligned or split between pro-Moscow and pro-Peking factions. While favoring closer links with the non-aligned countries of the "South," they had few concrete ideas on how to do this. And their political initiatives were even rarer and more futile.

It was not until the 1980s that something resembling a consensus emerged. This was less a positive adhesion than a passive acceptance of various already old *fait accompli* and a slide toward the center. It was becoming increasingly difficult to arouse Japanese voters against a security treaty that had been around for decades without bringing about any noticeable harm. It was even harder to convince people that Americans were somehow enemies while Russians were conceivably friends. Even the existence of an army was gradually accepted, either as a present need or a temporary expedient until universal peace could be attained. These concessions were made first by the DSP and Komeito and then grudgingly by the JSP and JCP.

Although such a consensus did remove some of the sting from Japanese politics, it was hardly enough to serve as the springboard for a brilliant foreign thrust, let alone notable initiatives. And, even when it did permit enough agreement on the ends to try something, there were serious hitches as regarded the means. Within the LDP, it was not sufficient to approve some common policy because most of the leading politicians acted almost as free agents when it came to foreign affairs. Each had his own views, and expounded them, and thought little of whether they coincided with "official" policy or not. This was further exacerbated by factional quarrels which spread into this field as well. The foreign minister usually came from a different faction than the prime minister and, if for no other reason than to embarrass the latter, could be counted on to push his own views. Meanwhile, some faction head or aspiring prime minister might travel to foreign capitals, meet dignitaries and make speeches, all this with scant concern as to what the government was doing.

The bureaucracy was no more united. Even within the Ministry of Foreign Affairs there were divisions among those in the offices working with the United States and those whose career involved dealing with the Soviets, Chinese or Arabs. To enhance their own status, they tried to improve relations with their clients, although it was usually the much larger American lobby that won.[21] Meanwhile, the Foreign Ministry had to contend with other ministries. Its goals were often at variance with those of MITI or the bureaus handling tasks like finance, air transport and shipping or agriculture. Since so much of its work impinged on economic matters, it was often at odds with ministries that were larger or had better political connections.[22]

Finally, there was considerable discrepancy between the official policies of the bureaucracy and government and what was being done on the spot by business interests. It was often they who caused intractable problems by provoking antagonism against Japan, creating a need to balance economic operations with aid or stirring up trade friction and conflicts. Until they could be brought around to a better disposition, it was impossible to solve much of this. And, since it was a question of exports (and money), they were not always that easy to persuade.

The lack of consensus was only aggravated by certain

cultural traits which made it yet harder to develop a true policy. Decision-making, demanding broad participation and agreement, was repeatedly hampered as efforts were made to get as many as possible to come around. This led to much adjusting of positions and horse-trading among the decision-makers which doubtlessly satisfied their needs. But it made Japanese policy very opaque and uncertain. It was difficult for others to know just what the Japanese wanted. This was not helped by the often ambiguous wording that was used and further confused matters. Finally, these time-consuming activities often took so long that decisions were only ready when they were no longer valid or had been overtaken by events. The outcome was a diplomacy that could be characterized as "ad hoc, reactive and equivocating."[23]

This frequently reduced Japan's foreign relations to a succession of declarations of intent that did little more than express uplifting sentiments or pledge cooperation with actions initiated by others. It was exceedingly rare that the measures were concrete and actually embodied appropriate machinery for ensuring that they were achieved. This was admittedly done for development aid, although even there annual budgets and bureaucratic red tape complicated the process.[24] Ultimately, there were committees of relevant politicians and bureaucrats to look into the major trade conflicts. But there never was a suitable tool for dealing with sensitive political issues, let alone sudden crises.

For Japan to play a leading role, it was not only necessary to have policies but also people who were sufficiently aware of the international scene to contribute to their wise formulation and effective implementation. This was always a glaring gap. There were amazingly few Japanese politicians who had lived abroad for extended periods or done much more than undertake periodic junkets to places of interest. Very few spoke foreign languages, aside from Chinese for some of the older generation and English for younger ones. Even when they traveled, they customarily formed self-contained groups guided and cared for by Japanese posted abroad. This tended to impede rather than encourage any direct or substantial contacts.

Only one prime minister ever showed much concern for foreign affairs during the whole postwar period. That was Yasuhiro Nakasone. Fortunately, some of the potential prime ministers acquired even more familiarity with the situation as foreign ministers, such as Shintaro Abe and Kiichi Miyazawa. But this personal interest was only of so much use since it was still the Foreign Ministry that shaped most policy. Moreover, considering that the electorate did not rate foreign issues very highly and devoting too much time to them actually seemed to work against a politician, there was scant reason to expect dynamic leadership from the top.

Within the ministries there were, of course, many who had gone abroad and they were particularly numerous in the Ministry of Foreign Affairs. But their foreign exposure was often quite shallow. While many knew the language of the country, some did not. And they tended to live in splendid isolation with little contact with the local population and most of that limited to their counterparts and officialdom. Those who were most attuned to local conditions were naturally the MFA employees. But they frequently appeared too accommodating to please the Japanese politicians or public who regarded them with much less trust than, say, MITI officials who were more in touch with domestic conditions and plainly working for the good of Japan.

The situation beyond the government and bureaucracy was no better. Relatively few academics were of any use.

They traveled less than might be expected since the horizons that interested them were local, busily fighting for a place in their own ivory tower. Journalists were stationed in all major capitals and followed crucial events for the rest of the nation. But they were periodically reshuffled and few developed enough expertise. Only the businessmen really spent much time in other countries and knew some of the realities of these places. Yet, their interests were too narrowly commercial for them to grasp the broader implications. Most ordinary folks never went abroad or, if they did, rarely strayed from their organized tours.

In short, Japan had a dearth of people who knew or cared about the rest of the world. This admitted shortcoming was supposed to be overcome by a process of "internationalization." It consisted of Japan becoming more like other countries, for which read "Westernization," and thereby developing a feeling for how others thought and behaved. This, alas, progressed little further than wearing similar clothing and eating similar food or reading poor translations of certain foreign works. Indeed, those who were truly "internationalized" by extensive visits abroad, education in foreign countries or marriage to foreign nationals were regarded with suspicion.

It was out of the question to maintain such an imperviousness to foreign influences and develop a cogent foreign policy. And this led one to wonder whether the Japanese really did want to play a more active role or undergo more internationalization than was absolutely necessary.

Foreign policy was not ranked very highly by anyone in Japan, be it the parties, bureaucracy, business community or ordinary people.[25] It came far behind the only goal the country really threw itself into, namely economic aggrandizement. This was revealed by the puny size of the Foreign Ministry, which had only about half as much staff as far smaller countries like Germany, France or Great Britain. It was shown more strikingly by the paltry funding provided, a mere quarter of those countries on a per capita basis. And it was manifested in the unwillingness to boost development aid or military expenditures. Surely, if Tokyo wanted to play a significant role, this could not be done without an appreciably greater commitment in men and money.

Even more to the point, the Japanese did not really wish to get embroiled in international issues. It was a much more comfortable position to be a bystander and let more intrepid countries intervene when things had to be righted. Such involvement might also lose it friends or, worse, clients. Moreover, to the still insular Japanese, most foreign quarrels and altercations appeared terribly inconsequential. They were indifferent to the problems of others and tended to trace failures to some congenital weakness of the people concerned. Little good could be gained by external entanglements and that is what much of foreign policy was regarded as.

Admittedly, there was some expansion in resources and a heightened show of interest outwardly. Under the surface, however, the public mood was turning in the opposite direction. It was painfully evident that the Japanese were becoming more nationalistic. The war had lowered their esteem to the point that they abjectly followed exotic models and towed the line of alien leaders. With the rise of Japan as an economic power and the decline of their former mentors, it was felt that there was not much to learn. The more the United States and Europe got into trouble and needed Japan, the more Japan questioned whether it should go out of its way to help them. More generally, there was a turning inward to seek the true essence of Japan, an essence it was assumed must be—if nothing else—different. With this, the move toward internationalism was overtaken by the move toward isolationism.

What this means to Japan's partners was most clearly stated by a particularly keen observer, Karel van Wolferen, a long-time journalist in Tokyo. "It would, of course, be extremely difficult for foreign governments to proceed on the assumption that no Japanese government exists which can cope with the external world by changing policies. This is nevertheless a necessary conclusion."[26] And the corollary is that, no matter how the other governments try to influence Japan, by cultivating it or threatening it, by tempting it or bullying it, by using diplomatic language or pounding on the table, they will only induce minimal movement. This will frustrate them more and more and also make it harder for Japan to join the rest of the world.

NOTES

1. Speech to the 84th Session of the National Diet, January 21, 1978. This speech was not atypical of Japanese prime ministers who rarely devoted more than a few sentences to specific issues no matter how significant.
2. The flirtation with an "omnidirectional" policy under Fukuda was so brief and shallow as to be meaningless.
3. Indeed, these disputes were so nasty that it proved impossible to have any American president visit Japan until 1976.
4. Some better examples of the growing literature on this phenomenon are William J. Barnds (ed.), *Japan and the United States, Challenges and Opportunities*, Stephen D. Cohen, *Uneasy Partnership, Competition and Conflict in U.S.-Japanese Trade Relations*, I. M. Destler and Hideo Sato (eds.), *Coping With U.S.-Japanese Economic Conflicts*, and Leon Hollerman (ed.), *Japan and the United States: Economic and Political Adversaries*.
5. Just how cool relations were is shown by the fact that for a decade from the mid-1970s the Soviet foreign minister refused to visit Tokyo and lower level contacts in either direction were few and far between.
6. See R. K. Jain, *The USSR and Japan (1945-80)*

7. Speech to the Diet, October 4, 1977.
8. This was Prime Minister Hayato Ikeda. But the label could have applied equally to other prime ministers and many more ambassadors.
9. See Cohen, *op. cit.*, and Woronoff, *World Trade War.*
10. See Woronoff, *Japan's Commercial Empire.*
11. In addition, they might be construed not as aid but as "neocolonialism." See Jon Halliday and Gavan McCormack, *Japanese Imperialism Today.*
12. Examples of this activity are provided in William E. Bryant, *Japanese Private Economic Diplomacy.*
13. This process can be followed in the Defense Agency's annual *Defense of Japan.*
14. Just how far they were expected to go was predicted with stunning inaccuracy by Albert Axelbank, *Black Star Over Japan.* But his fears of a return of militarism were, and still are, widely shared and often wildly exaggerated.
15. An analysis of Sato's "self-reliant defense" and Ikeda's "minimum defense" can be found in Frank Langdon, *Politics in Japan.*
16. According to Masashi Ishibashi in his book *On Unarmed Neutrality:* "I am perfectly aware that unarmed neutrality is unrealistic. But if the JSP were to lower this policy placard and become 'sensible,' there would then be nothing to stop Japan from turning toward militarism."
17. These surveys were taken by the Prime Minister's Office. The 1984 results showed that 83% recognized the necessity of the SDF, 71% accepted the Japan-U.S. Security Treaty and 72% objected to an increase in the defense budget.
18. As a leading newspaper explained, "by focusing its attention on the 1% of GNP ceiling, the Diet failed to develop constructive debate on what the defense of Japan should be." (*Maininchi*, January 3, 1986.)
19. Unlike countries which can conceive of being drawn into a war, Japan has no real civil defense strategy. It has not built shelters or stored food and medicine. It does not even have contingency plans. It would be incapable of reacting swiftly or effectively in an emergency.
20. For the trends of official foreign policy, albeit in much simplified and glorified form, see the annual Diplomatic Bluebook of the Ministry of Foreign Affairs.
21. On the Ministry's internal operations, see Harrison M. Holland, *Managing Diplomacy.*
22. These complications are highlighted in Chikara Higashi, *Japanese Trade Policy Formulation.*
23. See Seizaburu Sato, "The Foundations of Modern Japanese Foreign Policy," in Scalapino (ed.), *The Foreign Policy of Modern Japan,* pp. 367-89.
24. See Alan Rix, *Japan's Economic Aid.*
25. For the people's views, or lack thereof, see the annual Public Opinion Survey on Diplomacy, Prime Minister's Office.
26. *Far Eastern Economic Review,* May 9, 1985, p. 32.

PART FOUR

THE OUTCOME

10

The Japanese Way

What Japan Is Not

From even the most cursory examination of actual events, it is quite obvious that Japan is *not* a rather large number of things it is widely considered to be. It is not a liberal democracy in which sovereignty emanates from the people. It is not a haven of equality and fairness or a place where the rule of law prevails. It is hardly a classical capitalist economy based on *laissez-faire*. It is not really a nation state in a certain sense. And it is far from being as "modern" as assumed.

First of all, Japan is not a liberal democracy as provided for by its own constitution. The various organs entrusted with running the state have ceded most of their prerogatives to others who were supposed to serve them, although the politicians at least remain part of the *de facto* ruling triumvirate. But much of the power has been usurped by the bureaucrats, which is more than just a coterie of civil servants, and big business, which is more than just a lobby. Meanwhile, the people have lost much of their authority although they are still entitled to vote and, in theory, could reverse the situation overnight. It would thus be ludicrous to speak of government "of the people, by the people and for the people."

Part of this derives from the fact that the political parties, not written into the constitution but so essential as to be presupposed, did not develop along the lines expected. Rather than forming around policies, which would then be debated and distilled into laws, they organized around individuals who then served as brokers for special interests. To be an effective broker, one must hold office, and this explains why politicians would stop at nothing to get elected and reelected. Once having established themselves, and by working with business and pressure groups, they could perpetuate their rule. This allowed one party to seize—and nearly monopolize—power. While not rejected by the popular will, it proved impossible to have a very authentic democracy without some alternation.

Consequently, many of the things that are associated with political parties are lacking or misshappen. Programs and policies, when they even exist, are essentially windowdressing and scarcely affect the politicians' actions. Higher principles and ideologies ceased guiding them which means that opportunistic deals have became the order of the day. As these deals are largely unknown, they cannot be prevented or repudiated by the electorate. Elections thereby degenerate into general plebiscites of satisfaction or dissatisfaction with an unmovable ruling party. As for the candidates, they were chosen on the basis of personality and party affiliation as well as their proven ability to deliver the goods wanted by their clientele. It is the all-important clientele, which reciprocates by providing necessary campaign funds, that has replaced the people as a whole as the source of legitimacy.

Meanwhile, some of the fundamental pillars of democracy (written into the constitution just in case) were deformed and debased. There is very little equality to speak of and this loss is not even severely censured, so natural or inevitable it seems to most. There is plainly no equality between men and women, either in society, the workplace, or politics. There is no more equality between

Democracy in action. The LDP inner circle.

Credit: Foreign Press Center/Kyodo

those who could pretend to be true Japanese and those whose credentials are less impeccable. In the midst of a resurgent gerontocracy, years of experience and age counted more than many other valid attributes and youth is largely marginalized. Finally, those who do not like the system—and cannot do much to change it—are cast aside or ignored.

Even legality became a casualty of the times. It is commonly assumed that a constitutional state must be anchored in legislation which is universally applied to all without special exceptions and which cannot be changed arbitrarily. Yet, while Japan developed a very dense network of laws, it never came to accept the rule of law. For every law, there are numerous exceptions if one is sufficiently important to be exempted or can get away with evading them. Most of the laws are interpreted through regulations that could be applied almost case-by-case. On the other hand, those without influence or on the wrong side of the authorities may suddenly find that even petty rules are being applied with exceptional rigor.

It is often argued that, by imposing its influence over the government, the business community could at least guarantee the existence of a relatively pure capitalist system. Instead, as Adam Smith himself had warned, the worst threats to *laissez-faire* came from businessmen who wished to use the system in their own interests rather than subject themselves to the "economic laws." Thus, in Japan, the system was continuously denatured and distorted so as to defend special interests and help those who were strongest. This was done with the blessing, and often at the behest, of the national bureaucracy which found it could also gain from such intervention.

A closer look at Japan's economy shows that it bears little resemblance to pure capitalism. Most obvious, it was long a closed market and many barriers remain today. Imports were thereby obstructed and, creating a second wall, foreign investment was blocked. Production amount and prices are only partly determined by supply and demand for manufacturing and financial services are regulated by the state, while the rates for agricultural produce are left to political deals. There is no true labor market, since many employees are hired for "life" while others have to accept poor wages just because they work for smaller companies. The most blatant breach is that major companies regularly form cartels, oligopolies and monopolies, and manipulate vast sectors of the economy to their benefit.

In fact, there is even some doubt as to whether Japan could qualify as the most elementary unit of modern polity, a nation state. There is no question that the Japanese are relatively homogeneous with a strong sense of belonging. This is coupled with a very acute sense of exclusion which works against those who are regarded as outsiders. This latter instinct is so much stronger than the former that it inspires a deep feeling of being separate and distinct, indeed, almost unique. This in turn nourishes a feeling of superiority to other races and peoples and an insistence on placing their own interests higher than those of others.

However, this is not enough to guarantee internal cohesion. Despite the verbal patriotism, it is amazing to what extent Japanese society is marked by fragmentation and distances of all sorts. There are huge gaps between men and women, young and old, different geographical regions, urban and rural districts, and so on. This is further compounded by distinctions based on education and even specific schools attended, companies or bureaucracies joined or other professional alignments. Within these already rather small segments, there is further division as factions arise. The strongest unit is always the smallest and the core group always prevails over peripheral units unless a very slow and grudging consensus can be reached with others. Thus, if not for the overriding antipathy to foreigners, which periodically inhibits the internal divisions, it is not certain that the Japanese could muster enough solidarity to hold together.

Finally, it is open to question just how "modern" Japan is. Modernism is hard to determine and has never been adequately defined. Still, it is generally assumed to include many of the characteristics and institutions which were just mentioned as being inadequate, namely, democracy, political parties based on policies, an informed electorate, rule of law, multiple links among citizens and so on. Japan has not quite made the grade here. In addition, its educational system is archaic in many ways, social relations are stilted and hierarchical, there is little thought of leisure or spiritual uplift and not even much concern for a social safety net. The only points where it has clearly caught up are material things like industrial production and technology. This means that many of the manifestations of a "modern" Japan are illusory. These illusions do not always result from honest mistakes or accidental misunderstandings. Rather, they are part of a conscious effort to appear modern. Many of the alien concepts and institutions just referred to were put up for show to make the outside world believe that Japan could follow the latest trends and sometimes even outdo the originators. This is a very old tradition by now and has almost become second nature, so it cannot entirely be regarded as a deliberate attempt to mislead. Nevertheless, it creates an enormous gulf between *tatemae* and *honne,* with superficial appearances far more advanced than reality.

Over the past century or so, part of this sham modernization was induced by Westerners who insisted Japan could not join the "civilized world" as an equal as long as it did not have things like elections, political parties and a formal constitution. The institutions it is working under at present were dictated to it even more directly than those which applied in the prewar period. But the irrepressible urge to excel, to surpass the others, was equally at fault. That sparked the countless local claims that Japan's democracy, capitalism, social compact and so on were not only as good but better than elsewhere. It also resulted in strange Potemkin villages set up to make foreigners believe things were really superlative. This could be a new town, a portopia, a technopolis, an academic city which, although the only of its kind, was supposed to herald a stunning transformation of the nation.

Meanwhile, beneath the surface, things continued much as they had before and there was no brutal rupture with the past. The old ways, like bamboo, were bent but did not break and quickly snapped back once the pressure was removed. In many cases, they blocked or smothered the new ways. Naturally, these outmoded practices, customs, traditions and ticks of daily life formed a none too suitable infrastructure for a borrowed or imposed foreign super-structure. And the indigenous stock was often so different from the transplanted grafts that it rejected this Western-ism and modernism or turned them into something else.

Thus, it proved difficult to introduce democracy, equal-ity, legality, accountability and a host of other things because the necessary foundation was lacking. Even with the best will, neither the emperor nor General MacArthur could decree them into existence as long as certain ele-ments were missing in Japanese culture. These ingredients are so special and crucial that the audacity of trying to create them artificially, or do without, immediately be-comes evident.

One is a solid tradition of individualism since Western-style democracy grows out of an individualistic culture in which man is the center of things and the state is freely created by him and designed to serve him. Not only was there little of this in Meiji Japan, there was not much more sense of human dignity or ability to function in society as an individual just after the war. It is only now, after more than a century, that the stirrings of individualism are being felt. But they are still not embraced or considered healthy and positive by the population at large. In fact, many manifestations appear antisocial and egoistic as, all too often, they are. Without the emergence of a more natural and generally acceptable individualism whole sections of the constitution relating to rights and obligations are hol-low and the essential governmental organs must function awkwardly.

The hitch is not only that the principles and ideals apply

to individuals but that most of them were perfectly alien to Japan when first introduced. Liberty, equality, justice, democracy were so exotic they could not even be rendered in the Japanese language, let alone absorbed in the daily life of the people. Even today, there is far from adequate understanding or widespread approval of many concepts which underlie the constitution. Thus, they are regularly disregarded in society's workings or, if aspired to, create continual friction between politics as practiced and what they should be in theory. This only makes *tatemae* and *honne* more distant.

Moreover, some crucial principles were not even included in the Japanese Constitution (or Western ones) because they were implicitly assumed, like charity and compassion. This implies that beyond any formal rights and obligations, citizens should think of one another and make efforts to help the weaker or needier members. Such virtues are not a prominent part of the Buddhism adopted in Japan, which never stressed benevolence, and even further removed from feudal practices which catered to the strong while keeping the weak in their place. While that could create a sturdy structure, it was not based on active solidarity which becomes necessary under a democratic regime.

Another missing element is rationalism. This, too, is rarely connected with democracy and could not be written into any constitution. Yet, without it, most of the basic organs, and especially the checks and balances that keep the system in equilibrium, cannot function smoothly. It is impossible to run a parliamentary system unless, to some degree at least, participants try to reason logically with one another in order to seek the best outcome for all concerned. If they are moved more by emotional or social motives, such as loyalty to leaders, harmony with sponsoring groups or rigid adherence to an abstract ideology, they cannot think up the compromises that are always necessary.

While much of this can be set down neatly in writing, and the Japanese as dutiful pupils can learn the do's and dont's by rote memory, the whole system crumbles if it goes no deeper. It is indispensable for people to be guided by the principles and ideals to the extent that they hardly realize it and any other behavior appears unnatural or improper. They must also have such a stake in them that they exercise constant vigilence and take decisive action to defend the system. This defense, moreover, cannot be limited solely to cases where democracy works in their favor but also when it goes against them. Alas, such traditions scarcely exist and, for many, winning is all that counts.

No matter how crucial, it would be naive to blame Japan's defective democracy solely on a lack of suitable traditions or an inability to adopt new customs quickly enough. If the will were there, this could have been done. And, in fact, it was done to some degree. But there were certain groups which did not want democracy to take root. They had a preference for the old ways which they found more congenial. They also sought a compliant and obedient citizenry and labor force. Most of all, they wished to preserve whatever exceptional powers they may have possessed. These circles once included the nobility and military. Now it is primarily the politicians, bureaucrats and businessmen. They strove actively, more so than the masses, to stem the tide and turn the nation in other directions. And they got away with it.

That is why the theory of convergence did not work out as expected by most foreign (and many domestic) analysts. Obviously, many of the same influences were at play in Japan as in all other advanced and even developing nations. There was a trend toward urbanization that broke some of the ties with the older, rural society. There was a trend toward nuclear families which undermined the earlier extended family that controlled its members more closely. There was the impact of freer lifestyles and the many new gadgets that made physical labor less important and enhanced the value of knowledge. There was even a new educational system that turned out millions of graduates. Due to this, there was mounting pressure to become "modern," however that may have been defined.

Unfortunately, the exponents of convergence forgot the most important element. These trends and influences were not automatic. They did not spontaneously fashion modern people who lived in modern ways and therefore demanded equality, democracy, leisure, welfare, or anything else. Perhaps they fostered a desire for such things. But citizens did not get them simply for that. They had to fight every inch of the way. And, if they did not, they gained little more or lost some of what they had. This is the story of Japan.

That the Japanese did not reach the mark is not terribly surprising. After all, it took the Western countries centuries to get there, building on ancient Hebrew, Christian, Greek and Roman traditions. It also cost much sacrifice and bloodshed to seize a Magna Carta, overthrow an aristocracy or break away from a colonial empire. The martyrs for democracy were countless and even today those who would give their life for its underlying principles are legion. Despite this, some Western countries relapsed and few other countries managed to join them. Within a world community of over a hundred-and-fifty nations, only about a dozen, or two dozen at most, boast a working democracy.

However, just because Japan did not fully succeed does not mean that it was a complete failure. It was not. It did make some progress over against earlier periods. The various principles and processes were adopted in theory and obtained a degree of validity in practice, despite the many imperfections. While disappointed, the people did not break faith or turn toward a totalitarian system. Democracy was praised throughout society and even won lip service from the very elite that subverted it. In addition, just because this second attempt fell short of the goal does not mean that a renewed effort would not bring Japan yet closer to the ideal.

What It Is

It is much easier to say what the Japanese system is not than what it is. There are many reasons for that. After all, there are few enough analysts who even realize that it is not just a carbon copy of some Western prototype but a full-fledged system with its own institutions and *modus operandi*. Very few studies have therefore been made to see exactly what happens and then delineate the process. And, in some ways most confusing, the Japanese system still has to be described using terms which must either be freshly minted or give a false impression because they are foreign and mean something else in the Japanese context.

Probably the best place to start is not with the basic organs, namely the legislature, executive and judiciary or even the political parties, bureaucracy and business community. The fundamental building block is the small group, a group of individuals revolving around a more dynamic, magnetic or influential person who created it or inherited it. These are relatively autonomous groups which then enter into relations with similar groups to form larger composite units. Once reaching a critical mass, such units can recruit new members and receive a vitality of their own. These composite groups then enter into loose coalitions with others whose assistance they need for one reason or another.

The best example is obviously the ruling party, since it was patched together from several earlier parties and still consists of factions which cooperate and quarrel, merge and split. The socialist parties reacted similarly, and are an even more extreme case. Other parties only showed greater coherence if they were sufficiently small or were created by a higher group. The business community also consists of countless individual companies, joined together in four different federations and dozens of associations. Only the bureaucracy displays more unity, created by the constitution and urged to cooperate by the government. Yet, each individual ministry or agency has its own traditions, recruits its own staff, generates its own policies and, in general, puts its own interests first. What holds each of these units together, more than any internal bonds, is the ceaseless competition with rivals.

When cooperation arises among the small groups, it is often due to a need for allies to overcome such rivals. The LDP's factions hold together because they do not want power to slip into the hands of the opposition. This implies winning elections for which the advice of the bureaucracy and financing of business interests are necessary. While none of the three partners has a great affinity for the others, they realize that they can gain by forming a loose coalition. And it is this combination of the ruling party, an elite bureaucracy and big business, each element of which is actually a composite group, that runs Japan . . . no matter what the constitution may say.

The relations between the threesome vary, as was best shown by the reference to the game *janken*. Sometimes the politicians win due to political power; sometimes the bureaucrats win due to administrative competence; sometimes the businessmen win due to money. It depends on what is needed most and how strong each group is at a given time. But there is some rough parity and a feeling that they must hang together. This does not extend to the rest of the groups in the nation. Some of them are favored with patronage if they can provide the votes or money which are needed by the politicians, such as the agricultural cooperatives and the medical association. Others are placated if they can cause trouble for the politicians or bureaucrats, including some of the "citizens' movements." But there is little concern for the lesser groups that make up society, even such large ones as the trade unions. And certainly no real care is discernable for the sensibilities of the many citizens who have not organized.

This makes a mockery of democracy. For it is power, and not popular support, that determines how each unit is treated. This power springs from various sources. One is the ambit of a group's connections, not in the sense of how many citizens are represented but how much influence it wields. For example, the key question is not how many voted for a party as opposed to how many politicians can be mobilized no matter what the voters wanted. After all, the parties and politicians usually take their decisions without consulting—or even informing—the electorate and the prime minister and ministers owe their position solely to the LDP. The second factor is the extent to which they have grasped the levers of control which can be used to expand their constituency through patronage. That is the crucial tool of the ruling party and bureaucracy. The final element, which often outranks the others, is money. That is the trump card of business.

This sort of arrangement, combined with an exceptional disregard for policy and principles, reduces politics to little more than a division of the spoils. The foremost concern of the politicians and bureaucrats is for their own income and perks and, subsidiarily, to help influential members of their clientele who also pursue primarily material goals. This can be wangled through public works, subsidies, tax incentives or rebates and the like. That is why so much of the action consists of an allocation of resources or, more vulgarly, "pork barrel" politics. The impact of business circles on the process naturally pushes this to an extreme since they manipulate both the politicians and bureaucrats in directions that help them even if it means neglecting the needs or wishes of the general public.

These manipulations and arrangements have created a power structure that is increasingly solid. It is topped by LDP faction heads, senior bureaucrats and leading businessmen. Further down come the other parties, the bureaucracy as a whole and the overall business community, even smaller entrepreneurs. There are also the farmers and medical practitioners and some others. While most workers would not be included, the labor aristocrats employed by major companies are honorary members. Some trade union leaders (as opposed to the rank and file) stand on a lower rung. The base consists of the broad masses of ordinary workers, especially those in smaller firms, women as a whole, youth and the elderly, members of minorities and dissidents.

Until recently, this nascent hierarchy was relatively open since it was possible to enter any of the categories by dint of education or hard work. That is increasingly less possible. Most of the political parties now coopt members and are closed to outsiders otherwise. It is still feasible to get into an elite bureaucracy or company by passing the test, or rather graduating from a good school. But it takes money, either for tutoring or "backdoor entrance," to get in and the best schools are being filled with children from the upper middle class. Meanwhile, wealth has been accumulating and is being left to heirs who start off well above their counterparts. Better families, or those which think they are, have become more careful in screening the marital plans of their offspring. Thus, only four decades after the war, an aristocracy by birth is emerging.

While the group, especially the small group, is the primary building block and unorganized individuals are negligible quantities, there is a definite role for organized individuals. Members of groups are absorbed into the struggle for a share in the spoils to an extent that is rare elsewhere, once again because the distribution is not tempered by higher values. They must do everything they can to enhance the position of their group while undercutting that of competitors and rivals. When they do cooperate, either within the group or with allied groups, this is largely on the basis of an exchange of favors. Already an ancient tradition in Japan, the modern counterpart again differs by being overwhelmingly material, if not cash then certainly a consideration worth cash. This may do away with some of the personal egoism typical of the West, but it is replaced by an equally fierce group egoism.

While leadership is not as brazen or charismatic as in the West, it is just plain silly to assume it does not exist. Every group has acknowledged leaders, be they faction heads, bureaucratic superiors, company presidents and executives and the like. Indeed, even past leaders often hang on creating a multilayered leadership, in the case of former prime ministers who became elder statesmen, chairmen who manipulate presidents and spiritual advisors of religious groups or cultural associations. Even if disguised or attenuated by a consensual approach, there is never any doubt that decisions must be endorsed at the top and the most important points are never really discussed at any other level. A subordinate who should try to step out of line would quickly be put back in place, not only by those who are higher up but those on the same level or further down who feel he should wait patiently like the rest.

While most individuals only act through the group, some exceptional persons play a more autonomous role. They are usually not part of any one group but have privileged access to several. These are the assorted fixers *(kuromaku),* the middlemen, mediators, brokers, string-pullers and so on. Among their functions are to get factions to agree on the party president, encourage companies to collude on output or price or bring politicians into contact with the right businessmen. While of varying degrees of respectability, it would be impossible for Japanese society to operate without them. They have to bridge the gaps that arise between groups due to the intense loyalty and cohesion which prevents them from dealing freely with one another. This is such an enormous and delicate task that it is not always accomplished.

The group-orientation generates so much friction that it is patently absurd to speak of "harmony" as the final outcome. What occurs in practice is an alternance of cooperation and confrontation. The small groups are so compact and inward-looking, and members so used to dealing with one another, that it is admittedly easier to reach decisions. But this makes it much harder to come to any agreement with another group. If they have common interests, or need to cooperate in order to oppose some other coalition, then again the relationship may be smoother. But the further one moves from the small group to larger composite ⸢groups and then broader coalitions, the harder it gets to compromise and the more likely it is that the whole setup will fall apart. Indeed, the most salient features of social life are factionalism and fragmentation. They arise from two basic causes. Small groups will disintegrate if they grow too much or, more frequently, if two or more heirs lay claim to the succession.[1]

Large groups which coalesce from several smaller ones break up when the components fail to get along.

Factions are therefore at the root of many aspects of the Japanese system. Like it or not, they make it extremely difficult to attain any lasting unity and instead foment constantly shifting alliances, marked by divisions and secessions and occasional betrayals. On the other hand, the existence of small groups generates tremendous energy as units pair off and compete with one another to attract more voters, improve services to their clientele, sell more products or do something else better than the next. Positive or negative, this makes the political, social and economic scene particularly agitated and unpredictable. Whenever there is talk of "harmony," it usually means that the stronger side has imposed its will on the weaker for the time being or that the various contestants decided it was not worth fighting it out for the moment since the chances of altering the balance were too slim.

The result of all this is a situation in which might makes right. Those with access to power, either through control of the machinery, patronage or money, freely manipulate the system in their own interest. The only limits to what they can do are the efforts of other groups to counteract them. Any conflicts are thus settled by applying force to see which is stronger or, in an increasingly effete society, cutting deals which preserve the interests of the strong at the cost of the weak. Since the weak have ordinarily accepted this without striking back, there is not even that much crude force involved. To speak of such a solution as "fair shares" is naive since the shares are meted out strictly in accordance with a group's position in the power structure.[2]

Amidst this, there are certain factors which seem to indicate the presence of real potential for democracy. Some of them can be traced to the postwar reforms. Far more actually stem from older traditional techniques. They are best illustrated by the decision-making process, which is sometimes regarded as "bottom-up," and the urge for consensus. Yet, while they do provide some role for broader circles, they are not quite equivalent to democratic procedures.

For example, even if the opinions of all and sundry may be asked, and juniors are expected to draw up detailed proposals, it is always the seniors who decide. Moreover, since the method used to reach a decision is often *nemawashi,* namely personal deals, worked out behind-the-scenes and based on an exchange of favors, this can actually subvert democracy. Consensus, by aiming for the consent of everyone concerned as opposed to a mere majority, creates such an impossible condition that it is rarely attained. So, to fill the gap, it is usually the leaders who negotiate an interim agreement until their followers or the population at large can be brought around to thinking the same way.

Thus, when all is said and done, Japan's present political system hardly resembles the liberal democracy that was introduced by the postwar constitution. Instead, it looks much more like the arrangements that prevailed under the Meiji Constitution and, in some respects, perhaps even the regime that was imposed by the Tokugawa or existed in olden times. It consists of an alliance of three groups which formed to maintain a stable power base and gradually spawned a new social elite. The participation of the masses is sporadic, marginal and ineffectual. The underlying tone is one of support by the followers for any decisions of the leaders, this supposedly for the good of the nation. So much stress is placed on "loyalty," "mutual obligations" and "harmony" that one may well wonder what century this is. Meanwhile, references to "rights," "justice" or "popular sovereignty" are carefully expunged or regarded as faintly seditious.

This is not surprising. After all, this is the soil in which the Western ideas were planted. The parallel system grew more rapidly and vigorously because it drew its sustenance from rich sources of folk customs and local practices. Some of them were clearly feudal, techniques that had been known for centuries before the Meiji Restoration and carried over even after the modernization process was formally inaugurated. This was partially supported by Shinto, the native religion, which could be used to sustain the existing regime. Confucianism retained a noteworthy influence with its stress on hierarchy, proper relations between rulers and ruled and access to status through examinations. But the most decisive element in some ways was probably Buddhism. For it taught people not to be concerned with things of this world and to accept whatever fate held in store.

Still, it must be remembered that these were not the only Japanese traditions. There was much more equality, especially in village society and family life, before strict rules were imposed by the Tokugawa. The idea that followers had to accept control passively was repeatedly belied as one dynasty overthrew the other and then lesser *samurai* from outlying fiefdoms ousted the *shogun* and restored the emperor. Even more striking were the earlier rebellions of peasants or religious sects and then the rise of bourgeois, workers' and peasants' parties in the Taisho era. Women were not always quite as subservient and suffragists fought under the harshest conditions.[3]

So, one must be very careful about claiming that the present Japanese conduct arises out of "typical" traditions. What actually happened is that the ruling classes selected those customs and values which served their

Japan's last best hope. Nakasone—samurai or savior?

Credit: Foreign Press Center/Kyodo

purposes and tried to inculcate them further. Those which were harmful or simply spurious were denied or attributed to foreign sources. With time, and certain subtle pressures, most Japanese came to believe that they were acting as they should rather than as they were coached and brainwashed to behave. Such manipulation, by the way, is another time-honored tradition.

Rectifying Names

One of the most intriguing events in the declining Tokugawa era was an intellectual movement that sprang from the Confucian urge for a "rectification of names." The country was ostensibly ruled by an unbroken line of emperors. Yet, the emperor had no power. The *shogun*, who replaced him, was supposedly the "barbarian-subduing generalissimo." Yet, he failed to repel the Westerners. The *samurai* had ceased being warriors and become petty officials while the merchants, theoretically on the lowest rung, usurped some of the power and prestige. Terms no longer coincided and functions were misplaced. The world had become unhinged and order could not be restored until this terminological confusion was corrected.

As the postwar phase draws on, it is hard to repress a similar queezy feeling that words are meaningless or misleading and that the functions they should denote have been radically altered. This is only aggravated by the fact that most of the words used now have been borrowed from alien languages, where they described alien models, and rarely fit the indigenous phenomena properly. This applies, alas, to most of the key expressions in this book or any other written about the political system, whether in a foreign language or Japanese. To restore intellectual order, it is again necessary to rectify names. This is a more difficult task than ever since we have gotten so used to these words that we hardly notice how unsuitable they are. Still, there is no excuse for not making a try!

It is obvious that the Japanese system is not a textbook example of "democracy." There is no separation of powers and, in fact, the three essential organs hardly exist and have been replaced by others. Most important, the role of the people is minimal. This might make it a "semi-democracy" or "half democracy," as many local scholars claim. On the other hand, it is clearly not a "dictatorship." There is no one person in charge but a multitude, more even than is generally qualified as a "collective leadership." But they are not so numerous that they cannot get to know one another personally and cooperate informally. Perhaps the best available term is control by an "oligarchy," all the more so since this form of rule already existed in Meiji days.

However, this time the oligarchs are acting less on their own behalf than as representatives of the loose communities from which they emerged, basically the ruling party, bureaucracy and big business. This means that they could be replaced by others, either if their action were disowned or they simply aged and were succeeded by their juniors. To some, such an organization smacks of "corporatism." But that was an artificial structure created to support specific regimes while this has arisen more spontaneously and does not owe allegience to anything higher. Given its strong economic penchant, perhaps we should maintain the commercial analogy and speak of "Japan, Inc." until something better comes along.

Some would call this a "class" society.[4] But the three principal categories are still relatively open and their members are only differentiated by having opted for one career or another. Moreover, their leaders are not following broader "class" interests so much as narrow and practical professional ones. In addition, this overlooks the fact that the operative units are the small component ones which authorize the action of those above. Since small groups are so pervasive, and so powerful, there is good reason to speak more of "small-groupism."

Although dispersed rule, divided between loose communities that are further broken down into small groups, would seem to preclude a national "totalitarianism" or "fascism," it does generate other forms of "authoritarianism." There is no doubt that the pressure to comply with group decisions is tremendous within every social unit. Most striking is probably the regimentation of factory workers. But nobody is really left much latitude and instead has to fit into patterns that crush individualism and impose a conformity that scarcely exists in many dictatorships. However, since much of this is self-inflicted, one might best reapply the phrase "tyranny of the majority."[5]

While small groups can cooperate, they can also compete with others, including those they supposedly cooperate with. The friction and animosity this generates makes any reference to a "non-adversarial" society ludicrous. At most, it is a non-confrontational one since efforts are made at reaching a solution without use of verbal or physical violence, although that is not always feasible.[6] Indeed, if anything can explain both the brilliant achievements and the abysmal failures of Japan, it is this infernal rivalry. That is why it is viewed with very mixed feelings by Japanese who complain of, more often than they praise, the "excessive competition" (kato kyoso).

So much loose talk of "cooperation" inevitably exudes warm and human connotations which are probably misplaced in this context. Little of this is done to pursue common goals or implement policies of general concern. It is much more a question of giving those who support the politicians what they want in their own, usually egoistic interest. That is perhaps why Nobutaka Ike wryly described the system as "patron-client democracy."[7] Aside from being a rather odd mixture, this overlooks the fact that since then the clients have largely reversed the relationship and it is the patrons who have to do their bidding. This might make it a "client-patron" establishment.

The "laws" governing this society are amazingly lax, subject to interpretation and exceptions, or simply replaced by something less formal like regulations and administrative guidance. This, in the Western context, would mean accepting arbitrary rules. But it is not quite as arbitrary as that since the decisions depend on the relationship between those concerned and this, in turn, on the power structure or previous relations. While it can never be said with full assurance how things will turn out, there is usually a pretty good idea of what will and will not be permitted because one knows who is involved. Thus, above law, one must place the person (in the Japanese sense) and perhaps speak of the "rule of personal relations."

That most of the action is directed toward material and concrete advantages can probably be traced back to "feudalism," as is done by many intellectuals. This seems to explain as well the role of local dignitaries or company executives in mobilizing the votes of their followers and the granting of gifts that accompanies some of this. Still, while an exchange of favors is quite traditional, the use of money to buy power is an aberration. But, it has become so widespread as to justify complaints of "plutocracy" and "money politics."

Socially, there is no doubt that, in addition to the feudal elements, there is much that can be traced to Confucianism. This includes the distinctions of sex, age and social condition. It undergirds the social hierarchy and explains why the primary point of entry is an examination for which no sacrifice is too great. Philosophically, it provides a fulcrum for attempts to reinforce the loyalty of employees or heighten the diligence of workers. Indeed, there is almost no end to the fine virtues that can be borrowed. But it is no longer an integral worldview based on the words of the sage so much as a collection of precepts from which those in power can pick and choose. This would make the present society "pseudo-Confucian" at best.

Perhaps the most unexpected social characteristic, notable because it has long been eclipsed in other places where it once existed, is the respect for elders. This comes both from Confucianism and indigenous customs. But its renaissance in the twentieth century is much more a result of careful nuture by those who run parties, bureaucracies and companies in such a way that higher priority is given to loyalty and stability than ability and drive. Only through an arrangement where batches of employees are taken in annually and promoted almost automatically could such a feature survive. After forty years of postwar practice, it is impossible to speak of the Japanese system without mentioning "gerontocracy."

As for the economy, there has been much debate as to what form it has taken. It is patently not "capitalist" as understood by the classicists. But it is not "communist" or "socialist" nor, despite the considerable coordination, "collectivist" or "communal." After all, businessmen run the economy and not politicians or bureaucrats, let alone workers. And most of the deviations arise from collusion between companies. Under such conditions, this anomoly might well be labelled "monopoly capitalism," as the Marxists would have it. But even then there are quibbles. For most major companies no longer belong to capitalists but to other companies or to one another and, thereby, to those who operate them. This wrinkle might be regarded as "managerial capitalism."

Putting all this together, one comes up with . . . a blank. There is simply no other system that is quite like it. There are some parallels elsewhere, but very partial ones. And the greatest similarities are not with other countries but with earlier eras. This inspires untiring efforts to prove that Japan is somehow special, that it runs by its own rules and cannot be compared to others. In such a vein, it was suggested that one speak of "Nihonism." It would perhaps clarify things to refer to Nihonistic democracy, or Nihonistic capitalism or Nihonistic society. But, in so doing, one should not go to the extreme of assuming that the system is unique. Despite all the differences, there are commonalities which make it merely a variation on a theme and not a completely discordant note.

This is admittedly just a poor beginning to the sweeping rectification that is necessary. It would take hordes of scholars to coin the terms for countless other formations and concepts not even mentioned here, like government, political party, politicians, platform, electoral campaign and many others. Until this is done, words should be used very cautiously and conceding that they may not really describe what they should.

Indeed, since words are so treacherous, it is far better to adopt the approach that was attempted here, namely to carefully explain what happens, and how, and why, so that the subject may define itself through its behavior.

NOTES

1. See Chie Nakane, *Japanese Society*.
2. A system based on "fair shares" is one of the more curious conclusions drawn by Ezra Vogel, *Japan as No. 1*, pp. 97-130.
3. See Mikiso Hane, *Peasants, Rebels and Outcastes*.
4. For an interesting attempt at defining Japan's class structure, see Rob Stevens, *Classes in Contemporary Japan*.

5. Some in a position to compare regard the degree of conformity imposed on the average Japanese citizen as far greater than is expected of people in the Soviet Union or China.
6. For examples of conflicts and forms of resolution, see Ellis S. Krauss (ed.), *Conflict in Japan*.
7. See Nobutaka Ike, *Japanese Politics, Patron-Client Democracy*.

11
Losing Control

A Country With Problems

Arguably, it does not really matter so much whether the political system is truly Western-style democracy or some Japanese variant, or perhaps not even democracy at all, as long as it works to the satisfaction of those concerned. It has often been said that the Japanese system is supremely efficient due to close relations and smooth cooperation between the major actors. It has also been claimed that Japan was able to overcome a vast number of problems which fazed lesser countries. And it is assumed that the goals pursued must be popular due to a consensual approach. But it would be very mistaken to assume that Japan is a country without problems.[1]

Many of the problems arise because so much effort has been devoted to a rather narrow range of activities, most of them economic. Naturally, as long as the government's role is restricted, it can accomplish more and perhaps prove superior within this artificially constricted scope. But it is bound to be less effective as soon as it strays beyond its traditional boundaries and what is happening outside the pale may be even worse. Thus, to see how well the country is doing, it is absurd to ape the Japanapologists and start with the economy. It makes much more sense to consider what has been neglected.

Due to the insatiable demands to improve the nation's

productive machinery, it was necessary to overlook most alternative forms of spending. One, the most evident, was social overhead. As noted, the Japanese lack some of the most common amenities, including such elementary things as proper sewage, paved roads with sidewalks, parks and gardens, and so on. There is a shortage of schools, hospitals, libraries and museums. And, most appalling, the housing situation is disastrous as regards number of units, size, quality, location and cost. In this category, Japan tends to lag behind most other industrial countries, including some which are nowhere near as advanced.[2]

Looming up as the most serious future handicap is a lack of welfare. This applies to health insurance, social security and most particularly care for the aged. Once again, the quantity and quality are inadequate to meet the existing or prospective requirements. Worse, at the very time when the needs are rising sharply, the coverage and benefits are being cut back rather than expanded. This is bound to make life for a large portion of the population extremely painful and could even result in more noticeable forms of misery, as shown by the appearance of derelicts, bag ladies and the like.

Even in the one area where most progress was made, industrial production, the efforts were grossly skewed toward "modern" sectors. Those which did not qualify were left on their own and many suffered. More generally, small firms and their employees fared very poorly while some suppliers and subcontractors were crudely squeezed. Female workers, a swelling contingent, were used and then discarded, only to be rehired subsequently and paid obscenely low wages. Those who could not work were of slight value in the scheme of things and there was little concern for their fate.

Moreover, and this cannot be overlooked even in the most materialistic society, the excessive stress on work and production made it difficult to lead a normal life. Most people simply did not have the time to pursue personal interests. Leisure was inadequate to mix with one's family or engage in community activities, let alone to heed an inner call. While people became richer financially and purchased more consumer goods, they still remained poor as regards culture, religion or just friendship. This affliction was worst for the younger generations which rejected traditional morality and often replaced it with materialism as ideals and idealism were crushed in the grind.[3]

Japan's external relations were stunted as well. Its contacts with foreign countries were almost exclusively through trade and investment with economic exchanges largely replacing human ones. This eventually created not harmony but friction and conflicts, with an ever lengthening list of partners aggrieved by the continuing trade deficits and unwillingness to open its markets or offer greater assistance. Meanwhile, the number of close and reliable friends and allies has shrunk. This would be most worrisome if ever the fragile peace were to collapse and it became necessary to defend the country. For Japan was in no position to meet its own security needs.

These are all glaring lacks and omissions that will have grievous consequences in the years to come. But they might conceivably have been justified if at least the economic gains were sufficient and unquestioned. Even that is no longer the case.

Economic progress has always been measured in productive terms such as the amount of output, quantities exported, gross national product, and so on. On the basis of such a materialistic yardstick, there was reason for contentment during the 1950s and 1960s since all these indicators rose swiftly. Japan could proudly boast of a growth rate that often exceeded 10%. However, in the 1970s, it slumped drastically and growth is expected to be slow throughout the 1980s and beyond. Although the projected 3-4% is nothing to be ashamed of it will not bring much improvement. Thus, while desperate efforts are made to boost production (and other concerns are ignored), the rewards may no longer justify such exorbitant sacrifices.

Slow growth has already taken its toll in straitened living standards. Companies reacted by reducing wage hikes and this resulted in rather negligible increases in disposable income for most families. People therefore purchased less and sometimes saved more. By buying less, consumption has inevitably failed to replace exports as the primary source of growth. This further depressed a stagnant economy where it is hard to find enough jobs to accommodate the labor force, including women who have to work to supplement family income. Meanwhile, with tax revenue growing slowly, the government resorted to deficit financing and thereby created a raging fiscal crisis that shows no sign of abating.

Thus, over four decades of conservative rule, the country has passed from a relatively dynamic, bouyant and flourishing economy to one in which most people's lives are hardly improving and some, especially the elderly, face very painful constraints and hardships. At this point, economic issues blend into political ones, for most of the present difficulties can be traced to the only party that has been in office most of this time. And it is here that the lack of political advancement becomes most baffling.

Although Japan's economic machinery expanded, and lifestyles evolved, the political system hardly changed at all. The country is still run by relatively small, inward-looking and almost closed elites which fail to notice the trials and tribulations of the broad masses. Much of the political action takes place behind-the-scenes in a process where crucial decisions are not even taken by elected officials. The average citizen's fate is affected more by what bureaucrats and key businessmen decide is appropriate. It might be possible to influence them through the political machinery. And, in theory, the Liberal Democratic Party could be chucked out. But would the opposition do any better?

While the masses of ordinary people were already upset about the material problems, the lack of housing, leisure or job security, more and more were becoming annoyed by the rampant political abuses. They were tired of ritualistic elections that brought no real change. They had enough of incompetent or dishonest politicians and bureaucrats. And they were frustrated by their inability to impose their will on the nation's leaders. That was not assuaged by periodic gestures, such as Prime Minister Nakasone's promise to conduct "easily understandable politics" and "politics addressing the people." Nor was it erased by fervant claims that people were the center of all concern, as in this gambit by Nakasone.

"Above all, I want to strive for the creation of a society in which people's hearts are in harmony, a society which abounds in civility and love. I especially want to bring the light of politics into the home, and I place the highest priority on the home. Wherein lies actual happiness for the people? It is when the family hurries home and, joined around the dinner table, they are together in an aura of contentment. Is it not this indescribable feeling of love which is the very essence of happiness?"[4]

For this only made the rhetoric shriller and more overpowering and also more unreal. In fact, despite ages of practice, many Japanese were getting sick of the official *tatemae* and irked by its clash with an increasingly uncomfortable *honne*. The appearance, which everyone was expected to convey, was a happy and prosperous Japan united in its glorious march into the future. The reality was a nation with nagging problems, few of which showed any sign of going away. The appearance was a political system based on democracy, where the people reigned supreme. The reality was almost its opposite, an infernal machine used by the powers-that-be to control and direct the population.

This rather sorry state, which can be demonstrated very readily with economic statistics and a cursory reading of the newspapers, is no secret to the population. Although there is a definite preference for considering the more pleasant side of things, the citizenry is acutely aware of the problems and does not regard them as theoretical but ever more as personal threats. This can be seen from any number of polls and surveys taken by the government, media and others. In addition to often worried responses, there has been a trend for the reactions to become more negative with time.

In a survey by the Prime Minister's Office, more than half of the respondents felt that the national administration did not reflect the popular will while only somewhat over a quarter felt that it did. About a third of the people thought the nation was proceeding in an undesirable direction as opposed to somewhat less who thought it was moving in the right direction. Among the reasons for indicating that it was heading in the wrong direction, the most prominent were the recession and rising prices, defense policy, the social climate, education and social welfare.[5]

Regarding the narrower framework of economic activities, a survey conducted by the Economic Planning Agency came up with similar results. It asked a simple and straightforward question: "Is your life getting better than before?" Over half of the respondents answered "not at all" or "maybe not" and such pessimistic views have been expressed for years already. The causes for this negative attitude were many, the main ones being discontent over prices, tax inequality, insufficient savings, distrust of the pension system and concern about employment after retirement.[6] Meanwhile, income inequality began growing and more people felt they were no longer "middle class."

More striking even than the dissatisfaction with the present situation is the mounting anxiety about the future. Another survey of the Prime Minister's Office revealed very widespread misgivings about the course things were taking. Of those polled, 43% replied that society would become dimmer and only 12% that it would become brighter; 42% replied that it would become unstable and only 11% that it would become stable: 23% replied that it would slow down and only 7% that it would become more affluent. Even more astounding was the outcome of a comparative poll conducted by Gallup International. It noted that only 6% of the Japanese questioned were hopeful about what was going to happen between then and the year 2000 while 64% were fearful, the worst showing of ten industrialized nations.[7]

However, just because the system was no longer working to the satisfaction of large numbers of ordinary citizens does not mean that it displeased the elite. While the masses complained of less power, income and welfare, this was counterbalanced by increased prestige and authority as well as wealth and security in the three groups that formed the establishment. Big companies continued to prosper, top bureaucrats had little worry about the future, and LDP politicians seemed assured of more years in office. This was not only, or even largely, because they had proven their ability and value but because they controlled the means for redistributing any benefits in their own interest and passing the losses on to others. If this elite had been just a few persons or a specific class, it would have been under greater pressure. But it was reasonably broad. And those at the top were wise enough to let some of the spoils trickle down to others, such as subcontractors of major companies, lesser state employees, politicians in general, farmers and some professionals.

Moreover, the fact that things were difficult and hardship more visible did not really disturb them. From time immemorial the Japanese masses had been easier to manipulate, and responded best to their leaders, when they were under pressure. This was so evident that, even when there was no reality to it, politicians and managers invoked imaginary dangers or created fictitious enemies in order to restore order in the ranks and revive the fighting spirit. If anything, they had been dismayed by the relaxation and indiscipline that spread with growth and prosperity. Now they were secretly relieved that their underlings were being reminded that life is full of challenges which must be responded to with unity and loyalty.

The Machine Jams

At this point, as so many others during the story, it is tempting to quote the old saying that "people get the kind of government they deserve." If the Japanese were willing to accept control by an elite even when they had the power to vote them out, and could not see that the elite had taken advantage of them, they had no right to aspire to more than second-rate citizenship and a life of drudgery. The reproach is entirely justified and pity is out of place. But it does not alter the fact that Japanese society was so constructed that the outcome was anything but surprising. Ancient customs and traditions that could not be discarded and social patterns and hang-ups among the leadership and masses prompted them to take certain steps even when they were not really convinced of their validity. The machine, once set in motion, was hard to point in some new direction, let alone put into reverse.

Some of the reasons are structural. As shown repeatedly in this book, the various components of the establishment interact with one another and reach understandings when each has something to gain. Otherwise, they tend to block one another and the result is a stalemate. During the 1950s and 1960s, there was plenty of leeway for adjustments in an expansive economy with few social or political problems. In the radically different climate of the 1970s and 1980s, the sparring can go on indefinitely as urgent decisions are left in abeyance for years (and even decades). But the problems do not go away. They fester and swell and make it yet harder to reach an acceptable compromise. This odd machinery which keeps turning without generating solutions was astutely analyzed by Karel van Wolferen.

"Japanese social and political order is maintained by a system with semi-autonomous components, each endowed with discretionary powers to undermine the state. These components—certain groups of bureaucrats, some political cliques, clusters of industrialists and many lesser groupings such as the police, the judiciary and the gangsters—are involved in a continuous balancing act with one another. A hierarchy, or rather a complex of overlapping hierarchies, is maintained, but it has no top. There is no supreme institution with ultimate jurisdiction over the others. And thus there is no place where, as Harry Truman would say, the buck stops. The buck keeps circulating."[8]

Other causes are social or psychological. And, in a crisis situation, the drawbacks only become more acute and overwhelming. This arises almost automatically from the acceptance of a consensual approach. While the original decision-making process is inordinately complicated and time-consuming, this is nothing compared to the difficulties of seeking later modifications, adjustments or reversals. One explanation is that a fundamental rule of the game is that once the consensus is reached, the issue is settled and no longer thought about rationally. Instead, everyone is expected to throw himself wholeheartedly into the struggle and persevere. Questioning the consequences of such action is tantamount to treason.[9]

Even if it were agreed to review the consensus for some reason, it is now necessary to place blame for any possible mistake. This is not easy under any conditions. It is even harder when most important figures were involved in forging the decision and even more so when their further support is desired. Also, when the original decision was taken, the potential advantages were still uncertain. If the compromise has to be altered, those who benefited will not wish to give up what they have for what, in times of difficulty, may be very theoretical gains.

Moreover, to revise a consensus and get society moving in another direction, some form of leadership is essential. But the nation's leaders have undergone a remarkable sea change since the early postwar period. That witnessed the rise of younger bureaucrats and businessmen who replaced their purged seniors. Even many of the politicians were new in the sense that they had not been prominent in the earlier parties or came in from the bureaucracy or grass-roots. These men often got where they were by personal ability and drive. They knew what they wanted and did not hesitate to press for it. At present, more and more of the politicians, bureaucrats and businessmen are the successors of such people. The way in which they rose was not to show ability or initiative but obedience and loyalty.

Meanwhile, the style of leadership has evolved dramatically from the early period when forceful individuals shaped the parties, cabinets, administrations or companies to their own needs. To keep these ever larger, ever more structured and institutionalized behemoths moving, it was necessary to develop a more collective-type leadership and to spread responsibility and participation wider. This hastened the move to consensus-type arrangements which became typical of Japan. Admittedly, it is a consensus of those who count and not everyone. But, with time, the number of those consulted—and who can block the process—has augmented notably.

The heaviest weight, however, came from the accentuation of gerontocracy. It is not that seniority has grown stricter or stronger; it is probably less rigid than in the past. The big difference is rather that today's elders live much longer than their predecessors. When most people only reached the age of forty or fifty, seniors were just one generation older than juniors, who were still quite spry and adaptable when they took over. Now, with a much longer life expectancy, leaders tend to stay on into their seventies and eighties. They are two or more generations older then the bulk of the population. And new leaders only arise when they are already quite old men in their fifties and sixties.

These various factors, plus others referred to before, combine to make the present leadership one of the least dynamic and innovative that can be imagined. "Leaders" not only lack the essential training, they have been formed essentially as followers and those who showed some sign of genuine ability may well have been discarded. Groups are increasingly timorous and afraid to entrust their fate to strong hands. When occasionally a more forceful person sticks out, he is often hammered back in. Having waited so long to rise to a position of authority, the ultimate heirs are usually out of touch with present needs and realities.

Entrusting Japan's future to the past. Yet another cabinet of dreary old
men.

This already unfavorable general situation is further
aggravated by certain specific conditions.

One fundamental problem derives from the fact that,
while the business community is still relatively virile and
aggressive, the politicians and bureaucrats have become
weaker and more docile. They are manifestly unable to
defend their own turf and put the businessmen in their
place and, caught up in their internal affairs and rivalries,
too busy to do much more than perpetuate their rule. But
they do not really fulfill even their restricted functions

very competently or efficiently. This obviously makes it harder to introduce the necessary reforms.

It also highlights the rather odd combination of a "hard" economy arising out of a "soft" polity and dominating it. Since the business leaders know best where they want to go, there is reason to believe that they will continue counselling the same direction as before even if it is to the disadvantage of a large portion of the population. Only a rebirth of political will and foresight, conditioned by greater respect for popular sovereignty, could reverse the situation and bring about a change in tack. But such an outcome can hardly be expected.

It is already unlikely because the politicians still have no clear idea of which policies they want, let alone of which policies might be more appealing to the population and also workable. It is ruled out even more categorically by the continued supremacy of the Liberal Democratic Party. In a system with an alternation of parties in office, the new government can always blame past blunders and failures on its opponents and proceed to make changes. The LDP has no one to blame mistakes on other than itself. True, there are different prime ministers, but their predecessors are still around and too many decisions result from consensus to be attributed to anyone in particular.

So, change emanating from within the elite is not very likely. Instead, it would have to be promoted by a counter-vailing force, some group or combination which could replace or at least influence the ruling triumvirate of politicians, bureaucrats and businessmen. In previous regimes, this existed in the form of the military, aristocracy, advisors or the emperor himself. But there is no counter-pole in present-day Japan and little chance that one will emerge in the foreseeable future. The only bodies that can influence policy are not genuine power centers but mere pressure groups whose sole desire is to obtain backing for their vested interests.

While heightened influence of the opposition parties, or a possible coalition and a more improbable replacement, cannot be rejected out of hand, they do not seem imminent. In addition, even if they came about, it is uncertain how much change they would bring. Junior partners in an LDP coalition would only have a small voice. And the basis for such cooperation would have to be general agreement on policy, namely a consensus not far removed from the present one. This is a consensus which even the Socialists and Communists are gradually approaching at the very time when what Japan needs most is a real alternative.

This shows the fatal drawback to so many of Japan's alleged virtues, such as loyalty, harmony and dedication. They tend to inhibit the generation of alternatives which must be sought elsewhere. Alas, in a nation based on relatively closed, inward-looking elites, not much heed is paid to what others have to say. Thus, dissidents and rebels, poets and philosophers, or merely scribblers and "critics" whose vocation it is to come up with new ideas often remain voices in the wilderness.[10] It takes a very long time for them to attract attention. If what they suggest is too discomforting it will probably just be ignored. If what they suggest sounds more acceptable, it will probably be diluted and then absorbed into the consensus.

Youth has always provided a welter of new ideas. They were not always wise or useful, but they were at least different. Such ferment arose in the 1960s and students, despite their excesses, energetically contributed to exploring other paths. Nowadays, young people are hardly active in any discernable manner on the social, political or intellectual scene and have apparently become as conservative as the rest. What effect this will have is uncertain. But it is already distressing to know that those who rise to the top in the more distant future may be even more devoid of principles and idealism than today's leaders. The final source of new ideas is the outside world. While Japan remains stable and increasingly immutable, there is an incredible profusion of ideas and concepts which could suggest other solutions. These ideas, however, are often too contradictory and sometimes also too confusing to be positively received. Some specific points, such as additional trade liberalization or more development aid, may be accepted if foreign powers exert enough pressure. But the ascendency of the outside world is no longer sufficient to incite a thoroughgoing rethinking or reshaping of policy.

Only one other protagonist remains, the population at large. There is little chance that it would react sharply enough to impose new policies or philosophies on a government it has failed to direct for decades. Nor is it likely to switch parties. For, as is painfully evident, the people as a whole have become increasingly conservative. This is not a move to the right so much as to the center. Everyone is bunching together in the middle and avoiding extremes, right and left, whether it concerns economic, social or political action. This induces a preference for well-trodden ways and a fear of new and uncertain paths. There is no stomach for experiments, adventures or risks. The popular attitude can best be summed up as a desire for continuity and an unwillingness to "rock the boat."

So, Japan is again locked into "single-minded pursuit" in which one set of goals prevails over, and effectively stifles, all others. In the past, this has happened for national unity, loyalty and stability, international prestige and colonial empire. Now it is directed toward a more pedestrian, and theoretically more rational, drive for economic advancement. This time as we̶̶̶ ̶̶̶̶̶fillment has proven more elusive than expected and remains just beyond the reach of those who run the state. In fact, the more they strive for it, the more remote it becomes.

For the various reasons mentioned, it is very hard to change either the goals or the tactics. Instead, the elite resorts to other means of hiding any failures or making people feel that it has been a resounding success. None of them are very different in form from what leaders the world over do when in the same position. But they often have a more pervasive influence on the Japanese since they tie up with certain traditions and mental fixations.

In a variation on the "big lie," the elite simply denies that anything has gone wrong. (Since this involves not just individual fibs but an all-embracing web of pretensions, it might be called the "big *tatemae*.") Politicians, proudly make speeches which revel in a bright today and more brilliant tomorrow, only tacitly admitting difficulties by stressing how they will quickly be taken care of. The bureaucrats glibly present a highly attractive scenario of how Japan "overcame two oil crises to attain stable growth." They also speak of an affluent society in which consumption is sluggish because people already have everything they want. The businessmen are the only ones who hint at more ominous threats, but that is mainly to convince the population to restrain its expectations and make even greater sacrifices.

Then, in a variation on "bread and circuses," the establishment stages extravaganzas to demonstrate to the world, and its own citizens, just how much progress has been accomplished. This started with the Osaka Exposition in 1970, which perhaps had some justification. But it was followed endlessly by other shows like the Okinawa Ocean Exhibition and Kobe Portopia. The latest is the Tsukuba display of high tech prowess. Meanwhile, every petty advance is blown up to make it look unique and extraordinary, be it for an academic city, a new media community or a technopolis. That they offer little more—and sometimes less—than quite ordinary events abroad is hardly noticed in the barrage of publicity. In addition, it is conveniently forgotten that nothing much resulted from earlier ambitious programs that promised garden cities, regional plazas or a remodeling of the archipelago.

An even more impressive campaign is launched to persuade the population to look forward to an imaginary future when all problems will have disappeared due to the strivings of the nation and the marvels of modern technology. This future is not the next ten or twenty years. It is not even strictly the year 2000. For these visions of approaching bliss are englobed in a concept of the 21st century which is insistently pressed by the leadership as if today's cares and woes are insignificant or must be borne bravely for the sake of a better life to come.[11] One prime minister after the other proclaimed his vision of this brave new world, although none bothered explaining how Japan would get there. This quote from Prime Minister Nakasone is just one among many.

"Years have passed since it was first suggested that the 21st century would be the Japanese century, but I believe there are three conditions which must be fulfilled before we can truly realize that hope. The first is whether Japan can continue to earn the recognition of the international community as a cooperative and trustworthy country, the second whether the Japanese people can maintain their diligence, and the third whether we can create a society which, in addition to its material affluence, treasures the sublimity of man's spirit, has a respect for civility and the other person, maintains its unity, and wins the respect of the world's peoples. I know that times are difficult. Yet a brighter future lies ahead. I see in the distance a vision of

Japan as a richly verdant Pacific archipelago off the east coast of Asia, the home of a new culture integrating the best of East and West."[12]

Obviously the most effective stratagem remains a slighting reference to the rest of the world. If there are problems in Japan, there are also problems elsewhere. In fact, or so it is said, things are far more distressing in other countries and Japan has fared much better. This is not always true. But it does not matter as long as the establishment controls the media and the media continue to paint a very bleak picture of what is going on in other parts of the world.

These are patently efforts to deny or run away from the problems rather than to tackle them. For this the leadership should be criticized. But the citizenry does not really bother because there is a deep streak in the Japanese character that makes the populace highly susceptible to such gambits. Most people do not like to think of unpleasant things and prefer to dress them up and make them look better. There is a sneaking feeling that talking about problems only makes them worse or, at any rate, makes those concerned feel yet unhappier about their sad fate. This reaches its paroxysm in the still irradicable conviction that Japan is inherently different, that it does not obey the same historic laws as other countries, that it will always come out on top. Somehow there will be a divine intervention, a heavenly wind (*kamikaze*) or another miracle to solve its problems.

Thus, the machine rolls on and on, seemingly unstoppable, in a direction that appears to be preordained because it can scarcely be altered by human intervention. But that is not truly the case. Any number of other openings exist and, with enough exertion, the machine could be turned around or brought to a halt. This, however, calls for action, not blind or sporadic action but conscious and sustained action. That, alas, is not part of the cultural heritage while a dose of fatalism is. As long as people think nothing can be done, that it is inevitable, *shikata ga nai* . . . , then it truly is.

The Impending Crisis

Fortunately, most Japanese reflect, the system appears to be solid and the elite well in control. In fact, the system is too solid and the elite too well in control to permit the adjustments which are necessary to adapt to major changes in the surrounding environment. Strength thereby becomes a weakness and the system turns brittle because it prevents many essential acts which could release some of the stresses and strains. Instead of offering hope to those who are not pleased with the situation, it makes them assume that no possible improvement can be obtained from the formal political machinery or the existing remedies.

The result is an endless series of minor and dispersed events, often enough involving such petty or innocuous matters that they pass unnoticed, which take place under the surface. Since they usually occur within social categories that are too weak or indecisive to buck the establishment, they are not deemed worthy of attention. And sometimes they can hardly be perceived because they consist of an internalized reaction which barely affects formal behavior, such as a mood of indifference, abstention or disaffection. This recourse is not unlike that of the crypto-Christians who had to renounce their principles publicly but kept the faith in secret or untold numbers of common folks in Tokugawa days who went through all the motions but hid their true feelings.

Politically, the response of many citizens has been to reduce their involvement in the formal machinery of party politics. Very few go out and campaign for politicians and policies and not many become party members even when the fee is nominal. It has become harder to turn out the vote and voters must be tempted and cajoled to back certain candidates. But they have not sought alternative methods either. The earlier student and leftist activism, the local and prefectural campaigns for reformist candidates, the grass-roots participation have all faltered. A growing, exceedingly "silent" majority seems to have conceded that the people are not sovereign or even a significant factor in the nation's governance.

In return, they do not want to be bothered by the authorities or obliged to pull their weight. Although the national budget runs a continuous deficit and social security schemes are underfinanced, they make it clear that they do not want to pay any more taxes. Tax evasion even for what was approved has become endemic. Many of the other laws and regulations are so systematically violated, such as those on zoning, parking, fire, safety, labor and antitrust that it is regarded as an imposition to be reminded of their existence. Japan is under fire for its trade surpluses and closed market, but no special interest willingly accepts discipline for the good of the rest. The nation could not defend itself in a war. And, if one were to break out, most citizens would not try to repel the invaders but run away.

This negativism reaches even further. Many individuals no longer accept the need to be good citizens in more ordinary ways. Community service has so little appeal that most big city or urban districts failed to grow into real neighborhoods. There are few voluntary activities that draw people together and there is not much interest in beautification or improvement. Families have also been disintegrating as social units, this time due less to personal desires than the implacable demands of work. Most husbands are away from morn' to night and some do not even show up for weekends. Now many wives have to work as well. Children, who might unite them, are busy studying. All this weakens the vital cells of society.

They are then more subject to many social ailments Japan had seemed immune to. Crime has been spreading constantly, involving not only gangsters and their ilk but formerly law-abiding citizens. The fastest growing contingent has actually been youth, which bodes ill for the future. There are ever more complaints of violence in the home and classroom, violence directed against once unquestionable symbols of authority, parents and teachers. Meanwhile, the family is falling apart in another way, due to divorce of married couples or, more commonly, lack of affection between a husband and wife who do not bother separating. In this atmosphere, prostitution and a virulent sex industry, drug addiction and alcoholism only flourish.

These more sensational deviations, however, are not the most widespread or, in certain ways, the most pernicious. The most insidious threat is that countless "decent" Japanese have given up on any formal or constructive solution to their problems and begun to seek their own salvation. Despite unceasing calls for more work and discipline, loyalty and sacrifice, the younger generations have resolutely turned toward their personal lives and interests. For the first classes, this involved a quite benign and perfectly understandable desire to be with their home and family, spawning *my-homu* and *nyu famarii* trends. But more recent ones have shown little interest in anything but their material comfort, not even leisure or sports so much as wasteful and childish forms of conspicuous consumption.[13]

While the student radicals frequently opted out with a vengeance after failing to reform society, most of their successors have accepted society as a given, something they cannot really affect, and then created their own private world. They still operate in groups more than as individuals, but these are relatively passive and negativistic associations of friends and acquaintances, fellow commiserators who are just as unhappy with the situation as they. Today's social units are smaller than ever, more dispersed than ever, and more cut off from the rest of the population than ever. The rejection of conventional and traditional mores is almost total, although they do not stress this, since they give little thought to what others think or do.

This is increasingly a counter-culture by default. It is not utopia, some hopeful or promising improvement on the old. Rather, it is a nirvana, a place of refuge away from the maddening crowd. What happens to presently constituted society is no longer a major concern. And if that society were to crumble, it would not be of much interest either. Having figured out that the supposedly "real" world was not *honne* but *tatemae,* many Japanese have no hesitation in inventing whatever sort of realities appeal to them while remembering to clothe them in more respectable, if quite illusory, appearances.

Since so much of this takes the form of omission rather than commission, passive approval of the accepted ways and covert endorsement of something else, visible participation in existing institutions and secretive alienation from them, it is not easy to grasp what is happening. Nonetheless, there are abundant manifestations of disintegration within the supposedly solid structure of the Japanese state. Anywhere else, they would be regarded with deep foreboding and efforts would be made to stem them in time. At the peak of its power, the present elite tends to ignore them if not furtively cover them up.

This, too, has a long tradition. Most of the past dynasties and regimes were equally oblivious to the tensions and contradictions that undermined their effectiveness and turned away their potential supporters well before some internal or external enemy gave the decisive blow. In extreme cases, the rot proceeded so far that it became evident to the population at large that the system was crumbling. Unable to reform itself, and also unable to preserve the system, the elite watched as bits and snatches of the realm broke away. The most recent examples were the decline and fall of the Tokugawa Shogunate, Taisho democracy and the nationalist regime.

As a matter of fact, Japan has been characterized by repeated cycles of decay and collapse followed by renewal and vitality which relapses back into decay that paves the way for another collapse. This has often been accompanied by an opening and closing of the social hierarchy to other segments of the population which breathed new life into the elite. On occasion, there was a further element of acceptance of foreign ideas and models and an urge to learn from abroad, only to be cut off later on. Japan again appears to be moving toward the latter portion of the cycle which leads from renewal to decay.

Defeat in the Pacific War ushered in a period of turbulence *and* progress which was interrupted by two rollbacks. One was the "reverse course" just after the Occupation. Far more significant are the present conservative tendencies which stubbornly resist essential changes in policies that have proven ineffective. This is accompanied by a growing concentration of power within an elite that is self-satisfied and inward-looking and which is increasingly ignored by the rest of the population. Meanwhile, there has been a harking back to "traditional" ways, not necessarily because they are better or more appropriate but because they are old and seemingly more Japanese. This combines with a sharper rejection of foreign influence and a withdrawal from the outside world.

This could mean that the only way change will come

about is through another collapse followed by another rebirth. In the past, the system's demise has sometimes been precipitated by foreign intervention. War cannot be excluded. But trade wars are already a certainty and would further shake the nation's economic underpinnings. Internally, spreading disaffection could gradually sap the people's will, making them work less, study less, contribute less, and cooperate less. It might take some time, and Japan's decadent phase has occasionally lasted decades. But society, the economy and the state would gently sink into the morass.

The scenario would not resemble collapse in the West. There would be little open dissidence or revolt. The outcome would not be an explosion but rather an implosion as the essential pillars rot and nothing remains to support an overburdened structure. Japan's noble postwar experiment would then conclude, not with a bang, and maybe not even with a whimper. . . .

NOTES

1. These problems are described in Jared Taylor, *Shadows of the Rising Sun,* and Woronoff, *Japan: The Coming Economic Crisis* and *Japan: The Coming Social Crisis.*
2. That economic progress could have social drawbacks is shown in Hugh Patrick (ed.), *Japanese Industrialization And Its Social Consequences.*
3. These broader manifestations of social unease are taken up in Tadashi Fukutake, *Japanese Society Today* and *The Japanese Social Structure.*
4. Speech to the 97th Session of the National Diet, December 3, 1982.
5. *Japan Times,* April 23, 1984.
6. *Japan Economic Journal,* November 27, 1984.
7. *Japan Times,* February 5 & April 5, 1984.
8. *Far Eastern Economic Review,* May 9, 1985, p. 32.
9. On the complexities of Japanese decision-making, see Vogel (ed.), *Modern Japanese Organization and Decision-Making.*

10. As Ellis Krauss remarked of the student radicals, "their tragedy, and Japan's potential danger, is that such talented and concerned men cannot find institutionalized channels to translate their opposition effectively into constructive reform." (*Japan Radicals Revisited*, p. 173.)
11. Woronoff, *Inside Japan, Inc.*, pp. 252-73.
12. Speech to the 101st Session of the National Diet, February 6, 1984.
13. This is best typified by the "crystal" generation.

Acronyms

BOJ	Bank of Japan
DA	Defense Agency
Domei	Japanese Confederation of Labor
DSP	Democratic Socialist Party
EA	Environment Agency
EPA	Economic Planning Agency
FTC	Fair Trade Commission
JCP	Japan Communist Party
JHC	Japan Housing Corporation
JMA	Japan Medical Association
JNR	Japanese National Railways
JRCC	Japan Railway Construction Corporation
JSP	Japan Socialist Party
KDD	Kokusai Denshin Denwa
Keidanren	Japan Federation of Economic Organizations
Keizai Doyukai	Japan Committee for Economic Development
Komeito	Clean Government Party
LDP	Liberal Democratic Party
MAFF	Ministry of Agriculture, Forestry and Fisheries
MFA	Ministry of Foreign Affairs
MHA	Ministry of Home Affairs

MHW	Ministry of Health and Welfare
MITI	Ministry of International Trade and Industry
MOC	Ministry of Construction
MOE	Ministry of Education
MOF	Ministry of Finance
MOJ	Ministry of Justice
MOL	Ministry of Labor
MOT	Ministry of Transport
MPT	Ministry of Post and Telecommunications
Nikkeiren	Japan Federation of Employers Associations
Nissho	Japan Chamber of Commerce and Industry
NLC	New Liberal Club
NTT	Nippon Telegraph and Telephone
OECF	Overseas Economic Cooperation Fund
SCAP	Supreme Commander for the Allied Powers
SDF	Self-Defense Force
Shaminren	Social Democratic Federation
Sohyo	General Council of Trade Unions
Zenchu	Central Union of Agricultural Cooperatives
Zenno	National Federation of Agricultural Cooperative Associations

Bibliography

1. Prewar Period
2. Politics
3. Bureaucracy
4. Business
5. People
6. Economic Issues
7. Social Issues
8. Foreign Policy and Defense
9. General

1. Prewar Period

Beasley, W.F., *The Modern History of Japan,* London, Weidenfeld & Nicolson, 1981.

Borton, Hugh, *Japan's Modern Century,* New York, Ronald Press, 1955.

Crump, John, *The Origins of Socialist Thought in Japan,* London, Croom Helm, 1983.

Hall, John Whitney, *Japan: From Prehistory to Modern Times,* New York, Delacorte, 1970.

Ike, Nobutaka, *The Beginnings of Political Democracy in Japan,* Baltimore, Johns Hopkins Press, 1950.

Lockwood, William W., *The Economic Development of Japan,* Princeton, Princeton University Press, 1968.

Minichiello, Sharon, *Retreat from Reform: Patterns of Political Behavior in Interwar Japan,* Honolulu, University of Hawaii Press, 1984.

Sansom, Sir George, *History of Japan,* Stanford, Stanford University Press, 1958, 1961, and 1963.

Scalapino, Robert, *Democracy and the Party Movement in Prewar Japan,* Berkeley, University of California Press, 1955.

————, *The Early Japanese Labor Movement,* Berkeley, Center for Japanese Studies, 1983.

Silberman, Bernard S., and Harootunian, H.D., *Japan in Crisis, Essays on Taisho Democracy,* Princeton, Princeton University Press, 1974.

Storry, Richard, *A History of Modern Japan,* London, Pelican Books, 1960.

Ward, Robert E. (ed.), *Political Development in Modern Japan,* Princeton, Princeton University Press, 1960.

2. Politicians

Baerwald, Hans H., *Japan's Parliament,* Cambridge, Cambridge University Press, 1974.

Curtis, Gerald, *Election Campaigning Japanese Style,* New York, Columbia University Press, 1971.

Fukui, Haruhiro, *Party in Power: The Japanese Liberal Democrats and Policy-Making,* Berkeley, University of California Press, 1970.

Hrebenar, Ronald J., *Japanese Political Parties and their Electoral Environment,* Boulder, Westview, 1986.

————. (ed.), *The Japanese Party System,* Boulder, Westview, 1986.

Ike, Nobutaka, *A Theory of Japanese Democracy,* Boulder, Westview, 1978.

————, *Japanese Politics: An Introductory Survey,* New York, Alfred A. Knopf, 1957.

————, *Japanese Politics, Patron-Client Democracy,* New York, Alfred A. Knopf, 1972.

Itoh, Hiroshi (ed.), *Japanese Politics—An Inside View,* Ithaca, Cornell University Press, 1973.

Kishimoto, Koichi, *Politics in Modern Japan,* Tokyo, Japan Echo, 1977.

Langdon, Frank, *Politics in Japan,* Boston, Little, Brown, 1967.

Maki, John M., *Government and Politics in Japan, The Road to Democracy,* New York, Praeger, 1962.

Masumi, Junnosuke, *Postwar Politics in Japan,* Berkeley, Institute of East Asian Studies, 1986.

McNelly, Theodore, *Politics and Government in Japan,* Lanham, University Press of America, 1984.

Pempel, T.J. (ed.), *Policy-Making in Contemporary Japan,* Ithaca, Cornell University Press, 1969.

Quigley, Harold S., and Turner, John E., *The New Japan, Government and Politics,* Minneapolis, University of Minnesota Press, 1956.

Richardson, Bradley M., *The Political Culture of Japan,* Berkeley, University of California Press, 1975.

Richardson, Bradley M., and Flanagan, Scott C., *Politics in Japan,* Boston, Little, Brown & Co., 1984.

Samuels, Richard J., *The Politics of Regional Policy in Japan,* Princeton, Princeton University Press, 1983.

Scalapino, Robert A., and Masumi, Junnosuke, *Parties and Politics in Contemporary Japan,* Berkeley, University of California Press, 1968.

Steiner, Kurt, *Local Government in Japan,* Stanford, Stanford University Press, 1965.

Stockwin, J.A.A., *Japan: Divided Politics in a Growth Economy,* London, Weidenfeld & Nicolson, 1975.

Tanaka, Kakuei, *Building a New Japan,* Tokyo, Simul Press, 1973.

Thayer, Nathaniel B., *How the Conservatives Rule Japan,* Princeton, Princeton University Press, 1969.

Tsuneishi, Warren M., *Japanese Political Style,* New York, Harper & Row, 1960.

Ward, Robert E., *Japan's Political System,* Englewood Cliffs, Prentice-Hall, 1978.

Watanuki, Joji, *Politics in Postwar Japanese Society,* Tokyo, Tokyo University Press, 1977.

3. Bureaucracy

Campbell, John Creighton, *Contemporary Japanese Budget Politics,* Berkeley, University of California Press, 1976.

Horne, James, *Japan's Financial Markets, Conflicts and Consensus in Policymaking,* Sydney, George Allen & Unwin, 1985.

Johnson, Chalmers, *MITI and the Japanese Miracle,* Stanford, Stanford University Press, 1982.

Kubota, Akira, *Higher Civil Servants in Postwar Japan: Their Social Origins, Educational Background and Career Patterns,* Princeton, Princeton University Press, 1969.

Park, Yung H., *Bureaucrats and Ministers in Contemporary Japanese Government,* Berkeley, Institute of East Asian Studies, 1986.

Spaulding, Robert M., Jr., *Imperial Japan's Higher Civil Service Examinations,* Princeton, Princeton University Press, 1967.

Tsuji, Kiyoaki (ed.), *Public Administration in Japan,* Tokyo, University of Tokyo Press, 1984.

4. Business

Allinson, Gary D., *Japanese Urbanism: Industry and Politics in Kariya,* Berkeley, University of California Press, 1975.

Azumi, Kaya, *Higher Education and Business Recruitment in Japan,* New York, Teacher's College Press, 1969.

Bryant, William E., *Japanese Private Economic Diplomacy,* New York, Praeger, 1975.

Mannari, Hiroshi, *The Japanese Business Leaders,* Tokyo, University of Tokyo Press, 1974.

Marshall, Byron K., *Capitalism and Nationalism in Prewar Japan, The Ideology of the Business Elite,* Stanford, Stanford University Press, 1967.

Woronoff, Jon, *Inside Japan, Inc.,* Tokyo, Lotus Press, 1982.

———. *Japan's Wasted Workers,* Tokyo, Lotus Press, and Totowa, Rowman and Allenheld, 1983.

————. *The Japan Syndrome*, Tokyo, Lotus Press, and New Brunswick, Transaction Books, 1985.

Yanaga, Chitoshi, *Big Business in Japanese Politics*, New Haven, Yale University Press, 1969.

Yoshihara, Kunio, *Sogo Shosha*, Oxford, Oxford University Press, 1982.

5. People

Apter, David E., and Sawa, Nagayo, *Against the State, Politics and Social Protest in Japan*, Cambridge, Harvard University Press, 1984.

Hane, Mikiso, *Peasants, Rebels, and Outcastes*, New York, Pantheon Books, 1982.

Koschmann, J. Victor, *Authority and the Individual in Japan: Citizen Protest in Historical Perspective*, Tokyo, University of Tokyo Press, 1978.

Krauss, Ellis S., *Japanese Radicals Revisted*, Berkeley, University of California Press, 1977.

Krauss, Ellis S., Rohlen, Thomas P., and Steinhoff, Patricia G. (eds.), *Conflict in Japan*, Honolulu, University of Hawaii Press, 1984.

Kuroda, Yasumasa, *Reed Town, Japan: A Study in Community Power Structure and Political Change*, Honolulu, University of Hawaii Press, 1974.

McKean, Margaret A., *Environmental Protest and Citizen Politics in Japan*, Berkeley, University of California Press, 1981.

Moore, Joe, *Japanese Workers and the Struggle for Power*, Madison, University of Wisconsin Press, 1983.

Najita, Tetsuo, and Koschmann, J. Victor (eds.), *Conflict in Modern Japanese History, The Neglected Tradition*, Princeton, Princeton University Press.

Scalapino, Robert A., *The Early Japanese Labor Movement*, Berkeley, Institute of East Asian Studies, 1983.

Steiner, Kurt, Krauss, Ellis, and Flanagan, Scott G. (eds.), *Political Opposition and Local Politics in Japan*, Princeton, Princeton University Press, 1980.

Yanaga, Chitoshi, *Japanese People and Politics*, London, Chapman & Hall, 1957.

6. Economic Issues

Halliday, Jon, *A Political History of Japanese Capitalism*, New York, Pantheon, 1975.

Kosai, Yutaka, and Ogino, Yoshitaro, *The Contemporary Japanese Economy*, Armonk, M.E. Sharpe, 1984.

Nakamura, Takafusa, *The Postwar Japanese Economy*, Tokyo, University of Tokyo Press, 1981.

Shinohara, Miyohei, *Industrial Growth, Trade, and Dynamic Patterns in the Japanese Economy*, Tokyo, University of Tokyo Press, 1982.

Shinohara, Miyohei, and Yanagihara, Toru, *The Japanese and Korean Experiences in Managing Development*, Washington, World Bank, 1983.

Uchino, Tatsuro, *Japan's Postwar Economy*, Tokyo, Kodansha International, 1983.

Woronoff, Jon, *Japan: The Coming Economic Crisis*, Tokyo, Lotus Press, 1979.

Yamamura, Kozo, *Economic Policy in Postwar Japan, Growth versus Democracy*, Berkeley, University of California Press, 1967.

———. (ed.), *Policy and Trade Issues of the Japanese Economy*, Seattle, University of Washington Press, 1983.

7. Social Issues

De Vos, George (ed.), *Institutions for Change in Japanese Society*, Berkeley, Institute of East Asian Studies, 1984.

De Vos, George, and Wagatsuma, Hiroshi, *Japan's Invisible Race: Caste in Culture and Personality*, Berkeley, University of California Press, 1971.

Dore, R.P., *Land Reform in Japan*, London, Oxford University Press, 1959.

Farley, Miriam S., *Aspects of Japan's Labor Problems*, New York, Institute of Pacific Relations, 1950.

Fukutake, Tadashi, *Japanese Society Today,* Tokyo, University of Tokyo Press, 1981.

————, *The Japanese Social Structure,* Tokyo, University of Tokyo Press, 1982.

Hanami, Tadashi, *Labor Relations in Japan Today,* Tokyo, Kodansha International, 1979.

Patrick, Hugh (ed.), *Japanese Industrialization and Its Social Consequences,* Berkeley, University of California Press, 1976.

Pempel, T.J., *Policy and Politics in Japan, Creative Conservatism,* Philadelphia, Temple University Press, 1982.

Rohlen, Thomas P., *Japan's High Schools,* Berkeley, University of California Press, 1983.

Steven, Rob, *Classes in Contemporary Japan,* Cambridge, Cambridge University Press, 1983.

Woronoff, Jon, *Japan: The Coming Social Crisis,* Tokyo, Lotus Press, 1980.

8. Foreign Policy and Defense

Axelbank, Albert, *Black Star Over Japan, Rising Forces of Militarism,* Tokyo, Tuttle, 1972.

Barnds, William J. (ed.), *Japan and the United States, Challenges and Opportunities,* New York, New York University Press, 1979.

Cohen, Stephen D., *Uneasy Partnership, Competition and Conflict in U.S.-Japanese Trade Relations,* Cambridge, Ballinger, 1985.

Destler, I.M., and Sato, Hideo (eds.), *Coping with U.S.-Japanese Economic Conflicts,* Lexington, D.C. Heath, 1982.

Halliday, Jon, and McCormack, Gavan, *Japanese Imperialism Today,* Middlesex, Penguin Books, 1973.

Higashi, Chikara, *Japanese Trade Policy Formulation,* New York, Praeger, 1983.

Holland, John K., *Managing Diplomacy, The United States and Japan,* Stanford, Hoover Institution, 1984.

Hollerman, Leon (ed.), *Japan and the United States: Economic and Political Adversaries,* Boulder, Westview, 1980.

Jain, R.K., *The USSR and Japan (1945-1980)*, Atlantic Highlands, Humanities Press, 1981.

Langdon, F.C., *Japan's Foreign Policy*, Vancouver, University of British Columbia Press, 1973.

Morley, James W. (ed.), *Japan's Foreign Policy (1868-1941)*, New York, Columbia University Press, 1974.

Nish, Ian, *Japanese Foreign Policy (1869-1942)*, London, Routledge & Kegan Paul, 1977.

Rix, Alan, *Japan's Economic Aid*, London, Croom Helm, 1980.

Scalapino, Robert A. (ed.), *The Foreign Policy of Modern Japan*, Berkeley, University of California Press, 1977.

Woronoff, Jon, *Japan's Overseas Empire*, Tokyo, Lotus Press, and Armonk, M.E. Sharpe, 1984.

————, *World Trade War*, Tokyo, Lotus Press, and New York, Praeger, 1984.

9. General

Benedict, Ruth, *The Chrysanthemum and the Sword*, Tokyo, Tuttle, 1954.

Gibney, Frank, *Japan: The Fragile Superpower*, New York, Norton, 1975.

Kawasaki, Ichiro, *Japan Unmasked*, Englewood Cliffs, Prentice-Hall, 1969.

Kinmonth, Earl H., *The Self-Made Man in Meiji Japanese Thought*, Berkeley, University of California Press, 1981.

Murakami, Hyoe, and Hirschmeier, Johannes, *Politics and Economics in Contemporary Japan*, Tokyo, Kodansha International, 1979.

Nakane, Chie, *Japanese Society*, Harmondsworth, Penguin Books, 1973.

Reischauer, Edwin O., *Japan: Past and Present*, Tokyo, Tuttle, 1946.

————, *Japan: The Story of a Nation*, Tokyo, Tuttle, 1970.

Taylor, Jared, *Shadows of the Rising Sun*, New York, William Morrow, 1983.

Vogel, Ezra F., *Japan as Number One,* Cambridge, Harvard University Press, 1979.

———— (ed.), *Modern Japanese Organization and Decision-Making,* Berkeley, University of California Press, 1975.

Wray, Harry, and Conroy, Hilary (eds.), *Japan Examined, Perspectives on Modern Japanese History,* Honolulu, University of Hawaii Press, 1983.

Index

Abe, Shintaro, 57, 59, 79, 85, 87, 100, 372.
administrative guidance, 118-9, 123, 126, 224, 268, 273, 275-6, 283, 321, 402.
Administrative Management Agency, 297, 300.
administrative reform, 43, 170, 172, 188, 245-6, 261, 291, 293, 295-302.
amakudari, 137, 164-5, 171-2, 232, 237-8.
Antimonopoly Law, 125, 167-8, 274, 276-7.
Asanuma, Inejiro, 199.

Bank of Japan, 129, 130, 234, 237, 240.
banks, private, 126-8, 159, 161, 166-8, 172, 234-6, 239-40, 351; state, 125, 128, 230, 236-8.
Board of Audit, 120, 136, 307, 312, 315-6, 322.
Buddhism, 24, 76, 199, 332, 386, 397.
budget, 29-30, 102, 123, 127, 248, 358, 361-3, 366; deficit, 43, 240-7, 288, 425.
burakumin, 20, 190, 335-6.
bureaucracy, 20-1, 26, 32-3, 40, 50, 77-8, 92, 100, 106-49, 148, 154, 157, 164-5, 171-3, 187, 209, 213, 224-8, 231-2, 237-8, 256, 298, 301, 325, 336, 382, 390-2, 410-3, 415-8, 421; failings, 120-3, 131-47, 266-8, 270-3, 283-6, 307-12, 315-6; influence, 114-24, 313, 363; recruitment, 110-3, 262; size, 109-10, 296, 300.

business community, 25, 32-3, 50, 81, 92, 114, 150-74, 199, 209-10, 213, 223-6, 230-4, 235-6, 245-6, 262, 270-1, 320-5, 354-6, 370, 372, 390-2, 410-3, 415-8, 421; big business, 231-3, 235-6, 239, 245-6, 276-7, 279, 296-8; political influence, 152-3, 155-74, 267-9.

centralism, 24, 30, 106, 108-10, 147, 255-6, 292, 300.
China, 20, 23, 43, 67, 332, 336, 345-7, 349, 354-5, 367-8.
Christianity, 25, 199, 329, 332, 424.
citizens' movements, 184, 203, 264-8, 362.
class structure, 20, 25-6, 178, 233, 278, 280, 283, 387, 392-3, 399, 400, 412-3, 427-8.
coalition, 46-7, 72-5.
Confucianism, 20, 24, 110, 397, 399, 402-3.
connections, 85, 87, 91-2, 111, 327.
consensus, 26-7, 47-8, 76, 88, 90, 330, 360-5, 369, 406, 414-6, 418-9.
conservatism, 186, 189-90, 204, 255, 369, 420, 428.
constitution, 21, 23-4, 28-34, 42, 114, 174, 175, 178, 180, 256, 265, 328-39, 357-8, 380, 386; revision, 49, 328-30.
construction industry, 137-8, 155-6, 158-9, 162, 165, 246, 307-13, 316-7.
consumers movement, 145, 184, 233, 239, 251, 270-8, 277, 356.
convergence theory, 14, 387-8.

Ibuka, Masaru, 259.
Ike, Nobutake, 401-2.
Ikeda, Daisaku, 70, 199.
Ikeda, Hayato, 42-3, 49, 51, 55, 88, 101, 170, 183, 199, 222, 297, 350, 358.
Imperial Rule Assistance Association, 23, 40.
Inayama, Yoshihiro, 153, 155, 170, 245, 277.
independents, 47, 71-2, 95, 326, 335.
individualism, 190, 235, 260, 385-6, 393-4, 425-6.
Indonesia, 321, 355.
investment, overseas, 169, 216, 354, 356.
International Labour Organisation, 214-5, 282, 284, 292, 338.
Ishibashi, Tanzan, 42, 52, 55.
Ishihara, Tadashi, 154.
Ishikawa, Fusae, 71.
Ishizaka, Taizo, 152, 172.

Japan Chamber of Commerce and Industry, *see* Nissho.
Japan Committee for Economic Development, *see* Keizai Doyukai.
Japan Communist Party, 39-41, 44-7, 60-5, 72-3, 78-9, 93, 163, 182-3, 200-3, 207-9, 250, 253, 262, 292, 298, 313, 315, 325, 329, 337, 343, 362, 368-9, 419.
Japanese Confederation of Labor, *see* Domei.
Japanese National Railways, 108-9, 125, 129, 138, 145, 197, 243, 293, 300, 307-8, 316.
Japan Federation of Economic Organizations, *see* Keidanren.
Japan Federation of Employers Associations, *see* Nikkeiren.
Japan Housing Corporation, 108, 308, 311, 316.
Japan, Inc. 124, 172-3, 400.
Japan Medical Association, 197-8, 291-2, 299.
Japan Railway Construction Corporation, 108, 138, 243, 308, 311, 316.
Japan Socialist Party, 39-41, 44-7, 60-5, 72-3, 78-9, 93, 163, 182-3,

200-3, 207-9, 250, 253, 256, 262, 292, 298, 312, 325, 329-30, 332, 336, 343, 360, 362, 368-9, 419.
Japan-U.S. Security Treaty, 41-3, 61, 64-5, 182-3, 198, 202, 209, 343, 357, 360, 368, 376.
judiciary, 30, 180-1, 264-5, 272, 275-6, 321, 324-5, 334, 338-9.

Kaifu, Hachiro, 320.
Kaneko, Mitsuhiro, 69.
Kanemaru, Shin, 58-9, 86.
Kasuga, Ikko, 66, 74.
Kawasaki, Ichiro, 327.
Keidanren, 151-3, 155-6, 159, 161-2, 172, 199, 245, 251, 267-8, 277, 280-1, 290, 293, 296, 356, 363.
keiretsu, 235-6, 274.
Keizai Doyukai, 153-6, 278.
Kishi, Nobusuke, 42, 54-5, 57, 77, 85, 88, 122, 182-3, 199, 209, 319, 329, 357.
Kodama, Yoshio, 198, 320-1.
Kokusai Denshin Denwa, 125, 138, 147, 315.
Komeito, 41, 44-7, 70-5, 78-9, 86, 93, 163, 199, 253, 299, 360, 369.
Komoto, Toshio, 51, 57, 74, 79, 86, 100, 158-9, 174, 245.
Kono, Yohei, 71.
Konoe, Prince Fumimaro, 28.
Kosaka, Tokusaburo, 158.
Korea, 18, 23, 321, 336, 345-6, 349, 351, 355, 367.

land reform, 28, 195.
leadership, 86-90, 393, 413-21, 424.
Liberal Democratic Party, 40-7, 48-60, 74-6, 77-82, 93, 98-103, 115-6, 121-3, 129, 155-64, 169-72, 186-7, 195-9, 201-3, 209, 238, 244-5, 316-27, 390-2, 409-10, 418; decisionmaking, 98-103, 115; party reform, 53-4, 56; president, 51-4, 56-7, 324; program, 48-9, 186, 255-7, 267-8, 281, 290, 292-3, 297-8, 328-36, 346, 359-61, 368-70.

local politics, 46-7, 69, 75, 84, 103, 109, 135, 137, 243, 250, 254, 256, 311, 314-7.
Lockheed affair, 51, 59, 71, 318-20, 323-5.

MacArthur, General Douglas, 26, 28, 40, 178, 342.
Macrae, Gordon, 221.
Makieda, Motofumi, 256.
Management and Coordination Agency, 300.
Mansfield, Mike, 345.
Marubeni, 245, 320-1.
Matsuno, Raizo, 319, 323.
media, 83, 204-10, 423; *see also* press.
Meiji era, 19-22, 28, 32, 114, 124, 132, 181, 195, 396-7.
Middle East, 347-8, 355.
Miki, Takeo, 43, 51, 53, 55-7, 74, 77, 86, 170, 199, 358.
militarism, 23-4, 151, 178, 358-9, 363.
ministers, 99-102, 108, 116-20, 122-3, 165, 338.
Ministry of Agriculture, Forestry and Fisheries, 108-9, 129-30, 138, 248-51, 272, 299.
Ministry of Construction, 108-9, 129, 138, 165, 311.
Ministry of Education, 138, 255-6.
Ministry of Finance, 108-9, 111-2, 126-31, 138, 145, 165, 222, 234, 237-8, 240-7, 290, 293, 310, 316.
Ministry of Foreign Affairs, 130-1, 354-5, 368, 370-4.
Ministry of Health and Welfare, 129-30, 145, 270-2, 289-94, 316.
Ministry of Home Affairs, 109, 139, 159, 244; *see also* Home Ministry.
Ministry of International Trade and Industry, 108-9, 128-31, 138, 145, 147, 165, 171-2, 222-7, 229-31, 264-8, 270, 274-7, 279-80, 370, 372.
Ministry of Labor, 129, 278, 281-3.
Ministry of Posts and Telecommunications, 127-30, 138, 147, 197, 238, 315.

Ministry of Transport, 108-9, 129-30, 138, 147, 317, 320.
Minobe, Ryoichi, 46.
minorities, 18, 184, 190, 329, 335-7.
Mitsubishi, 22, 245.
Mitsui, 22, 245.
Miyamoto, Kenji, 67-9, 85-6.
Miyazawa, Kiichi, 59, 86, 89, 100, 245-6, 372.
modernization, 21, 383-5, 388.

Nagai, Michio, 82.
Nagano, Shigeo, 154-5.
Nakane, Chie, 26.
Nakasone, Yasuhiro, 43, 49, 51, 56-9, 74, 77, 82, 88-9, 101, 122, 155, 159, 170, 187, 231, 245, 259-60, 297-8, 302, 322, 324, 330-2, 357, 360-1, 372, 398, 410.
Nakagawa, Ichiro, 49, 51, 57, 59, 315.
Nakauchi, Isao, 262.
nationalists, 23-5, 49, 77, 107, 181, 198-9, 329-30.
National Tax Administration Agency, 160, 322.
"new leaders," 79-81, 85-7, 89, 158.
New Liberal Club, 41, 44-7, 71, 73, 75, 83, 164, 262, 298, 325.
Nikaido, Susumo, 58-9, 74, 86, 321.
Nikkeiren, 153, 281, 283-4, 293, 296, 338.
Nippon Telegraph and Telephone, 108, 125, 129, 138, 293, 300.
Nissho, 154-6, 162, 246, 280, 363.
Nissho-Iwai, 319.
Nixon, Richard, 345-6.
Nosaka, Sanzo, 67.
nuclear energy, 184, 201-2, 314, 362-6.

Ohira, Masayoshi, 43, 51, 55-7, 78, 100, 120, 187, 199, 243-4, 291, 297, 306.
oil crisis, 170, 172, 185, 241, 275, 347.
Okita, Saburo, 82.
old age, 286, 288, 291, 294-5, 407.
Opposition, 42-3, 47, 60-76, 102-3,

121, 123, 163-4, 186, 209, 238, 244-5, 292-3, 324-5, 330-5, 357, 360-2, 410, 419.
Organization for Economic Cooperation and Development, 214-5, 292, 345, 352, 368.
Osano, Kenji, 198, 320-1.
Otsuki, Bumpei, 153, 155, 245, 281, 284, 296.

Pacific War, 23-4, 28, 287.
pacifism, 60, 62, 64, 201-2, 357, 360-3.
"people," 20, 25-6, 28, 83, 113, 123-4, 157, 168, 181-94, 232-3, 234-6, 239-40, 244-5, 250-1, 264-6, 269, 273-4, 286, 290-1, 294-5, 299, 313, 326-7, 356, 362-5, 371-5, 379, 391, 410-3, 420-3, 424-8.
Philippines, 321-2, 355.
planning, 221-2, 231.
police, 42, 146, 179-80, 183, 198, 338.
political parties, 22-3, 39-104, 115, 182-3, 187-9, 379-80, 390, 425.
politicians, 22-3, 32-3, 39-40, 51-3, 76-103, 114-24, 127, 140-1, 144, 157-66, 171-3, 184, 187-9, 208-9, 213, 227, 232-3, 238, 243-4, 298, 308-12, 314-28, 328-35, 371-2, 412-3, 415-6, 421-3.
pollution, 43, 145, 184, 233, 263-9.
press, 29, 69, 189, 205-10, 318, 322, 332, 373.
pressure groups, 121-2, 143-4, 150-74, 194-204, 329, 356, 380, 419.
prime minister, 30, 42-3, 52-4, 56, 100-2, 116-20, 123, 130, 175, 189, 222, 227, 243-4.
Prime Minister's Office, 108, 120, 130, 269-70, 273, 290, 300, 337, 411-2, 422.
protectionism, 126, 166-8, 172, 215, 223-4, 226, 231-2, 248, 251-3, 277-8, 343-4, 351-2, 356.
public corporations, 108-9, 125, 127, 131, 37-9, 238, 243, 297-8, 300, 310-1.
public works, 168, 184, 203, 223, 227, 238, 242, 246, 301, 305-14.
purge, 40, 42-3, 49, 77, 256.

radicals, 40, 182-5, 192, 202, 426, 430.
Reagan, Ronald, 296, 344.
Reischauer, Edwin O., 35, 339, 345.
religion, 24-6, 29, 70, 199, 331-2.
"reverse course," 42, 62, 107, 182, 256-7, 278, 301, 428.
rights, 29, 335-8, 396.

Sakurada, Takeshi, 153.
Sasaki, Ryosaku, 66.
Sato, Eisaku, 43, 51, 55, 78, 85, 88, 122, 170, 183, 297, 317-8, 359.
Sato, Eishiro, 153.
Sato, Takayuki, 320-1, 326.
Science and Technology Agency, 129-30.
Self-Defense Forces, 109, 178-80, 329-31, 358, 360-1, 364-6, 368.
seniority, 85-7, 111, 133, 136, 157, 165, 381, 403, 415-6.
Shidehara, Kijuro, 28, 41-2, 178.
Shiina, Etsusaburo, 54-5.
Shimasaki, Hitoshi, 336.
Shinto, 24, 199, 332, 397.
Small and Medium Enterprise Agency, 279-80.
Social Democratic Federation, 63, 65-6, 73.
Sohyo, 62, 78, 163, 200-1, 256, 281, 284, 291, 298, 329, 332.
Soka Gakkai, 70-1, 76, 78-9, 199.
Southeast Asia, 349, 351, 354-5.
Soviet Union, 23, 42, 66-7, 347-8, 367, 369-70, 375.
Sunoda, Sunao, 341-2.
support organization, 94-5, 160, 323.
Supreme Commander for the Allied Powers, 24, 27-8, 40-2, 66, 106-7, 125, 182, 195, 253, 274, 278, 287, 342.
Supreme Court, 30, 180-1, 217, 276, 334.
Suzuki, Zenko, 43, 51, 53, 57-8, 74, 86, 88, 155, 159, 199, 245, 249, 297, 330, 357.

Taisho era, 22-3, 28, 33, 397.
Takairi, Yoshikatsu, 70.